Diamonds: Famous and Fatal

The History, Mystery and Lore of the World's Most Precious Gem

Diamonds: Famous and Fatal

The History, Mystery and Lore of the World's Most Precious Gem

Leo P. Kendall

Barricade Books • Fort Lee, NJ

Published by Barricade Books Inc.
185 Bridge Plaza North
Suite 308-A
Fort Lee, NJ 07024

Library of Congress Cataloging-in-Publication Data:
CIP Data pending
contact the Library of Congress for this information.

Printed in the United States of America.

10 9 8 7 6 5 4 3 2 1

Table of Contents

Preface

*T*he beauty, rarity and fascinating lore of diamonds have intrigued man through the ages. Even in pre-historic times men would pick up shining baubles for their beauty, for personal decoration and even to venerate.

Among the shiniest of these baubles was the diamond, particularly alluvial diamonds that had acquired a bright sparkle from the polishing they received as they tumbled through stone-covered stream beds on their way from the highlands where they originated to more accessible places where man could find them.

Granted, the diamond was by no means the only precious or semi-precious gemstone that caught pre-historic man's eye. However, its clear or tinted brilliance outshone all others. Nor was it the rarest of gems. In fact, quite the contrary: it is one of the most common of all gemstones.

One can but wonder what made the diamond the world's premier gemstone. Certainly it was not just its brilliance; man learned how to bring out the beauty in other, more workable, gemstones long before the techniques for releasing diamond's dazzle had been invented. Perhaps it was that hardness, coupled with diamond's beauty that accounts for some of diamond's mystique.

But even this hypothesis does not explain the inordinate interest in the malevolent power that some diamonds seemed to exert over their owners. Why were men so enamoured of the diamond that they were willing to maim, torture and kill for it? What can explain the many stories of the greed and corruption that surround diamonds more than any other gemstone? How important was the diamond in influencing the course of history? And does its influence continue to this day?

Although many books about the diamond contain a short section dealing with its history, few if any treating this aspect exclusively have been published in English. Certainly there has been no book that has dealt with diamond's history in the depth and manner that you are about to explore. Stories of how the diamond was perceived—as an indestructible tool and cutting instrument, a poison, a medicine, a currency almost beyond value, a love potion, and a king-maker - have been culled from writings that have appeared through the millennia. In fact, at times diamonds seemed to be all things to all people.

Since its discovery, the diamond has maintained a sublime, if not ominous, allure. Often considered to be the bearer of the most nefarious curses, its history is full of mysterious and fascinating episodes where diamonds appeared to have exerted a malevolent influence on their possessors, even to the extent of perverting the course of history.

The general history of the diamond is related in this book, with emphasis on those aspects which are fabulous, strange and malevolent. This history is interspersed with the stories of specific diamonds, famous and infamous, which will bear out and underline the bizarre beliefs and events which have characterized their histories. Some of the most spellbinding of the stories about diamonds had their origins in the bloody and, for most Westerners, mysterious history of India and the Middle East. A number of these tales are related in the following pages. Many of these same diamonds later found their way to the West where they had an important impact on the glamour and intrigue of Western courts.

You will not find information about the technical or geological aspects of the diamond except to the extent that it may be necessary to clarify an historical point. What you are about to read is not a text-book; it is a compilation of the myth, fact and fiction surrounding the diamond. These stories will entrance you with the diamond's fantastic history. It will be left up to you, the reader, to decide for yourself to what extent the diamond actually carried out these malign curses and how, or whether, it has influenced the course of history.

The "Moon of Mountains"

*D*iamond, "…a factor in tragedies innumerable, supplying the motives of war, setting father against son, blurring the fair image of virtue, making life a curse where it had been a blessing and adding new terror to death". With these words, E. W. Streeter, foremost chronicler of the history of diamonds, captured this intriguing gem's malevolent reputation—one that rivals its own beauty. It has stirred man's imagination for centuries.

Not all diamonds were cursed, for it's doubtful whether this scintillating stone would have attained its position as the world's premier gem, or become a universal symbol for love and betrothal if they were. The history of evil that has haunted so many famous diamonds can be attributed simply to greed or coincidence.

Still, one wonders. Can the diamond's bloody history be written off so easily? Isn't it possible that certain diamonds, combined with certain owners, have actually created the misfortunes associated with them through the ages?

Perhaps the ancient Hindus were right when they described the positive and negative influences a diamond had on its possessor. According to their treatises on precious stones, "…there are certain streaks of light within…that run parallel or in contrast to the lines of fate of the wearer. If they are parallel, the wearer has victory and joy; if they are not, the possessor is thrown into misery".

Perhaps a curse, once acquired, cannot be easily cast off. This would explain why diamonds present in the violent battles of the Mogul and Persian Empires seemed to carry their curse to each new owner. Of the many diamonds connected with these courts, the "Moon of Mountains," best illustrates this point.

By the year 1739 Mohammed Shah, Grand Mogul in title only, exercised very little real power outside the territories surrounding his sumptuous and decadent capital at Delhi. Much of the wealth gathered by more energetic ancestors sat untouched in the royal treasury, making Delhi a tempting, ripe plum awaiting anyone audacious enough to pluck it.

Nadir Shah, the Turkoman ruler of Persia, proved to be that harvester. He swept through the Khyber Pass into northern India, leaving pyramids of skulls in his wake, a testament to the fate of every army standing in his way. And a warning to any foolish enough to contemplate the same. He soon occupied Delhi and turned his soldiers loose in an orgy of rape and pillage.

In his booty was a great diamond called the "Moon of Mountains." No one knows where this diamond came from or how it acquired its name. The only certainty is that by 1739 it had been in the possession of the Mogul Emperors for many years.

Whether it came to them by conquest, as a tribute from some vassal prince, or was the end product of diamond mines near Hyderabad can only be guessed. In any case, it could not have been seen as more than a trinket, even at 126 carats, when compared with the gems and wealth the Moguls had amassed.

Following the conquest of Delhi, Nadir Shah returned to Persia carrying his spoils. According to legend, he had the "Moon of Mountains," along with a sister diamond, the 'Sun of the Sea', mounted took root in one of his thrones. But he had little chance to enjoy this brilliant symbol of his exalted position. The seeds of violence and avarice he'd sown were reaped by his followers.

In 1747 a group of Nadir's lieutenants, greedy for larger shares of the power they'd helped amass assassinated him. A period of internecine warfare followed, during which the booty from India was dispersed. It changed hands untold times, as first one and then another of the warring chieftains attained supremacy only to be deposed by a rival stronger or craftier than he.

In the 1750s a disreputable looking Afghan, probably one of the rebels involved in Nadir's assassination, turned up in Basra. Basra was a sizeable town located about seventy-five miles inland from the Shatt al Arab river, formed by the Tigris and Euphrates, where it empties into the Persian Gulf. In those days Basra was an emporium for merchandise from the East on its way to Western markets, as well as a haven for merchants of questionable scruples.

Shaffrass was one such merchant. He carried on a lucrative trade with his two brothers. It was to him the Afghan came to sell ill-gotten merchandise. Shaffrass and his brothers could hardly contain their astonishment when the Afghan removed a filthy rag from his travel-stained robe and opened it to reveal a royal ransom in precious stones.

Among the gems several stood out: an enormous emerald glistening like the back of some iridescent scarab, an exceptional blood-red ruby and a magnificent sapphire, known in Persia as the "Eye of Allah." But the gem that caught Shaffrass' attention was a diamond as large as a fig, whose fire dimmed the luster of the others to a mere flicker.

The Afghan, unaware of the true value of his treasure, offered the gems for a tempting price, but still higher than the brothers could pay. After a hasty consultation, they asked for a few days to raise the funds. The Afghan consented and a meeting was arranged. Knowing the devious ways of the Basra merchants, having engaged in much double-dealing himself to possess these gems, the Afghan began to suspect a trap and left Basra.

In the meantime the brothers Shaffrass had raised the money. Having come so close to a considerable fortune, they were enraged when the Afghan failed to appear. But their efforts to find him were fruitless; it was as if the same desert from which he materialized had swallowed him up again.

The Afghan had made his way up the Tigris to Baghdad. There he found a Jewish merchant who could meet his price. He immediately unburdened himself of his treasure for two thoroughbred Arabian stallions and 65,000 piastres. Had he been clairvoyant he might well have mounted one of his newly acquired chargers and returned straightaway to the trackless mountains of Afghanistan. Instead, he headed for the bars and brothels to squander his riches.

Quite by accident, Shaffrass landed in Baghdad at the same time. Only fate can account for the second meeting of these two among the teeming masses of the city's bazaar. The wily Armenian told himself that he would not let the Afghan out of his sight this time. One can only imagine his chagrin upon finding the fabulous gems had, once again, slipped through his fingers.

He plied the Afghan with drink to extract the name and address of the merchant to whom the jewels had been sold. He then hurried to the merchant's house to see what kind of bargain could be struck.

But none of the jewels were for sale, least of all the diamond that plagued his thoughts to the exclusion of all else. He haggled, finally offering double the amount he paid for all the gems, just for the diamond. It was to no avail. This time he had met his match and his bargaining got him nowhere. For a merchant such as Shaffrass this was unthinkable; every object had its price. Being thwarted only served to heighten his desire. Now he had to have the diamond at any cost.

By this time Shaffrass' two brothers had joined him. They decided to force the merchant to take them to it. In the dark of night they broke into his house, rousted him from bed and tortured the location out of him. They disposed of the unfortunate man to ensure that he would carry no tales, and returned to their quarters.

Early the next afternoon the brothers departed for the bazaar to complete their nefarious business. Their attentions were directed to the brothels, bars and opium dens that surrounded it in a web designed to ensnare the unwary businessman and relieve him of his day's profits. They were sure that they would find the Afghan there, squandering the remains of his fortune. Only his testimony could incriminate them when the murder of the merchant came to light.

He was found and persuaded to join them for dinner. This time the unsuspecting Afghan arrived as agreed and was, in the time-honored Eastern tradition, poisoned in his cups. The Shaffrass brothers bundled the bodies into a large sack that they dumped unceremoniously into the Tigris.

The brothers had all they desired. They had acquired a fortune in gems and disposed of anyone who could incriminate them. But greed has nothing to do with the rules of logic. The glittering diamond that had worked its spell on Shaffrass now caught his brothers as well. Each demanded it as his reward. Since there seemed to be no way out of this impasse, Shaffrass settled the matter. For the second night in a row, two bodies fed the appetite of the Tigris.

Now in sole possession of a treasure far beyond his expectations, Shaffrass wasted no time leaving the scene of his bloody exploits. He journeyed first to Constantinople, then through central Europe until, sometime in the mid-1760s, he finally came to rest in Amsterdam.

Using his ill-gotten gains, he established himself as a gem merchant. The high quality of his finer specimens attracted the attentions of European monarchs. The English and Russian sovereigns in particular, showed interest in the exquisite diamond at the center of his collection. But Catherine the Great, Empress of all the Russias, wanted it most of all, to boost her growing collection.

On the basis of the diamond's description, she paid for Shaffrass to journey to St. Petersburg where Lazarov, the crown jeweler, could examine the great stone. Negotiations began almost at once, with an offer of a 10,000 ruble annuity and elevation to the Russian nobility. But Shaffrass was nothing if not greedy. This offer was nowhere near his expectations and he held out for the exorbitant price of 600,000 rubles in cash.

Catherine was in no hurry. She knew she had time on her side. Shaffrass was incurring heavy debts in order to maintain a lifestyle

Catherine the Great

equal to the position and riches he felt would soon be his. Count Panin, Catherine's favorite minister, played him along, never acceding to his demands but never rejecting them. When Shaffrass' credit was exhausted, Panin put an end to the negotiations and informed him that he could not leave Russia or the capital until his debts were paid. This would force the sale of the "Moon of Mountains" on far more favorable terms.

But Shaffrass was not as simple as Count Panin believed. The diamond wasn't his only asset. From his lesser gems he managed to raise enough funds within St. Petersburg's Armenian community to satisfy his creditors. Not wishing to match wits with the Count again, he disappeared from the capital.

It was not until ten years later that the Russian Court heard from Shaffrass. He was reported to be in Astrakhan, a town on the Caspian Sea at the southern border of Catherine's realm. His murderous deeds had been discovered and he was no longer able to return home. He had married and was raising a family there.

Catherine had not forgotten Shaffrass' beautiful diamond and immediately dispatched negotiators to this outpost of her empire. While the amount paid varies according to the source, it is generally agreed that Shaffrass received a sizeable cash settlement plus an annuity and elevation to the nobility.

Lest the conclusion be drawn that the rewards of evil are high, the end of our story should prove otherwise.

Shaffrass was now the father of seven daughters, and a man of means. A goodly portion of his wealth was dispersed as dowries. However, not all his sons-in-law were satisfied with their share. One of them, figuring to gain more through inheritance, poisoned him in much the same manner as Shaffrass had removed his own two brothers.

With this act, the sanguine history of the "Moon of Mountains" seems to have drawn to an end. The diamond resided for many years among the Russian Crown Jewels. It disappeared sometime in the nineteenth century, carrying its curse with it.

Genesis:
Formation and
Earliest Records

Although the history of the "Moon of Mountains," and others yet to be related, makes the diamond seem the product of malicious supernatural forces, its birth was a natural process like any geological form. In the eons before life began to form, pressures worked within the heated matter and gases that would someday coalesce into our planet Earth. From this magma emerged the diamond, a substance the rarity, beauty and mystery of which has intrigued man like no other.

Perhaps a sparkling pebble, polished by the corrosions of the ages, entranced some ancient Dravidian, preparing his small plot on the sun-baked plateau of central India thirty centuries ago. Even in those primitive times, such a bauble may have aroused the greed and duplicity that has characterized the diamond's history.

Although the diamond was not the earliest gem known to man, it played a part in history very early on. Some legends place it in mythology. One of the earliest writings in which a diamond is mentioned is the Arthasastra, a scholarly treatise dealing with politics, war, punishment and taxes. It is attributed to Emperor Chandragupta Maurya's chancellor, who expelled the garrisons of Alexander the Great from Northwest India in the third century BC.

These writings would likely be inscribed on palm leaves sewn together, then folded accordion-like and kept in woven baskets. They contained some of the first descriptions of diamonds, and told of how they were found, in the area around the modern-day city of Benares on the Ganges River.

> The deposits are in mines, rivers, and various other...sources. The color of diamond is like to that of a cat's eye, that of a sirisa bloom, that of the urine or gall of a cow, like that of alum or alike the color of other precious gems. The diamond which is great, heavy, hard and resists heat, which is regularly formed and which is capable of making scratches on plates and dishes, which reflects light and sparkles, is the best.
>
> Those from which the corners are broken, which are irregularly formed and which are on one side curved, have less value.

The section of the Arthasastra dealing with taxes and the administration of justice also gives an indication of the high value placed on diamonds by early Indians. Even the mining of diamonds was taxed. Justice was swift for anyone caught stealing a diamond; they were fined eight times the value of the stolen gem and sentenced to death.

It is remarkable that such high value was placed on uncut stones. Yet, from the ancient text, it's obvious that the diamond's hardness was an attribute early discovered and highly valued. It was in evidence in early India as a cutting tool long before this use became known in Europe. In fact, cave inscriptions of the ancient Dravidians suggest diamond-pointed tools, while northern Europeans were still wandering the primeval forests clad in furs. There is even evidence that the early Chinese knew them, but only as tools for engraving jade.

Babylonian traders, who had reached India by the sixth century BC, may have become intrigued by some of these rare, sparkling trinkets. Indians had begun to enhance the natural form with polishing. As polished gemstones they would have been worthy of the legendary diamond throne offered to Alexander the Great by the Ethiopians.

* * *

While some experts believe gems were worn originally as adornment, the diamond was not valued in India for that reason, or for its hardness and beauty. It was attributed a mystical allure that has remained with it to this day.

It seems only natural that Hinduism, one of the oldest religions, originating in India like the diamond, should incorporate this gem into its philosophy. Indeed, one of the Sanskrit words for diamond, *Indrajudha*, means Indra's weapon. Indra is the Hindu warrior and thunder god. The more commonly used words, *vajra* and *acira*, meaning thunderbolt and fire or sun respectively, are all references to the brilliant flashes thrown off by this stone. Nevertheless, Venus, rather than the sun or the moon, was the planet to which the Hindus dedicated the diamond, probably because it was the brightest celestial body.

The Buddhabhatta, an ancient Hindu treatise on gems, relates the colors and powers of the diamond to the four Hindu castes. The *Brahmin*, or highest class diamond:

> ...should have the whiteness of a shell or of rock crystal...give power, friends, riches and good luck; the *Kashatrya* [should have] the brown color of the eye of a hare...prevent the approach of old age; the *Vaishya*...the lovely shade of a petal of the dadali flower...[and] bring success; the *Shudra*...the sheen of a polished blade...[and bring] all manner of good fortune."

However, the *Buddhabhatta* also says that "[A] diamond...the color of blood or spotted with red, would quickly bring death to the wearer, even if he were the Master of Death." To the Hindus a flawed diamond was unlucky enough to prevent even Indra from reaching his supreme heaven. If a diamond was pure red or yellow, it could only be worn by a king.

Even the natural shapes of diamonds were cause for speculation about its powers. Triangular diamonds were said to cause quarrels; a square stone induced terror; and death was said to be caused by a five-cornered gem. Only the six-cornered diamond was thought to bring good luck. It can only be guessed how many diamonds, which could've been turned into the most radiant of gems, were discarded or destroyed because of these beliefs.

Hinduism also encouraged offerings to images or shrines of the gods to obtain good fortune. The text of the *Haiti Smriti* instructs, "[I]f he worships with a diamond, even the impossible, or Nirvana, that is eternal life in the highest heaven, will be secured." Of the sixteen offerings recognized in Hindu ceremonial worship, it is the ninth that assures good fortune to the donor. It consists of gems and jewelry, and specifically includes the diamond.

However, the religious power of the gift is limited. The sacred character of the diamond wears off after twelve years. When the gifts are no longer worthy of religious use, they are sold to defray the running costs of the temple, and as income for the priests and their attendants.

Hindu shrines, particularly the eyes of idols, were often adorned with precious gems. Early Western travelers to India were fascinated by these jewel-encrusted statues, and carried fantastic stories to the West. Some were even turned into successful novels, like Wilkie Collins' *The Moonstone*.

A sixteenth century visitor to India, one Ralph Fitch, describes images of what was probably the black goddess Kali, the terrifying consort of Shiva, as garlanded with a necklace of skulls, "...their mouths monstrous, their eyes gilded and full of jewels, their teeth and eyes of gold, silver and glass."

The idol of the Hindu god Krishna in the great temple at Jagannath, was described by a famous seventeenth century gem merchant named Jean-Baptiste Tavernier. It had, "...two diamonds for his eyes and a pendant from his neck which reaches to the waist...the smallest of these diamonds weighs about forty carats."

* * *

Buddhism, which shares many beliefs with Hinduism but does not retain its rituals, provides another symbolic representation of a diamond. A Chinese Buddhist pilgrim named Heuen Tsang visited India in the period 629-645 AD. He describes a wondrous diamond throne that:

> ...stood near the Tree of Knowledge, beneath whose spreading branches Gautama Buddha is said to have received his supreme revelation of truth. This throne had

been constructed in the age called the *Kalpa of the Sages*...and its foundations were at the center of all things; it measured one hundred feet in circumference, and was made of a single diamond. When the whole earth was convulsed by storm or earthquake this resplendent throne remained immovable. Upon it the thousand Buddhas of the Kalpa had reposed and had fallen into the 'Ecstasy of the diamond'. However, since the world has passed into the present and last age, sand and earth have completely covered the 'Diamond Throne', so that it can no longer be seen by human eye.

Buddhists also esteemed the diamond as a symbol of the purity of life against whose properties man should constantly measure himself. This aspect of the diamond's symbolism is made clear in a passage from the Buddhist poem, *The Questioning of King Melinda*:

O King, as the diamond is pure throughout, so, O King, should the sincere man of virtue, constant in right endeavor, be ever pure in his manner of living. This, O King, is the first quality of the diamond he ought to have. Again, O King, as the diamond cannot be alloyed with inferior substance, so, O King, should the sincere man of virtue, constant in right endeavor, never mix in friendship with wicked men. This, O King, is the second quality of the diamond he ought to have. Again, O King, as the diamond is only set about with the most costly jewels, so, O King, should the sincere man of virtue, constant in right endeavor, only associate with men of highest excellence. This, O King, is the third quality of the diamond he ought to have.

* * *

The symbolic mysticism that developed around the diamond in India traveled with it to the West and was adapted by different religions. Judaism was quick to incorporate the symbology of precious stones into its rituals. The Book of Exodus, Chapter 28, verses 17-21, describes the precious and semi-precious stones used in the

21

Jewish High Priest's breastplate, and their symbolism.

> "And thou shalt set in it settings of stones...four rows of stones: the first row shall be a sardius, a topaz, and a carbuncle: this shall be the first row.

> "And the second row shall be an emerald, a sapphire, and a diamond.

> "And the third row a ligure, an agate and an amethyst.

> "And the fourth row a beryl, and an onyx, and a jasper: they shall be set in gold in their enclosings.

> "And the stones shall be with the names of the children of Israel, twelve, according to their names, like the engravings of a signer; every one with his name shall they be according to the twelve tribes."

Arguments have persisted through the centuries as to whether the stone in the above passage was really a diamond. Each would have had to measure about 2" by 2.5," a size more than half that of the largest known diamond, the "Cullinan." It weighed 3106 carats in the rough. Even the Jewish historian Josephus, writing in the first century AD, admits, "...they were an ornament not to be purchased by men because of their immense value."

Isidore Kozminsky who describes the "magical Shamir" provided a possible explanation. *Sjamier* is translated as "diamond" in ancient Hebrew. It "had the power of eating into the hardest substances at the will of its holder," and was supposedly the seventh of the ten marvels of Creation, given to man on the first Friday. Since it was forbidden to engrave the stones of the breastplate with metal, the Shamir was used. According to Kozminsky, Moses "...[traced] the tribal names with his forefinger on the Breastplate (and then) simply held the shamir over them...the letters were as by magic cut clearly into the stones without trace of fracture or flaw."

Some experts claim that in those times it would have been

impossible to engrave a diamond. However, the Bible also gives an indication that the art of diamond engraving came with the gem to the West. The Book of Jeremiah, Chapter 17, verse 1, says: "The sin of Judah is written with a pen of iron, and with the point of a diamond is it graven upon the table of their heart, and upon the horns of your altars."

In any case, Jewish scripture informs us that there were actually two breastplates. The first, described in the Book of Exodus and known as the Breastplate of Aaron, dates back to the Babylonian Captivity. The second, or Breastplate of the Second Temple, was constructed after the Captivity. The semi-precious and precious stones attributed to each of these breastplates varies.

However, it was only in the Authorized Version of the Scriptures (1611 AD) and in Luther's German version of the Bible that the Hebrew word, *yahalom*, denoting the sixth gem, came to be translated as "diamond." Before that time it was considered to mean green jasper, jade or onyx.

Even this holiest of diamonds had its negative aspects. Around the beginning of the fifth century AD, St. Epiphanius, Bishop of Constantia, described the diamond called "Declaration," worn on the breastplate of the High Priest at the feasts of Pascha, Pentecost and Tabernacles. The diamond was said to indicate to the Jews what fate God had decreed for them by its color or brightness. If they had erred in their worship and ways, the stone became murky, predicting pestilence and death. If it became blood red, they would die by the sword. However, if the stone shone bright and clear, the people of Israel knew they were free from sin and could celebrate the festival.

* * *

Christianity did not hesitate to adapt Judaic and pagan myths relating to the diamond, assigning its own religious meaning. Glorious sacrifice, as in the blood of Christ's crucifixion, was associated with the ruby; the emerald denoted the peace and happiness given by God; and fidelity to Christ and God were inherent in the diamond. The diamond also took its place in the center of the seven gems on a Catholic Bishop's crosier, his pectoral cross, candelabra and altar stones.

As with many religions, Christians used gems to decorate religious shrines and statues. One such statue was of the Blessed Virgin in the sanctuary of the church of Santa Casa in Loreto, Italy. The Infanta Isabel of Flanders gave a rich vestment for this statue, described by a seventeenth century English traveler as "...set thick with six rows of diamonds downe before, to the number of three thousand." Is this so different from the adornment of Hindu idols?

Or does the description of the city of Devaraka, home of the divine Krishna, differ so from the New Jerusalem described in the Book of Revelations? The Hindu Paranas describe Devaraka:

> It measured a hundred yojonas, and over all, was decked in pearls, rubies, diamonds, and other gems. The city was high, it was ornamented with gems: and it was furnished with cupolas of rubies and diamonds, with emerald pillars, and with courtyards of rubies. It contained endless temples. It had crossroads decked with sapphires, and highways blazing with gems. It blazed like the meridian sun in summer.

Revelations, Chapter 21, verses 17 through 21, gives a comparable description of the New Jerusalem:

> And he measured the wall thereof, a hundred and forty and four cubits, according to the measure of a man, that is of an angel.

> And the building of the wall of it was of jasper; and the city was pure gold, like unto clear glass.

> And the foundations of the wall of the city were garnished with all manner of precious stones. The first foundation was jasper; the second, sapphire; the third, a chalcedony; the fourth, an emerald;

> The fifth, sardonyx; the sixth, sardius; the seventh, chrysolite; the eighth, beryl; the ninth, a topaz; the tenth, a chrysoprasus; the eleventh, a jacinth; the twelfth, an amethyst.

And the twelve gates were twelve pearls: every several
gate was of one pearl: and the street of the city was pure
gold, as it were transparent glass.

A legend, which Christians may have adapted from the ancient
Persians, relates how diamonds and precious stones originated, and
became associated with original sin. The story goes that God created
only useful things in the Garden of Eden. But Satan took note of
Eve's passion for all the bright and beautiful flowers that abounded
there. Ever seeking ways to entice man to evil, he decided to imitate
their color and brightness.

Taking up great handfuls of earth, he molded them until he had
reproduced each of these colors in a precious stone. As a culmina-
tion of all things beautiful and enticing, he combined them in one
masterwork—the diamond. Although Eve resisted these temptations,
the brilliant gem so strongly appealed to man's avarice that it filled
the Earth with corruption and sorrow.

* * *

It is perhaps not surprising that astrology, a form of divination
developed by the ancient Chaldians and Assyrians, prescribes wearing stones assigned to one's zodiac sign to strengthen their influence
over human fortunes.

An analogy can also be made to the Judo-Christian custom of
dedicating stones to the guardian angles. Kunz tells us that "...the
color and appearance of the stone was not merely emblematic of the
angel, but, by its sympathetic quality...was supposed to attract his
influence to provide a medium for the transmission of his beneficent
force to the wearer."

However, astrology has no place for the diamond on its list of
zodiacal gems. This may be explained by the non-existence of diamonds as a gemstone at the time astrology was formulated, or, in
later times, by a lack of brilliance in its natural form.

The diamond figures in astrology, nevertheless. It is one of the
planetary stones assigned to Mars, along with the ruby and jacinth.
Both Saturn and the Sun dominate it, in astrological terms. From this
comes the association of the diamond with Sunday. Ancient
astrologers believed it had strong powers when worn by anyone born

under an ascendant aspect of the planet Mars. It was said to bestow "...fortitude, strength of mind, and constancy in wedded love; it repelled sorcery, poison, and nightmares, calmed anger, and strengthened friendship, (and was) often referred to as the Stone of Reconciliation."

These beliefs continued to grow throughout the Middle Ages. They were but a page in the history of this stone's formidable legacy.

Legend and Lore

Before the diamond came to be valued for beauty, it was most prized for mystical powers connected with its reputation for hardness and fire resistance. The word "diamond" derives from an ancient Greek word meaning unconquerable or untamable. It came about due to the belief that neither fire nor blows could subdue this indomitable substance. (Our modern word, *Madame*, derives from the same base.)

Its power was attributed to this hardness which was, in turn, associated with manliness. For this reason men, exclusively, wore diamonds as amulets until the beginning of the fourteenth century.

The diamond's qualities were also interpreted in another manner, as protection. At the writing of the *Buddhabhatta* anyone wearing a diamond was protected from snakes, fire, poison, sickness, thievery, water and enchantment. These powers were supposedly weakened or destroyed should the diamond be polished. However, it is known that diamonds were occasionally polished anyway, ground or shaped by Indian lapidaries.

Although of Indian origin, diamonds found their way via Ethiopia to Rome where they were set unpolished in fine steel or intricately woven gold-wire settings as a charm against insanity. They were relatively small—less than ten carats—because all larger diamonds were reserved for the Indian princes in whose domains they were found.

But it was not until the time of Pliny the Elder (AD 23-79) that the first pseudo-scientific account of the diamond's sources and properties was attempted in the West. In his thirty-seven volume *Natural History*, a compendium of mostly second-hand information, Pliny reports that, "[T]he most valuable thing on earth is the diamond. There are six sorts known and those of India and Arabia are of such an unspeakable hardness that when one places it on an anvil, and strikes it with a hammer, it strikes back with such power that the hammer and anvil are shattered into small pieces."

The belief in the diamond's indestructibility was held as late as 1476, when Swiss soldiers looting the tent of Charles the Bold found a cache. To determine whether they were genuine, the soldiers struck the diamonds with hammers, which destroyed them. For it is now known that although diamond is the hardest natural substance known to man, it's brittle enough to shatter or cleave when struck.

Pliny may have had intimations of this for he goes on to tell us that, "[T]he superiority (of diamond) over iron and fire can be surmounted when it is soaked in fresh, warm, goat's blood. Only then, when the hammer is handled with great power, will the diamond be broken up into nearly invisible splinters."

Pliny also stated that diamonds were always found with gold, a belief that may have come from the teachings of Plato. Louis Dieulafait writes that Plato "...described the diamond, which he distinguished from other precious stones, as being a kind of kernel formed in gold; and supposed that it was the noblest and purest part of the metal that had condensed into a transparent mass." This may sound like nothing more than fanciful thinking. Nevertheless, it is a fact that Brazilian, South African and Australian diamonds are found near sizeable gold deposits.

Pliny also relates a legend that may have originated with the Greeks in the fourth century BC. The story is often attributed to Alexander the Great. Pliny claimed that diamonds were found only in the East in a deep valley protected by seething masses of venomous serpents. The only way the natives could safely retrieve these diamonds was to throw pieces of carrion flesh, to which the diamonds adhered.

Mountain eagles then swooped onto the bait, carrying it and the diamonds to their aeries in the heights above. When the eagles completed their feast, the diamond gatherers would climb to the nests. There was no reason to fear the now-engorged eagles and they collected the diamonds from their droppings. Strangely enough, one element in Pliny's story is true. Diamonds do adhere to greased surfaces. It's a technique that is still used to extract them from the surrounding elements.

Versions of this story have been repeated throughout the centuries, first as one of Sinbad's adventures in *The Thousand and One Nights*, and later as part of Marco Polo's chronicles of his trip to China. It may have been invented to serve a practical as well as entertaining purpose, in the way fables were used to teach lessons. In those credulous times many a potential plunderer may have been deterred by such a story.

In supposedly more advanced times the same beliefs, and some even more incredible, held sway. A book appeared in fourteenth century England entitled *The Voiage and Travail of Sir John Mandeville*, in which Sir John states that a diamond would break into a sweat and become damp when near poison. He further states that the diamond, because of its supposed power over other stones and elements, could destroy magnetism.

This was believed until the time of Elizabeth I, when her physician, William Gilbert, finally laid it to rest. Even Leonardo da Vinci claimed that the diamond cured lunacy and nightmares, defended against sorcery and possession by devils, dispersed fear and quelled quarrels. He reiterated the claim that it made its wearer bold, courageous and invincible in battle.

Geronimo Cardano, an Italian mathematician and physician, took this last claim with a grain of salt. In 1585 he wrote, "It indeed renders fearless, but there is nothing that contributes more to our safety than prudence and fear; therefore it is better to fear."

The invincibility of the diamond wearer was widely believed in Europe during the Middle Ages, much to the sorrow of many brave men. Kings, princes, lords and knights wore diamonds, if they could afford them, mounted in the hilts of daggers and swords, or on their armor. If they dreamt about diamonds before a battle, so much the better, for they were sure to be victorious.

Because of these beliefs many valuable gems were lost on the battlefield or pillaged following a battle. But only gems received as gifts had this virtue; if the gem was purchased its talismanic power was lost. Losing a diamond was considered an omen, if, indeed, the mishap had not already occurred in the process of the loss.

One of the strangest beliefs held for centuries by ancient philosophers as well as those of the Middle Ages was that the diamond was alive and able to self-reproduce. Plato believed that gems "...were veritable living beings, produced by a sort of fermentation determined by the action of a vivifying spirit descending from the stars." Theophrastus elaborated further by claiming that precious stones were either male or female, an erroneous theory corroborated by Sir John Mandeville. "Diamonds are male and female," he said, "and they engender commonly and bring forth small children that multiply and grow all the year. I have oftentimes tried the experiment, that if a man keep them with a little of the rock, and wet them with Maydew often, they shall grow every year, and the small will grow large."

This idea survived as late as the sixteenth century when Francisci Ruei wrote about a noblewoman of the House of Luxembourg who had two diamonds that produced progeny. "The cause of this...would seem to be that the celestial energy in the parent stones...first changes the surrounding air into water, or some similar substance, and then condenses and hardens this into the diamond gem."

Some legends about diamonds can be traced to their religious or mystical origins. Such is that of the Magical Shamir that mystically carved the Jewish High Priest's breastplate. Ancient Jewish legend says that this magical diamond disappeared at Moses' death and did not reappear until the time of Solomon.

When Solomon decided the time was ripe to build a temple, his priests reminded him that it was unlawful to work the stones of the holy building with tools of iron, and that only the famed Shamir could be used.

The priests instructed him to force two demons, a male and a female, to appear before him and reveal the Shamir's hiding place. But the demons were unable to comply with Solomon's request. They begged him to release them and obtain the secret from the Prince of Demons, Ashmadai. In return for their release they told Solomon where Ashmadai could be found.

Ashmadai had made a well high in the mountains and sealed it with a great stone bearing his magical seal. Each evening, when he returned from Heaven to learn the earth's secrets, he would break the seal, drink from the well, reseal it and go his way.

Solomon released the demons, then sent his disciple, Benaiah, to the well with his own magical chain and ring, upon which were engraved the name of the Divine Being. Substituting drugged wine for the water without breaking the seal, Benaiah waited until the Prince of Demons drank from the well and fell into a deep sleep. Stealing forth from his hiding place, he bound Ashmadai with Solomon's chain. Ashmadai awoke and could not break the chain carrying God's name. He was brought before Solomon.

When asked to yield up the Shamir, Ashmadai replied that it was not in his possession and that Solomon must ask the Prince of the Sea and his servant, the moorfowl. Skeptical, Solomon asked what the moorfowl had to do with the Shamir.

"It uses it to split the barren mountain rocklands," Ashmadai replied, "in order that the seeds of the trees and plants which it drops into the crevices may mature and render these places beautiful and agreeable to the wants of man. Then it brings the Shamir back to the Prince of the Sea who trusts its oath."

With this information, Solomon sent out his men to locate the moorfowl's nest. The nest was discovered, full of the bird's chicks. This gave Solomon an idea. He instructed his men to cover the chicks with glass so that the moorfowl could see, but not reach, its young. The bird flew away and returned with the Shamir in its beak. It beat the stone on the glass causing it to break asunder. The king's men rushed from their hiding places and took the Shamir from the frightened bird, which then killed itself because it had broken its oath to the Prince of the Sea.

Solomon released Ashmadai, over whom he had proved his superiority, and proceeded with the building of the Temple.

* * *

Diamond stories have been many and varied throughout the ages and nearly all contain an element of unhappiness or grief. The origins of other legends are less clear than those found in ancient lore. Gnomes and elves have long been considered the guardians of mines and treasures of the earth. According to Kozminsky, "[I]t is said that these little fairies suffer much, and that when they grieve for those they have loved and lost, their tears change into diamonds, which remain as the jewel emblems of pure and unselfish grief."

Healing properties have long been attributed to gems based on their rarity and on the belief in their mystical influences. Although it has been conjectured that the therapeutic use of gems originated in India, the earliest evidence stems from ancient Egypt where it is known that gem powder was used in healing salves.

In fact, ancients held an almost universal belief in their curative properties. Their use was related to their color. Red stones were applied to halt hemorrhaging, yellow stones were applied against jaundice and liver disease, and green gems, such as jade, were applied against kidney disease.

Even the early Greeks, who contributed so much to medical science, believed in their curative powers. Theophrastus mentions this use of gems, around which a theory of Greek medicine known as *unami* had formed.

During the Middle Ages numerous "Lapidaries" appeared in which gems were claimed to effect wondrous cures. So many miraculous attributes were assigned to each stone that one could almost believe any precious stone could be used for the cure of all disease. Kunz tells of one seventeenth century prescription calling for a mixture of thirty-four ingredients, including jacinth, emerald, sapphire, topaz, garnet, pearl, ruby, white and red coral, and amber.

He goes on to state "It would indeed seem that a good dose of such a mixture should have provided a cure of all the ills that flesh is heir to by the simple and effective means of removing the unhappy patient to a better world." In any case, it is doubtful whether the patient would have survived the cost of the cure.

One of the most famous, or infamous, uses of gems in this manner took place in 1534. Pope Clement VII took gravely ill and was treated by his physicians with compounds concocted of various precious stones. When none of these remedies seemed to work he was finally administered a dose of powdered diamond. This treatment, too, was unavailing and he succumbed to disease, having ingested a reputed 40,000 ducats worth of these precious gems.

Another curious belief was that diamonds protected one from the plague. It was observed that peasants were the first attacked by the plague while the rich, who could afford to wear diamonds, were spared. That was seen as proof of its power. So strong was this belief that even Queen Elizabeth I of England wore a diamond on her bosom to guard against infection.

Queen Elizabeth I

Each gem was assigned a particular part of the body upon which it was believed it would exercise the greatest preventive powers over disease. The sapphire was prescribed for the ring finger, and the emerald for the index finger. Mandeville stated that, "[A] diamond should be worn on the left side of the body for it is of greater value there than on the right, for the strength of their growing is towards the North...the left side of the world, and the left part of a man is when he turns his face to the East." Anyone who understood this rhetoric, let alone believed it, probably needed protection.

Diamonds were also thought to be poisonous, at least under certain conditions. This belief was held not only in Europe but Burma, India and other eastern countries. The Hindus, however, believed this was true only of flawed diamonds; when pulverized, flawless diamonds were said to impart positive benefits such as strength, happiness, beauty and long life.

The cases of death attributed to diamond dust poisoning are numerous. The infamous *poudre de succession*, which Catherine de Medici supposedly tapped from a specially constructed ring into the drinks of those she wished to eliminate, was reputed to be powdered diamond, probably heavily laced with arsenic. Then there is the case of the Turkish Sultan Beyazid II (1447-1512) believed murdered by his son with a dose of pulverized diamond mixed into his food.

There is a simple tale that illustrates how seriously two of these commonly held fallacies about diamonds were taken. Benvenuto Cellini, the famed Renaissance artisan in gold, was convinced that he was being poisoned by diamond dust while imprisoned in Rome in 1538. He resigned himself to death. Then it dawned on him that he could test the hardness of the piece of grit in his food assumed to be a splinter of diamond. Only after he had succeeded in crushing the splinter between his knife blade and his stone did he regain the will to live.

By now we know the healing or poisonous effects assigned to precious stones are false. Most stones have elements which cannot be assimilated by the body and therefore pass through it. However, until modern medicine proved otherwise, our ancestors believed in all of the miraculous and deadly powers of gems.

Assigning a gem to a month as a birthstone has been traced back to Josephus and St. Jerome, at the beginning of the sixth century AD. Their writings allude to the stones used to carve the high priest's breastplate, the foundation stones of the New Jerusalem, and the twelve signs of the zodiac.

The wearing of gems as birthstones seems to have become commonplace only after the settling of the Jews in eighteenth century Poland. Marie Leczinska, the Polish queen of Louis XV may have popularized it, after she came to the court at Versailles. It was at this time that the diamond was substituted for the sapphire as a birthstone for April.

Much of the curious lore that surrounded the diamond in the Dark Ages was summed up in the *Lapadarium of Marbodus, Bishop of Rennes*, who probably composed this poem sometime between 1067 and 1081 while serving as master of the Cathedral School of Anjou.

> Foremost of all amongst the glittering race
> Far India is the Diamond's native place;
> Produced and found within the crystal mines,
> Its native source in its pure luster shines:

Yet though it flashes with the brilliant's rays
A steely tint the crystal still displays.
Hardness invincible which nought can tame.
Untouched by steel, unconquered by the flame;
But steeped in the blood of goats it yields at length,
Yet tries the anvil's and smiter's strength.
With these keen splinters armed, the artist's skill
Subdues all gems and graves them at his will.
Largest at best as the small kernal shut
Within th' inclosure of the hazel nut.
Another stone the swart Arabian find,
Broke without blood, of less obdurate kind:
Of duller luster and of lower price,
In weight and bulk it yet the first outvies.
A third gives Cyprus, girdled by the main;
The fourth Philippi's iron mines contain:
Yet all alike the obedient iron sway
As does the magnet, if this gem's away;
For in the presence of this sovereign stone
Robbed of its force an idle mass 'tis thrown.
In magic rites employed, a potent charm,
With force invincible it nerves the arm:
Its power will chase far from thy sleeping head
The dream illusive and the goblin dread;
Baffle the venom'd draught, fierce quarrels heal,
Madness appease and stay thy foeman's steel.
Its fitting setting, so have sages told,
Is the pale silver or the glowing gold;
And let the jewel in the bracelet blaze
Which round the left arm clasped attracts the gaze.

If the beliefs in which our ancestors put so much faith had been true, today's world would be filled to overflowing with glittering, omnipotent diamonds, manipulating all mankind with their powers of good and evil.

Lost and Found

*G*ems of all kinds, diamonds among them, were highly prized by the Romans, but few found their way past the opulent courts of the Middle East. The scarcity of gems during the early Roman Republic was such that the wearing of precious stones was restricted to official purposes.

This changed early in the first century BC with the expansion of Rome into Asia Minor. Following Pompey's final defeat of Mithradates VI, vast quantities of gems were brought back to Rome. Soon everyone, plebeian and patrician, wore them.

By this time gem wearing had become so extravagant that successive emperors were forced to restrict excess by law. But the legislation was honored more in the breach than the observance. Pliny described one lady attending a simple betrothal ceremony as covered with pearls and emeralds from head to toe.

Semi-precious and precious gems and pearls were mounted in the finest gold, in female hair ornaments, necklaces, bracelets and, most of all, in rings. The imperial Romans seemed to have a passion for rings. One man, according to Martial, wore six on each finger. There were rings for summer and winter, for the days of the week, signet rings, amulet rings, zodiacal rings and even rings that released a lethal poison when bitten, as Hannibal is reputed to have done.

Nearly all gems worn in rings were engraved, either intaglio or cameo. They were used by their wearers to seal documents or as personal expression, similar to the coats-of-arms of later times.

Engraved gems were passionately collected by wealthy Romans. Marc Antony exiled the senator Nonius for refusing to give up one such coveted gem. Even Julius Caesar was an ardent collector, depositing up to six collections in the temple of Venus Genetrix.

But this passion for engraved stones limited the types of gems to softer stones, such as carnelian, amethyst, sardonyx, chalcedony and red jasper. The diamond was undoubtedly set in rings in its natural form, described by Pliny as that of "...two whipping tops united at their broadest ends." But it was valued more for its mystical and symbolic powers than as adornment.

The diamonds' shape and luster was still not revealed, although some may have been slightly polished. Early polishing was first discovered by Indian lapidaries as a means of disguising surface blemishes. The dust of flawed diamonds was mixed with oil and the mixture applied to the blemish by means of a rotating leather wheel. Sometimes the top and bottom of the natural crystal was ground away, creating the first facets.

It is interesting to note that even though the use of diamond dust for grinding and polishing other stones was known to the Romans, Pliny persisted in his belief that the diamond was unbreakable.

* * *

The term "Dark Ages," the early Middle Ages up to the tenth century, characterized by ignorance and lack of progress, perfectly describes the knowledge of the diamond during that time. Gemstones were barely used in jewelry following the disintegration of the Roman Empire and subsequent disruption of trade with the East.

Although the northern Goths and Anglo-Saxons developed their own distinctive jewels, they consisted principally of gold work or cloisonné. This was a process whereby metal filaments were attached to a metal surface to form a design. The open spaces between the filaments were filled with colored enamel and heat-fused. But the use of diamonds was unheard of.

The nearer these civilizations were to the center of the former Roman Empire and Middle Eastern trade sources, the more abundant their gemstones. A spectacular treasure trove of this time was the "Treasure of Guarrazar" near Toledo, Spain. It included eleven pure gold crowns dating from the seventh century, adorned with Oriental pearls, emeralds and sapphires set *en cabochon*.

These crowns may have been votive offerings, to be hung above a church's altar, since nearly all jewelry of this period was of an ecclesiastical nature. It was only in the north of Europe and British Isles that jewelry continued to be used for personal ornamentation.

The influence of the Byzantine court at Constantinople kept alive many arts of jewelry design known to the Romans. Even these were strongly influenced by Oriental styles. Only in Rome and the Middle East were precious stones and pearls still used copiously in jewels.

Gems were used for personal adornment in the Middle East and India during the Middle Ages. As early as the first century AD the Greek historian, philosopher and geographer, Strabo, tells of the Indians' great love for jewelry. It was undoubtedly simpler for Indians to satisfy their desire for gems than for Europeans, due to the abundance of semi-precious and precious stones available in India, Burma, Thailand and Ceylon.

Jewelry's cool metals and stones must have refreshed the body in the Indian subcontinent. It was worn in place of clothing, particularly by women. Crowns, hairpieces, breastplates, multi-stringed necklaces with a thick chain to separate the breasts covered the head and torso.

There were bangles and arm cuffs, all of finely worked gold, bronze or fiance, set with carved or enameled stones and gems. The lower body was covered by a *cache-sex*, a stringed girdle of gold chains and beads of agate, carnelian, jade and lapis lazuli, which served much the same purpose as a loincloth.

From this girdle chains ran along the thighs and legs to silver foot bangles, anklets and gem-studded toe rings. Often the only cloth that complemented this intricate ornamentation was a fine muslin veil or a downy-soft Kashmiri scarf.

The outfit was ornamented by a symbolic jewel. One such piece was the Hindu *naoratna,* the "nine-gem jewel" referred to in the *rat-*

nacastras, or treatises on gems. This jewel consisted of diamond, ruby, pearl, coral, jacinth, sapphire, topaz, cat's-eye and emerald, each of which corresponded to various heavenly bodies. It "was designed to combine all their powerful astrological influences."

Magnificent gold and bronze armlets and bracelets with stone and cloisonné inlay were known in ancient Persia, as were pendants, fibulae, torques and earrings. Ancient Archaemenid jewelers made extensive use of precious stones.

The seventh century Persian king, Khosrau II, is reputed to have had a crown of pure gold covered with pearls the size of sparrow's eggs. It was set with grenadine rubies that lit his palace on dark nights, and emeralds capable of blinding vipers. It hung from the ceiling on a gold chain seventy cubits long, which allowed it to touch the king's head without weighing him down.

The onset of Islam in the seventh and eighth centuries modified the design and use of jewelry. Golden earrings, pendants, necklaces and rings encrusted with semi-precious and precious stones still played a secondary role to gold and enamel.

The rest of the gems in Europe were in the hands of the nobility or, more often, the clergy. Nobility wore them for adornment while the clergy incorporated them into ecclesiastic garb.

* * *

Lord Twining states that "[T]he English coronation... regalia...has a longer and more continuous history than that of any other country in Europe." Nevertheless, surprisingly little is known about the gems contained in the earliest crown jewels. Certainly the diamond-bedecked royal regalia we associate with the English Crown was not nearly so ornate during the early Middle Ages.

By the time of King Edwy, who reigned for only two years (955-957), we know that the royal crown was "... wrought with gold, silver and precious stones." But whether any of those gems were diamonds is unclear. In a Latin verse composed following William the Conqueror's coronation on Christmas day, 1066, the identities of twelve precious and semi-precious stones in his crown correspond to those on the Jewish High Priest's breastplate. But no diamond is mentioned.

Much the same is true of the French crown jewels in this period. Twining describes a golden scepter ascribed to Dagobert (crowned 628).

> On the summit was a golden eagle on which was sitting a youth, said by some to be Ganymede. The eagle's wings were set with four emeralds and a garnet surrounded by eight pearls. The eagle was based on a globe held by a hand with a little branch garnished with pearls, enamels and coral. Below the hand was a golden rod also enameled and set with stones.

However, Twining doubts whether any part of the scepter dated back as far as Dagobert. Once again, no specific mention is made of diamonds.

It was during this period that the right of the Church to crown the king was accepted both in France and England. To reinforce this right and deny any usurper crowned outside the Church, the ecclesiastic authorities claimed custody of the royal coronation ornaments.

In England, the monks of Westminster Abbey guarded these symbols of sovereignty. In France the royal regalia was housed in the Abbey of St. Denis. This way the coronation regalia acquired a religious importance.

It also made it almost impossible for the regalia to be used on other occasions. So it was commonplace for monarchs to commission a second set of royal ornaments, including personal crowns, for their secular use.

But why was the diamond so little used during this period? At the time diamonds came from alluvial deposits in India and only a small proportion were of gem quality. Furthermore, international trade came to a near standstill following the break-up of the Roman Empire.

Warfare between princes ravaged much of the continent. Pestilence and roving bands of brigands inhibited trade contacts. Few gems could complete the immense journey from India to the courts of Europe unhindered; and those that did were normally not diamonds. Why should a nobleman expend his limited funds on a rough diamond not only smaller than other gems, but lacking their color and luster as well? Why not own an emerald, sapphire or balas ruby rather than a diamond?

For these reasons rulers in Europe, India and the Middle East came to value other gems above the diamond. Rubies, emeralds and pearls were universally held in higher esteem. The Persians even placed more value on chrysolite—modern peridot—a crystallized iron-magnesium silicate. In India the ruby, not the diamond, was known as the "Lord of the Stones." As long as the diamond's true beauty and fire lay undiscovered, it was considered inferior to other gems.

* * *

It wasn't until nearly the end of the Middle Ages that diamonds came into their own as the world's premier gemstone. Although the Indians had been polishing them for centuries, diamonds were still greasy and without luster, valued more for their rarity and mystical powers than any intrinsic beauty. The hardest of gems, it was a rare brilliant flash from a polished surface that hinted at the fire within.

By the eleventh century, with the resurgence of cities and more stable governments in Europe, trade was beginning to revive. The growth of the gem trade was accelerated by the establishment in the Levant of vast commercial empires following the Crusades. They included Genoa, Pisa, Naples and Venice. These city-states overflowed with oriental luxury goods, formerly obtainable in minute quantities, and only by the wealthiest potentates and clergy. Silks, spices and precious stones were exchanged for the products of Europe, primarily textiles. Easier access to the East combined with the increased wealth of European nobility gave rise to readily available precious stones. They were more affordable, and saw an increased secular use.

Even so, the price of diamonds, and most other gems, reached such heights that a law was passed in England in 1283 that permitted only those of noble birth to wear jewels. This may appear to have been an attempt to reserve rare and precious articles for the nobility, but it was really to stop the export of funds from the country, since all jewels were imported.

By 1363 Edward III of England had taken this law one step further, by forbidding even knights to wear precious gems. The climax was in 1380 when Juan I of Spain restricted the wearing of jewels to royalty.

Perhaps it was Edward, Prince of Wales' fondness for gems, and the extremes he employed to purchase them, that prompted his father to promulgate this law. In 1356, following the battle of Poitiers, a crown belonging to King John II of France came into Edward's possession. Consisting of gold, diamonds, sapphires, rubies and great pearls, it was pawned, together with a gold star set with rubies, diamonds, sapphires and pearls for £2000, a princely sum then.

A royal crown containing diamonds was used at the coronation of Charles V of France in 1364. Prior to that, only emeralds, rubies and other precious stones had been used in such a piece of regalia. By the end of the fourteenth century Anne of Bohemia, consort of Richard II of England, was purchasing "...three rings each with one great diamond placed in the middle...costing £66 from one John Palying, a London goldsmith."

Some experts claim that women of noble blood were beginning to wear diamonds by the beginning of the fourteenth century, and theorize that these were worn primarily for ornamental purposes. It is safe to assume that no beauty of those days, any more than of later times, would wish to dull her charms by wearing the crude, lackluster diamonds then available. Something must have been making them more attractive. This theory, as well as one of the first tales of a diamond's disastrous effect on its possessor, is demonstrated by the story of Agnes Sorel and Jacques Couer.

* * *

The beginning of the fifteenth century saw the appearance of a Frenchman of uncommon commercial talent, one who was somewhat responsible for bringing the Hundred Years War to an end. He was introducing gems in large quantities to France. His name was Jacques Couer.

A merchant of immense ability, he grew up at Bourges where Charles, the French Dauphin driven from Paris by the English and their Burgundian allies, had established his court in exile. Couer

glimpsed the potential of the international luxury trade while working in his father's fur business. It was based on imports from Russia.
In 1432, armed with bold effrontery and modest capital, he set off
on a journey that was to begin one of the greatest trade empires of
its time.

Traveling to Narbonne on the Mediterranean coast, he boarded a
galley bound for Egypt and the ports of the Levant. There he noted
the smooth functioning and richness of the trade with the East,
almost entirely in the hands of the great Italian trading empires.

Despite the Italian's skill, he found a gap in their system. In their
years of growth, the Italians had neglected to capitalize on Cairo,
another potential center for the Eastern trade. Couer analyzed the
commerce in exotic goods—sugar, cotton, gems, silks and spices—
which flowed through this entrepot. He then made another discovery
of even greater importance: while there was gold in abundance in the
East, silver was in short supply. This offered some bold entrepreneur
the opportunity to export silver and buy gold, to be resold at home at
an unprecedented profit.

He returned to France and set to work immediately, establishing
a trading company and wool manufacturing enterprise in the South,
near Bourges. The produce was then sold to the Venetians who unwit-
tingly supplied the capital for their own competition. Couer used it to
finance his imports from Egypt. In a short time he had established a
flourishing trade with the East.

But Couer had not forgotten about the market for silver in the
East. To capitalize on this he acquired the rights to several abandoned silver mines dating back to Roman times. He was soon carrying on a lucrative trade in this precious commodity.

It is also possible that the mines were a ruse. He may have simply bought silver coins, whose export to the infidel East was forbidden by the Pope, melted them down and passed them off as produce
fom his mines. Whether or not this was the case, the trade provided
him with a vast income that he used to surround himself with the
sumptuous trappings of a merchant prince.

Couer's activities coincided with the truce in 1435 between
Charles, now King Charles VII, and his Burgundian opponents.
Couer's agents followed the King—who was now pacifying his limited

domains—setting up commercial activities in the towns brought under Charles' firm control. Couer also came into the King's good graces by lending him funds to cover the cost of the marriage of his son, the Dauphin Louis, to Marguerite of Scotland. This was the step which established him as financier to the King, a position he would be called to fill many times in the coming years.

Charles continued working to reclaim his kingdom. He needed money. In April of 1436, Charles' armies, partially financed by Couer, liberated Paris from the English and Couer was named master of the national mint. As further reward for his achievements, Charles named him *argentier du roi* (steward of the royal expenditure, and banker to the court) in 1439.

In 1441 he granted letters of nobility for "...him, his wife, their children, and all their posterity for the future," as well as making him commissioner to the estates of Languedoc. In 1442 Couer became a member of the King's council.

Even with these titles Couer continued to expand his personal trade empire, no doubt facilitated by his royal connections. He managed to obtain trade concessions for French merchants and the right to consular representation at the court of the Sultan of Egypt, as well as authorization from the Pope to trade with the infidel.

In 1449 he raised the enormous sum of 200,000 ecus—nearly a ton of gold—to finance the war efforts of Charles, which finally led to the recovery of Normandy. He had become so powerful that he was accorded a place of honor during the King's triumphal entry into Rouen.

It was perhaps natural that Couer, who had risen so rapidly and far from such humble origins, made enemies at Charles' court. Many of the highest officials were in his debt. This hostility reached its peak in 1451 when he was charged with speculation, extortion and, cruelest of all, having poisoned the King's mistress.

How had Couer come to such a state? It had to do with the mistress, Agnes Sorel, born in 1409 in the province of Touraine, who came to Charles' court while in her teens. Following Charles' defeat at the battle of Verneuil she became a maid of honor in the retinue of Marie of Anjou, Charles' wife.

A contemporary described her as follows: "Her forehead was high and open, her eyes blue and piercing, surmounted by long eyelashes and languishing lids, her nose of perfect shape, and her mouth small. Her neck, shoulders and bosom were of perfect symmetry and snowy whiteness."

A sparkling wit and high intelligence matched her beauty. Sorel immediately attracted Charles. When he was finally in a position to do so, he lavished jewels, titles and estates on her to show his appreciation for the love and excellent advice she gave him, for Agnes had often served as the inspiration this feckless king needed to carry out his destiny.

In the early years of their courtship, when Charles could trust no one, Agnes served as go-between to Jacques Couer. Couer was the only man in France capable of supplying the luxuries that Charles showered on Agnes. He held a near monopoly on trade with the East and provided not only Charles and Agnes, but the whole French court, with the goods they desired to enhance their positions and satisfy their taste for luxury.

What goods they were! Exotic fruits and spices for their tables, incense, perfumes and coral rosaries for the clergy, and all the silks, furs and linens the women of the court desired. For the first time, seemingly endless quantities of fabulous gems—rubies for the armor and fittings of nobles and knights, and gems to enhance the beauty of the court's ladies. But most of all, there were diamonds.

Until this time a diamond had been the prerogative of kings and, in a few instances, queens. Now they graced the arms, hands and bodices of many noble ladies. Joan Dickenson says of Couer that he "...made Agnes Sorel his mannequin. Upon her lovely neck, he placed the first diamond necklace ever made; upon her bodice were pinned gold brooches set with diamonds; and the sash of her gown was held with a diamond belt buckle."

But the relationship between Agnes Sorel, the most famous beauty of her day, and Jacques Couer, France's first merchant prince, was an ill-fated one. The jealousy and enmity that had been stewing in Couer's debtors found an outlet following the death of Sorel. The actual cause was probably childbed fever following the birth of Charles' fourth bastard.

It was the same Charles who had done nothing to save Joan of Arc, that now stood idly by while Couer's accusers gathered forces like a pride of hungry lions, intent on devouring the man who had provided them and their king with funds during their times of need.

Imprisoned for nearly two years, thwarted on all sides, Couer was found guilty in May 1453 by a tribunal consisting primarily of his accusers. He was pardoned from capital punishment largely through the intercession of the Pope but he was sentenced to make restitution of 100,000 ecus and pay a fine of 300,000.

All of his goods were confiscated. Ignoring his plea that it would be impossible to fulfill the sentence if everything was taken from him, he was kept imprisoned until such time as the demands were met. Only through the efforts of Jean de Village, one of his lieutenants was Couer able to make a spectacular escape from under the noses of his enemies. Making his way to Rome, he was welcomed by his friend and protector, Pope Nicholas V.

Although Nicholas died shortly after Couer's arrival in Rome, his successor, Calixtus III, extended his predecessor's protection and patronage. He gave Couer command of a sixteen-galley fleet for an expedition against the Turks. On November 25th, 1456, while on this expedition, Couer died on the Aegean island of Chios. On his deathbed he drew up a final letter to Charles claiming innocence of the charges brought against him.

Over the years this story has been embellished into one of the first accounts in which diamonds, and in particular those which Couer procured for Agnes Sorel, were blamed for the misfortune and dishonor showered upon their possessors.

* * *

Not long after Couer's death another event contributed to the ominous history of the diamond. In 1477, Maximilian, Archduke of Austria, was so taken with his bride-to-be, Mary of Burgundy, that he presented her with the first known diamond engagement ring, establishing a tradition that has grown throughout the centuries. A point seldom remarked upon, is that Mary died within four months of her marriage!

Diamonds were becoming more common, although their brilliance was still largely concealed. Craftsmen who regularly worked precious stones may have gained a glimpse of diamond's hidden, iridescent beauty, but were seldom daring enough to try enhancing it. What jeweler, assuming he could lay his hands on the necessary materials, would be willing to risk his reputation, fortune and even his life to experiment with this wondrous stone?

Yet there must have been some. A Paris jeweler named Robert van Berquem, wrote in 1661 that his ancestor, Louis van Berquem invented diamond polishing in Flanders in 1476. This statement was accepted for over two hundred years, even though diamond polishing had been practiced for centuries in India. There was also evidence that diamonds were being polished in Europe before the time of Louis van Berquem.

An inventory of the goods of Louis of Anjou, made between 1360 and 1368, reports a number of polished diamonds. There are also indications that a diamond polishers' guild existed in Nuremberg in 1373, although some experts dispute this. In any case, data indicates that by the fifteenth century diamonds were regularly being polished in Flanders and Germany.

Four men, specifically called diamond polishers, appeared as expert witnesses in a court case at Bruges in 1465 concerning an amethyst supposedly sold as a balas ruby. This craft was certainly established in France by 1477 for Guillebert de Metz describes the La Courarie section of Paris as "where the diamond cutters live."

The uncertainty regarding the birth of European diamond polishing may have stemmed from the secretiveness of early guilds. Also this craft was coming into the hands of the Sephardic Jews who were being driven out of Spain to the Lowlands, carrying important trade contacts with the East. It was in their interests to maintain a wall of secrecy around their trade to deflect attention. By 1483 diamond polishers were clearly noted in the citizens' register and on ships' bills of lading in Antwerp where diamonds were shipped.

The diamond was now ready to make its grand debut as the king of gems.

A Place in the Sun

*T*he Renaissance, a period of unparalleled experimentation and discovery in the sciences and arts, marked the rebirth of the use of diamonds. Although not yet predominant, the diamond firmly established its place among competing gems. Diamonds became popular in the exhibitionistic displays of jewelry and wealth that characterized the rich and powerful.

Prior to the sixteenth century they were seen in Europe in three basic forms. The most common, known as *en point*, was the natural octahedron, with polished surfaces. Then there was the flattened "table-cut," and finally, a form known as *en cabochon* in which the base was flat and the upper surface rounded and polished in a convex shape, but not faceted.

These forms, although superior to the totally rough, unworked diamond, did not fully uncover the brilliance for which the diamond later became famous. Yet they were enough to increase the prestige of the gem and cause it to be viewed with new interest by both jewelers and Renaissance nobility alike.

Sometime during this period, no one knows exactly when or by whom, the processes of sawing and cleaving a diamond were developed. They added to diamond's luster by creating faceted surfaces through which light could be refracted and reflected. Sawing was done by means of a metal thread coated with diamond dust and oil. This probably originated in India. But it was the Europeans who improved upon the process by substituting a rotating, soft metal disk for the thread. Theoretically, a saw cut can be made in any direction through a diamond except along its cleavage plane.

Cleaving may also have been an invention of the early Indians, although no record of the process exists before 1604. Cleavage is made possible by diamond's crystalline structure, which allows it to split without shattering parallel to any of its eight natural octahedron surfaces. However, if the cleavage place is not precisely determined the first blow of the cleavage knife or wedge may render the most valuable gemstone into nothing more than a pile of minute fragments.

In the chronicles of the time one cannot help but notice the rather vague descriptions of diamonds' size. Such terms as "large as a walnut" or "big as a goose egg" were common. Vossius states that the largest diamond at the end of the sixteenth century was a 47 1/2-carat stone bought by Philip II in 1559. The exact weight of the stone is open to question since as many as ten different carat weights were used in Europe and three in the East. It was to be three centuries before the carat was internationally standardized at 200 milligrams.

Another point worth clarifying is that up to that time, the terms polishing and cutting were used almost interchangeably to indicate the process by which a surface of the diamond crystal was ground away, either to conceal a flaw or to give it symmetry (such as the table-cut).

* * *

Even with these technical advances the diamond's competition was strong. It merely accessorized enameled gold and other gems. In the middle of the sixteenth century Benvenuto Cellini claimed the diamond had one-eighth the value of a ruby. The emerald was also considered more valuable, while the amethyst was about equal to the diamond.

That fickle dame, fashion, also determined the relative value of gems. Elizabeth I is said to have purchased pearls by the bushel to adorn her person. Since she set the fashion, everyone else at her court wanted pearls, thus driving up their price.

However, there was an enormous increase in the use of diamonds and other jewelry in the rest of Europe during the Renaissance. This may be attributed to many factors. First, the famous diamond mines of the Indian Deccan were reaching the height of their production. The Indian monarchs were ready to exchange diamonds for Western goods. This meant that increasing quantities were reaching Europe and were becoming attainable.

The increased availability of these gems would not, by itself, have induced their purchase; they still had to be seen as an item of value and beauty. This was accomplished through the efforts of the skilled artists and artisans with whom European nobility began to surround itself.

Sometimes these were artists the like of da Vinci, Botticelli, Durer and Holbein who only created designs, leaving their execution to artisans like Jean Duvet, and Etienne Delaune of Paris. Many other designers, trained as goldsmiths, such as Cellini, della Robbia and Verrochio, created and executed their own designs.

The most popular form of jewelry in this period was the *enseigne*, a type of medallion to be worn on men's hats, and unisex pendants worn on the breast or as the central ornament among gold chains and necklaces. These pendants were set with diamonds, sapphires, rubies and seed pearls or, in the larger ones, finished with pear-shaped, dangling pearls. In Elizabethan England particularly, they were devised in curious, intricately worked natural forms. One such, noted in an inventory of Elizabeth I's jewels, was "A jeuel of golde, being a shippe, set with a table dyamonde, of fyve sparcks of dyamondes, and a small perle pendaunte."

Rings were also a favorite form of jewelry. An inventory of Henry VII's jewels made in 1530 lists no less than 234. They hadn't been that popular since Roman times. Pictorial records of the period show all fingers, thumbs included, laden with rings. And the diamond was highly prized. It took one peculiar form in which the lower half of a natural octahedron was encased in a high bezel, allowing the sharply pointed top to protrude.

Henry VII

The point of the diamond was employed in a practice in vogue at the time: writing on glass. Sir Walter Raleigh, while in the company of Queen Elizabeth, is reputed to have written on a window with his diamond ring, "Fain would I rise, but that I fear to fall." To this, Elizabeth inscribed the rejoinder, "If thy heart fail thee, do not rise at all."

In addition to rings, *enseignes* and pendants, aigrettes, hairpins and earrings were all commonly worn. One pin, the property of the German Princess Amalia Hedwig, contained five diamonds and five pendant pearls. Earrings came into wider use in the mid-1500s when hair fashions no longer covered the ears. Their inclusion as part of male adornment seems to have originated in Spain, spread to France, and reached its peak in Elizabethan England. Most of these earrings were quite simple, containing only a diamond, ruby or pearl.

Necklaces, neck chains and collars were also prominently worn throughout Europe. Portraits by German, Flemish and English painters contain abundant examples. These neck dressings, usually of heavy linked or twisted gold chain, were worn primarily by men at the beginning of the sixteenth century.

Jeweled collars had been reserved for women. This situation changed with Henry VIII's predilection for magnificent collars set with precious stones and pearls, the most famous of which was a massive gold collar containing fourteen balas rubies, fourteen diamonds and a great dangling carbuncle, as seen in Hans Holbein's famous portrait.

* * *

The great crowned houses of the time, particularly those in England and France, set the fashions in jewelry and crown jewel collections. Upon his accession to the English throne in 1485 Henry VII was faced with an empty treasury.

Twining states, "By careful administration he built up an exceptionally strong financial position...it is said that on his death there was £1,800,000 in the Treasury, an enormous sum for that time." Thus Henry VIII inherited a vast fortune. Enough to satisfy his penchant for rich jewels and finery.

Giustinian, the Venetian ambassador at the English court, describes Henry's personal adornment shortly after the beginning of his reign.

He ware a cap of crimson velvet…and the brim was looped up all round with lacets and gold enameled tags.…Very close round his neck he had a gold collar, from which there hung a rough-cut diamond, the size of the largest walnut I ever saw, and to this was suspended a most beautiful and very large round pearl. His mantle was of purple velvet lined with white satin.…This mantle was girt in front like a gown, with a thick gold cord, from which there hung large golden acorns like those suspended from a cardinal's hat; over this mantle was a very handsome gold collar, with a pendant of St. George entirely of diamonds. Beneath the mantle he wore a pouch of cloth of gold, which covered a dagger; and his fingers were one mass of jeweled rings.

During his lifetime Henry was able to maintain this ostentatious display of jewelry through gifts, legacies and forfeitures. But his greatest source of income came through the confiscation of Church property, following an act of Parliament that dissolved the monasteries. With one stroke of his pen he acquired nearly 300,000 ounces of plate and jewels, enough to finance his lavish tastes for years to come.

Henry's vanity and passion for gems drove him to acquire jewelry by other means. He commissioned jewels, most notably from Hans Holbein, the German painter resident at his court. These commissions stimulated the art of jewelry design. Holbein, however, was not a jeweler. Most of his designs were executed by his friend, Hans van der Goes, otherwise known as Hans of Antwerp.

Henry purchased jewels too, the most notable was the magnificent pendant, known as the "Three Brothers," which had belonged to Charles the Bold, last Duke of Burgundy. This fabulous jewel consisted of three great balas rubies, separated by three enormous pearls with a fourth hanging pendant from the bottommost ruby. In its center was a diamond five eighths of an inch square at the base, said to have been the first diamond cut by Louis van Berquem's new technique.

The legend accompanying this jewel again illustrates the diamond's mystical powers and misfortune. The Duke carried all his treasure with him on his campaigns. This included his diamond pendant. It failed him utterly for he was defeated at the Battle of

Granson in 1475. The pendant was found by a Swiss soldier in the Duke's tent and sold for a pittance to the Magistrates of Berne.

They in turn, sold it to Jacob Fugger, of the illustrious merchant family, where it remained for many years. In the 1540's Henry VII began negotiations with Fugger's son for its purchase and died shortly thereafter.

The riches of the English crown continued to grow under Mary Tudor, and extraordinarily so under Elizabeth I. The pearls she so loved once cost her 12,000 gold crowns for a case. A visitor to England in 1598 gives the following description of her attire: "The Queen had in her ears two pearls with very rich drops...upon her head she had a small crown; her bosom was uncovered, and she had on a necklace of exceedingly fine jewels. She was dressed in white silk, bordered with pearls the size of beans...over it a mantle of black silk shot with silver threads....Instead of a chain, she had an oblong collar of gold and jewels."

Her hands sparkled with gems. Among the many portraits of Elizabeth is one in London's National Portrait Gallery. Her dress is covered in pearls. She wears a pearl girdle and a carcanet, at the center of which is an enormous sapphire. Diamonds and rubies alternate with clusters of pearls. One cannot help but marvel at her ability to move about under such a rich burden.

Not all Tudor gems were used for personal ornamentation. Many found their way into the collections of state. Foremost among these was the Crown of State. One from an inventory of 1520-21: "...a circlet garnished with eight balas rubies, eight sapphires and five pointed diamonds, twenty rubies and nineteen pearls."

In the inventory of 1532 it was noted that some gems in this crown had been removed, exchanged, or altered. This documents the practice of removing stones from the state crowns when not in use. It was standard until the time of Queen Victoria.

The crown of Edward VI, Henry's short-lived successor, was one of the richest, containing nine great pointed diamonds and a table diamond, as well as pearls, rubies and an emerald. Scepters, swords, bracelets and the ampulla, all used during coronations, were decorated with royal gems.

* * *

The display of the Tudor court when compared with French monarchs of the House of Valois may be likened to the ostentation of the *nouveau riche*. They ruled France after the accession of Philip VI in 1328. Although the fortunes of the House of Valois fluctuated, by the sixteenth century the luxury and magnificence of the Court had been restored.

Following his coronation in 1498, Louis XII is recorded entering Paris, wearing a tunic of gold cloth embellished with precious stones and a helmet upon which was a gold crown adorned with gems. But it was his successor, Francis I, who established the greatest splendor ever seen at the French court.

Francis was particularly fond of diamonds. They seemed to be more readily available in France than England, probably due to Jacques Couer in the previous century.

Various inventories of Francis' reign contain what would now be priceless diamond jewelry. One such item was a collar Francis himself had worn many times, that he gave to his Queen for her state entry into Bordeaux. It consisted of eleven table and point-cut diamonds, set in bezels on festoons of friar's knots, each separated by gold cord ending in pearls. From this collar hung a great triangular diamond, known as the "Eye of Brittany," valued at 108,240 gold ecus.

Countless diamonds were included in Francis' purchases and gifts. Among them were a great table diamond purchased in 1532, valued at 65,000 ecus, and a drop diamond worth 15,000 ecus which he presented to Anne Bolyn upon dancing with her after his meeting with Henry VIII.

Francis was also the first king to establish, with a Letter of Patent, dated 1530, a treasure of crown jewels to be passed on to his successors. Jewels valued at 272,242 gold ecus, were selected from his personal property to become the inalienable property of the state. However, it was not long before he had second thoughts about this bequest. He ordered the councilors charged with their safekeeping to cease keeping records of them. As a result, some jewels reverted to his private collection.

Although Francis' immediate successors did not have his love for jewels, they nevertheless realized their value to the state. Both Henry II and his son, Francis II copied Francis I's letter of patent, designating certain jewels as state and Crown property. The jewels were periodically altered, reset, or loaned to mistresses reluctant to return them.

* * *

During the sixteenth century crown jewels were regularly used as security for loans to finance wars, purchase dowries and pay ransoms. The practice had existed before, but to a lesser degree.

Pope Calixtus III financed the fleet sent against the Turks in 1456 with all of his treasure. Another Pope, Clement VII, was forced to pledge one of the finest diamonds in his tiara to pay for the dowry of his niece, Catherine de Medici, to Henry II. Diamonds often figured prominently in such transactions because of their portability and value. Elizabeth I acquired the diamonds of the House of Burgundy as security for a loan that hadn't been redeemed.

The famous, 30-carat "Mirror of Portugal" scored its first deadly triumph when it was given to Queen Elizabeth by Dom Antonio, pretender to the Crown of Portugal. It was collateral for a loan meant to help him regain his throne. When Elizabeth's financial aid failed, she withheld the gem, claiming she had kept her end of the bargain. For his part, Dom Antonio not only lost his claim to the throne, but was sentenced in absentia to death, on the charge he had absconded with the crown jewels.

Queen Elizabeth had a penchant for acquiring diamonds in this manner. Henry of Navarre, later Henry IV of France, had given her the crown jewels of Navarre as security for a loan. When Henry's emissary came to redeem the diamonds for 60,000 crowns, Elizabeth claimed she had loaned 300,000. Since there seemed to be no proof of either claim, possession being nine tenths of the law, Elizabeth simply kept the diamonds.

The crown jewels so meticulously acquired by the House of Valois were broken up during the reign of the last Valois king, Henry III. His treasury was drained by the cost of religious civil wars that plagued his reign. Only the crown jewels, by now valued at 12,200,000 ecus, were available as security for loans. In 1569 he pledged a diamond-studded mantle clasp, a large table diamond with pearl pendant, another large diamond set in a pendant, and five great rubies to the Venetians for 382,000 ecus. Between then and his assassination in 1589 Henry pledged all the crown jewels, only a few of which were ever redeemed.

Perhaps one of the strangest tales of Henry's transactions using crown jewels concerned John Casimir, Count Palatine. He demanded 8,000,000 livres to remove his mercenary troops from the royal domains. In order to meet his demands Henry pledged the crown jewels.

Casimir proceeded to display them in glass cases throughout France. This was the first time that the treasures of a royal house, claimed as state property by French kings, could be viewed by the people who'd paid dearly for them through taxation.

* * *

The popularity of precious gems precipitated an increase in their value, which in turn was followed by attempts to falsify them. Some were successful, even with kings. Gold artisan Benvenuto Cellini tells of a Milanese jeweler who managed to pass off a counterfeit emerald to Henry VIII. He didn't discover the fraud until several years later.

The deceit, or art, of creating false precious stones existed as far back as ancient Egypt. Pliny noted that the Romans and Indians counterfeited gems with success. Albertus Magnus and St. Thomas Aquinas both cited examples of hyacinth, ruby, topaz and emerald being duplicated.

By the sixteenth century, duplicating precious stones had become commonplace. Diamonds were no exception. Geronimo Cardano, a physician and mathematician who should have known better, claimed that by boiling "a limpid sapphire of faint color" in melted gold, a true diamond could be obtained.

Apart from such fanciful claims, it is known that diamonds were duplicated by two methods. In one, colorless varieties of sapphire and topaz with a hardness, density and refractive power similar to the diamond were cut into diamond shapes.

The other, according to Cardano, used poor quality pieces of the real gem. They were placed on top of a piece of crystal and joined by a colorless glue. A gold setting concealed the joined section. Only gold was permitted in the settings of precious gems.

* * *

An event that epitomized this sumptuous age of extravagance

and exhibitionism was the meeting between Francis I of France and England's Henry VII on the so-called Field of Cloth of Gold. This meeting took place in 1520, not far from Calais. Each king and his retinue vied to outshine the other in pageantry and apparel.

Henry was dressed in a doublet covered with diamonds and rubies worth 100,000 ecus. He wore his celebrated collar, then valued at 400,000 ecus. Francis, in turn, was bedecked in his finest jewelry containing the famous diamonds of the French crown jewels.

H. Clifford Smith tells us that "...the English and French nobles entered into boundless extravagance in dress, and so loaded themselves with jewelry that, in the words of Du Bellay, 'they carried the price of woodland, water-mill, and pasture on their backs'."

Diamonds were being worn widely during the sixteenth century, but not yet as the chief gem. It took the technical advances of a new age. The seventeenth century brought the diamond to its full glory.

Coming of Age

wo factors were responsible for the diamond's emergence as the premier gemstone of Europe during the seventeenth century. Foremost was the introduction of international trade to the famous Golconda diamond producing area near Hyderabad, India. Fabulous diamonds were absorbed by the thirsty European market in unprecedented quantities, due to ambitious merchant travelers such as the Frenchmen Chardin and, in particular, Jean-Baptiste Tavernier.

The vast influx of quality stones stimulated gemcutters to perfect cutting techniques. Improved techniques brought about the second factor contributing to the diamond's rise, the development of the rose cut. This giant stride in the working of a diamond finally revealed its hidden brilliance.

No one can say exactly when this discovery was made, or by whom, although the "Koh-i-Noor," originally a variation of the rose, was probably cut in the sixteenth century. By the beginning of the seventeenth century the rose cut-diamond was the norm. It soon eclipsed the point and table-cuts that had been its most usual forms. A domed, faceted surface on a flat base, was likened to an opening rose bud, hence the name. This shape complimented the diamond as never before. It leaped into fashion.

Cardinal Mazarin, minister to the French courts of Louis XIII and Louis XIV, is credited with promoting experimental Dutch jewelers in the mid-seventeenth century. Their work led to the refinement of the so-called true rose, or sixteen-faceted, cutting.

France set the trend when it came to seventeenth century jewelry design, especially that incorporating diamonds. Jewelry was much influenced by the change in clothing fashions and the new materials. Damask, silk and lace replaced velvet and brocade. According to H. Clifford Smith, "...the jewelry of the period assumed an open and lace-like character, suitable also for the display of precious stones."

Another factor influencing jewelry design was the vogue for flower cultivation. Botanical motifs for jewelry became all the rage in France and soon spread throughout Europe.

At the beginning of the century colored stones such as ruby, sapphire and emerald were predominant. The diamond was secondary. But the diamond's new splendor in the improved rose cut was reversing these roles, fast becoming the chief ornament.

* * *

France, particularly Paris, came to dominate jewelry design. This had to do with the improved fortunes of the French monarchy at the beginning of the century. Henry IV of Navarre, the first Bourbon king and a Protestant, found his kingdom divided in a civil war between the Popular League and the Protestants when he came to the throne in 1589. His conversion to Roman Catholicism in 1593 was a major step toward the reunification of the country.

But he was still hindered by poverty brought on by the costs of incessant warring, according to Twining. "[He] possessed no personal fortune and found the royal domain in France almost entirely alienated. Moreover, the Treasury was without funds. The new king had nothing on which to raise credit as the crown jewels were in pawn, the King's Cabinet in Paris had been pillaged by the League and only a small portion of the Royal Treasury was saved...."

The use of diamonds by Nicholas Harlay, Siegneur de Sancy, saw the King through these trying times. Sancy, as Harlay was known, was a clever financier. Although a fancier and collector of some renown, he also understood diamonds value for raising funds. He was a fervid monarchist, particularly in support of Henry IV. Sancy combined vocation with avocation, using his own diamonds to secure loans for the King, thus restoring order to the country's finances.

We first hear of Sancy using his gems in this manner in support of Henry III just before his assassination in 1589. A warrant dated that year:

> A great flawless diamond...weighing 37 or 38 carats or thereabouts set in a golden frame at the end of which hangs a great round pearl, flawless and perfect, of about 20-carats; also a great heart-shaped ruby set in gold at the base of which hangs a great pear-shaped pearl, for the price of 20,000 ecus. The large jewels were pledged and put into the hands of the said Sieur de Sancy that he might pawn them in Switzerland, Germany or elsewhere. If they were pledged for less than 24,000 ecus, His Majesty will only pay to the said Sancy the price for which they were pledged.

The funds raised were used to pay 12,000 Swiss mercenaries instrumental in securing Henry IV's crown under Sancy's command. Another diamond known as the "Great Sancy," a 53.5-carat gem was pledged to raise more funds.

As Henry gained control of his country he began to reconstitute the Crown Treasure. Among his purchases was that of a fine diamond in 1600, valued at 30,000 ecus, from the Duke of Epernon.

Henry's son, Louis XIII, succeeded him at his death in 1610. He was under the influence of his mother, Marie de Medici, or her protege Cardinal Mazarin, for much of his rule. While Louis XIII's wealth, and the value of the French crown jewels grew, it was up to his son and successor, Louis XIV, to bring glory and power to the French Throne. But this took time.

Louis XIV did not rule until 1651. He was five years old at the time of his father's death in 1643. In the interim his mother, Anne of Austria, was regent for him. But the real power lay in the hands of her advisor, Cardinal Mazarin.

Mazarin, born Giulio Mazarini in Italy, entered the service of France as an assistant to Cardinal Richelieu after serving as Papal

Nuncio at the French court. He was elevated to cardinal at the recommendation of Louis XIII in 1641. After the death of Richelieu in
1642 and the king the following year, he became principal minister.

The wealth that came from Mazarin's power and influence
enabled him to satisfy his love of gems, particularly diamonds.
During his years of power he amassed a fortune in these fascinating
stones, not always by the most scrupulous means.

Before his death in 1661 he dictated a will in which he
bequeathed to the Crown a set of eighteen large and beautiful diamonds. He stated they were to be known as the "Mazarin Diamonds."

Among them were the "Great Sancy" and the notorious "Mirror
of Portugal." In all, they totaled over 323 carats. Only one was under
10. In 1661 they were valued at 1,931,000 livres, truly a bequest
for a king. Yet these gems were only a portion of his total collection.
In addition to minor bequests, he left a spray of fifty diamonds to the
Queen, and a 14-carat rose diamond named "Rose d'Angleterre"
along with a perfect ruby to Anne of Austria.

It appears that Mazarin's conscience was not entirely clear about
the manner in which he acquired his wealth. Claude Fregnac states
that, "Upon his deathbed the cardinal asked his confessor to advise
him how to make his will, and was told that he should render to the
King all the things that belonged to him but...distinguish between
what the King had given him and what he had taken for himself; the
dying man replied: 'In that case it is necessary to give everything up
to the King'."

Louis XIV took complete control of the French government following Mazarin's death. And it may be said that he inherited not only
Mazarin's power but his obsessive love of diamonds. During the
remainder of his reign the King began to satisfy that desire on a scale
seldom equaled in the West. When the famed gem merchant and
traveler, Jean-Baptiste Tavernier, returned from his 1669 trip to
India, he was presented at court. Louis was so enamoured of
Tavernier's gems that he ordered his finance minister to purchase
1,167 diamonds, among which was the 112-carat "Blue Diamond of
the Crown." This would come to be known as the "Hope." He paid
897,730 livres.

Not long after, a further outlay of 504,340 livres was made to another traveler from India for an assortment of diamonds and jewels. This purchase nearly coincided with another of 170,000 livres for the jewels of the Queen of Poland died in 1667.

Twining tells us that "In 1678 Sieur Alvarez, a jewel merchant...was ordered to cut 665 diamonds from the King's latest acquisitions, of which twelve were large stones." It is no wonder that between 1661 and 1691 the French crown jewels jumped in value from 7,400,000 to 11,400,000 livres.

But by no means were all of Louis' acquisitions destined for the crown jewels. Many were bought as gifts to the King's mistresses and children, for it was known the King enjoyed a display of jewelry among his court. However, Queen Marie Therese, a chaste woman with no fondness for luxury, was seldom the recipient of such largess.

Saint-Simon described him on one occasion as follows: "...his garments were ornamented with the most beautiful of the crown jewels; he was bent under the weight of them, he was wearing twelve million, five hundred thousand livres." Clifford Smith states that, "...he made it the duty of the grandees of France and Spain to wear their whole property in the form of glittering gems...to carry the value of lands and forests upon their own and their wives' apparel when they appeared before the eyes of their sovereign."

Is it any wonder that the Duchess of Burgundy, after appearing before the King "...was obliged to take to her bed because the clothes she had worn on the previous evening had been too heavily laden with precious stones." If for no other reason than the dazzle of his court, Louis could rightly claim his sobriquet "Sun King."

* * *

Other European monarchs emulated the splendrous French court, with varying degrees of success. It was during this century, particularly in the reign of Alexis (1645-76), that the affluence of the Russian court emerged. In Poland, King Sigismund III (1587-1632) numbered among his hoard a girdle containing fifteen diamonds, three diamond rings and a large diamond pendant.

He gave his queen a diamond ring, two necklaces containing a total of nine diamonds, nine rubies and twenty-one pearls, as well as a third necklace, said to have been particularly beautiful, that consisted of two strands each of diamonds and rubies, below which hung a pendant with the words Zygmunt August in diamonds.

Frederick William, Elector of Prussia, presented his consort, Louisa Henrietta of Orange, with a number of table and rose-cut diamonds valued at 78,350 guldens. His son Frederick purchased gems on a modest scale in 1681, which gradually increased to 261,000 reichs thalers in 1697. In his treasure was also the "Little Sancy," valued at 300,000 reichs thalers, which became the premier stone in the Prussian crown jewels.

* * *

Only English royalty, who had begun the century so auspiciously, came anywhere near the opulence of the French court. But they were susceptible to the diamond's dangerous powers. James I succeeded the childless Elizabeth I as the first Stuart King of England in 1603. His treasury was full of the precious stones and other wealth accumulated from the reigns of Elizabeth and Henry VIII. Whether in reaction to an austere Scottish upbringing or the temptation of unlimited finances, he was soon wholeheartedly building the Treasury.

In March, 1604, he bought the "Great Sancy" diamond from the French Ambassador for 60,000 ecus. Lord Twining, usually eager to compile lists of crown jewel inventories, was forced to admit, "[T]he 1605 inventory of James I contains a number of jewels...too many to quote in full." Nevertheless, he lists some noteworthy pieces. These included sixty-four buttons set with diamonds and two pendants containing table diamonds, one of which may have been the "Mirror of Portugal" or the "Mirror of France".

Like the later Louis XIV, James encouraged the display of jeweled extravagance at his court. In 1608 John Chamberlain, wrote to a friend who missed a court ball, "...you should have been sure to have seen riches in jewels, when one lady, and that under a baroness, is said to be furnished for better than a hundred thousand pounds; and the Lady Arabella goes beyond her, and the Queen must not come behind."

Even near the end of his reign, during which he levied enormous taxes to replenish the depleted royal coffers, the King still insisted on lavish display. A notable occasion occurred in 1623 when Charles I, then Prince of Wales, was sent to Spain to conclude an alliance sealed by his marriage to the Spanish Infanta.

To impress the Spanish with the wealth of his court, James supplied the Prince with a vast array of jewels. Among them was a hatband studded with "...twenty faire dyamonds sett in Buttons of goulde in manner of Spanish work, whereof eight are four-square Table dyamonds, two flower-square Table Dyamonds cut with fawcetts, two large poynted dyamonds, one faire Hart Dyamond and three tryangle dyamonds."

In addition, he gave the Prince the famed "Three Brethren" jewel. It contained a diamond said to be the first cut by Louis de Berquem. It was called the "...Mirroure of Frawnce...qyhiche I wolde wishe you to weare alone in your hatte with a litle blakke feather." He also gave the "Mirror of Portugal" diamond from which hung the Cobham Pearl, as well as a large "Cross of Lorraine" studded with diamonds. This was topped off with four other diamond crosses and a variety of jewels. Yet all this ostentation was for naught, the embassy returned to England empty-handed.

James' prodigality left Charles I in near-straightened circumstances, confronted by a hostile Parliament unwilling to help him overcome his situation, while facing a war with Spain the Treasury could ill afford. Although James had decreed that the crown jewels were "...to be indivisible and inseperate forever hereafter annexed to the kingdom of this realm," Charles was forced in the first year of his reign, to begin the disposal of these jewels. Clifford Smith succinctly sums up the loss and destruction of the crown jewels under Charles:

> ...the King had commenced early in his reign the dispersal of the immense hoards of jewelry brought together by his predecessors; and by selling and pawning raised large sums of money, to make good the deficiencies caused by the rupture with Parliament. Subsequently, during the Civil War, to relieve his personal necessities, numbers of jewels were sold at home, and many more pawned and sent over to the dealers at Amsterdam, who broke them up for the intrinsic value of their gold and precious stones; while the remain-

der were put under the hammer by a commission appointed after the King's death to dispose of the works of art in the royal collection.

Charles' principal agent for these transactions was his wife, Henrietta Maria. In 1642, he was desperately in need of funds to finance his war against Parliament. Charles sent her to Amsterdam with a plate and jewels to sell. Although she had difficulty disposing of the larger jewelry, the funds realized from what she did sell—including her personal jewelry—were quickly converted to coin, guns and powder, and sent to the King.

In 1664 the Queen again departed England, this time for the court of her nephew, Louis XIV. She brought all the jewels in the Royal Treasury, some of which were Crown property. A portion of these went for just over one million livres.

She raised loans totaling 427,556 livres from the Duke of Epernon using one of Henry VIII's ruby collars valued at 130,000 livres as security. Most notably, she managed to sell the "Three Brethren" for 104,000 livres, and the "Great Sancy" and "Mirror of Portugal" to Cardinal Mazarin for 360,000 livres.

But all of Henrietta's fund raising could not turn the tide against her husband. Even though the infamous "Great Sancy" and "Mirror of Portugal" were no longer in the hands of the King, their power against him was still evident. Following several disastrous military reverses Charles was captured by parliamentary forces and beheaded on January 30th, 1649.

What gems and jewelry Henrietta Maria had not succeeded in smuggling out of England were now systematically destroyed by the fanatical Puritans of the Commonwealth. Had their actions known logic they would have realized the value of this treasure to the State.

However, some were auctioned, and much of the gold melted down for coinage. Many priceless jewels and gems were literally destroyed—smashed beyond recognition or value by Cromwell's zealots. Even the regalia of state was forcibly removed from the Jewel House and Westminster, and "totallie broken and defaced." Cromwell was determined that no symbols of the monarchy survive.

It is perhaps surprising that even the austere Cromwell could not resist effecting some of the trappings of royalty. Twining says that for his investiture as Lord Protector in 1653:

> …the Coronation Chair was brought over from Westminster Abbey, a sword of state was carried before him and a scepter was presented to him by the Speaker. In 1656 there were suggestions of his being made King, and it is said a crown was made for him. At his funeral in 1658 he lay in effigy at Somerset House with an imperial crown of gold and jewels placed on a cushion on his chair of estate and with a scepter of gold and orb in his hand.

Cromwell's Commonwealth did not long survive him. In May of 1660, the monarchy was restored. Charles II was crowned on April 23rd, 1661. The delay between the restoration and the crowning may have been necessitated by the making of new regalia. Even the crown that Charles wore, the frame of which belonged to Cromwell, contained gems hired from local jewelers worth about £500.

One of the most extraordinary events of Charles' reign concerned the attempt in 1671 to steal the crown jewels. The new Restoration regalia had been placed in the Tower of London under the keeping of an old man, Talbot Edwards. His job was not only to guard the jewels, but to show them to anyone willing to pay a fee.

One day Edwards was approached by a Colonel Blood. Blood was an Irishman whose rank derived from his service in the Commonwealth army. He passed himself off as a parson and managed to worm his way into Edward's confidence, so much so that he finally proposed the marriage of his "nephew" to Edward's daughter.

On the day the bridegroom was to meet his intended, Col. Blood arrived at the Tower with three companions, heavily armed beneath their robes. Blood persuaded Edward to show the crown jewels to him and his companions while waiting for his nephew's betrothed. Leaving one of their men on guard, they followed Edwards to the Jewel House where they seized and bound him.

The keeper resisted. He was knocked unconscious, stabbed and left for dead. However, while the conspirators were secreting the jewels under their robes they were surprised by the keeper's son, who raised the alarm.

Leaving the bulk of the treasure behind, the gang overpowered some guards who had heard the alarm and ran to waiting horses. But they did not succeed in eluding all the guards. In the skirmish, Blood and one of his companions were captured. Most of the jewels were retrieved.

Anyone caught under such circumstances could normally have expected a quick trip to the beheading block. What makes this episode so extraordinary is that quite the opposite occurred. The King, impressed by their audacity, decided to put the conspirator's talents to better use. He ordered the release of the offenders and placed Blood in his own bodyguard with a yearly pension of £500.

Charles II was constantly quarreling with Parliament and involving the country in foreign intrigues. One thing he learned was that adding gems to the crown jewels was tempting fate. For the coronation of his brother, James II, in 1685, we learn that gems were hired for use in the crown regalia.

The Queen's coronet contained 172 diamonds and the Coronation Crown, 419. By the time of the coronation of William III in 1689 the Crown of Estate contained "...38 very large diamonds, 523 great and small diamonds, 129 very large pearls...valued at £35,000...[all] were returned after the coronation."

No accumulation of jewels took place during the Restoration. They still played a prominent role, but were not purchased specifically to augment the crown jewels. Charles II bought some magnificent stones from the French gem merchant Chardin to present to his many mistresses. William III also bought a considerable number for use as presents to ambassadors.

This was a practice of the time, which Clifford Smith states, "...played a very important part in the diplomatic affairs of the day. Even the most trifling negotiation cost the Exchequer an enormous amount in presents...while foreign envoys were likewise obliged to disburse large sums for the same purpose."

By the end of the seventeenth century jewels that had previously adorned the doublets of husbands were now appearing on women. A poem of the time describes such a lady's toilet:

> Diamond buckles too,
> For garters, and as rich for shoo.

A manteau, ruby buckle
And brilliant diamond rings for knuckle.
A sapphire bodkin for the hair,
Or sparkling facet diamond there:
Then turquoise, ruby, emrauld rings
For fingers, and such pretty things;
As diamond pendants for the ears,
Must needs be had, or two pearl pears,
Pearl necklace, large and ornamental,
And diamond, and of amber pale.

7
Prince of Diamonds:
Jean-Baptiste Tavernier

"The diamond is the most precious of all stones, and it is the article of trade to which I am most devoted." With these blunt words Jean-Baptiste Tavernier, traveler and gem merchant extraordinaire, summed up the fundamental principle that guided his adult life.

More than anyone of his time, Tavernier was responsible for the abundance of diamonds that became available in seventeenth century Europe, and marked the glittering court of Louis XIV. His *Travels in India*, an account of his peripatetic journey through the Middle East and SouthWest Asia, recorded a wealth of information on seventeenth century India, and the use of diamonds.

By the time Tavernier was twenty-two he claimed to have traveled widely through Western Europe and acquired a proficiency in the most common and useful European languages. His combined interests in travel and commerce are easy to understand; his father was a geographer and merchant, and his uncle Melchior a well-known cartographer.

One imagines his youth spent sitting at the feet of his father and uncle, listening to their discussions of foreign lands and learned men. A perfect foundation for the life of commerce, travel and adventure that was to be Tavernier's.

71

Early in the year 1631 Tavernier set off on the first of six voyages that would carry him as far as the Dutch East Indies. His first trip, however, took him no further than Persia. Nevertheless, he was embarking on trade in precious goods with a quantity of turquoise he knew would find a ready market in Europe. By 1633 he was back in France. Although his activities during the succeeding five years remain a blank, he must certainly have been preparing for his next journey.

In 1638, Tavernier, accompanied by his brother Daniel, set off from Paris on his second voyage. This journey was meant to establish him as a merchant in rare and precious merchandise. By way of Marseilles, Alexandretta and Aleppo, he reached Isfahan in May 1639. Isfahan was the site of the court of Shah Safi II, King of Persia. Tavernier made a favorable impression.

He probably left the Shah's court toward the end of 1639. Possibly journeying through Dacca and wintering in Agra in 1640-41, Tavernier was now set to make his first foray into India. He reports that the country was at peace in this twelfth year of Shah Jahan's reign.

It provided him the opportunity to record extensive notes. From these records, later published, much has been learned of the customs, money, weights and measures, and travel in the Middle East and India.

By the close of the year he was in Goa on the Malabar Coast. Goa had been annexed by the Portuguese more than 130 years earlier. It served as a base for Tavernier's explorations. He made his first visit to the already famous diamond trading center at Golconda, and possibly to the nearby diamond mines. In any event, he returned to Paris in 1643.

In an account of his third and longest journey, Tavernier gave more detailed descriptions of his travels and transactions. This time accompanied by two Capuchin monks, he arrived in Isfahan in 1644, where he spent some months in trade. By January 1645, he was at Surat but did not tarry long. Golconda drew him like a magnet into this center of the world's diamond trade, for, as he says, "[I]n order to acquire a thorough knowledge of it [diamond] I resolved to visit all the mines, and one of the two rivers where diamonds were found."

The first mine he visited was at Ramalakota, about eighteen miles south of Karnool. Here, he tells us, diamonds were extracted from veins "...some of half a finger and some of a whole finger in width....small irons, crooked at the ends...were thrust into the veins to draw from them the sand or earth...[in which] they afterwards find the diamonds." Tavernier claimed that the diamonds of Ramalakota were the "cleanest and whitest-watered" to be found.

At the time of this visit merchants wishing to work the mines paid the King of Bijapur a royalty that amounted to between two and four pagodas per day, depending on the number of miners employed. In addition, the King received two percent of the value of all diamonds found.

Each parcel of land measured about 200 paces in circumference and was worked by fifty to one hundred men who received three pagodas per annum. It was no wonder that for such miserly wages the miners did not "...show any scruple, when searching the sand, in concealing a stone for themselves...." This was no easy matter for they wore only a small loincloth.

The usual method of concealment was to swallow the stone, although Tavernier relates how one enterprising fellow attempted to secret a two-carat gem in the corner of his eye. Apparently such theft was considered a part of each merchant's risk and not severely punished.

However, workers who were honest, or not daring enough to attempt theft, could also be rewarded. Tavernier wrote, "[I]f by chance a stone is found which weighs above 7 to 8 mangelins, it is taken to the master of the mine, who by way of recompense gives a sarpo (i.e. a saropa, or complete dress of honor)...of the value of 25 to 30 sols and generally with it half a pagoda in silver, or else a pagoda, when rice and a plate of sugar are not given."

The merchants were on guard against theft by their workers employing "...twelve to fifteen watchmen...to see that they were not defrauded," but were much more trusting in their dealings with other merchants. Traders who visited to make purchases were entrusted with packets of gems worth thousands of pounds for seven or eight days "...in order that [they] may examine them with care."

Tavernier was also impressed by the expertise of children

between the ages of ten and sixteen, usually the sons of merchants, who appraised and bought diamonds.

> When anyone brings a stone he places it in the hands of the eldest of the children...he looks at it and passes it on to him who sits next. Thus it goes from hand to hand till it returns to the first one without anyone saying a word.

> He then asks the price of the specimen...and if by chance he buys at too high a price he is responsible. In the evening these children count up what they have purchased, and...separate them according to their water, weight, and cleanness. Next they price each as they expect to dispose of them to strangers, and by this they see how far the value exceeds the cost of purchase. They then carry them to the great merchants...and all the profit is divided among the children.

Most of the merchants with whom Tavernier dealt, although sharp bargainers, were scrupulously honest in their dealings and in their obligation to pay the King's percentage. All transactions were overseen by a functionary of the King, who arbitrated disputes and recorded transactions to calculate the royal percentage. The Frenchman also appears honest but did not hesitate to deal with those who weren't. One such transaction ultimately worked in his favor.

A poorly dressed merchant offering mounted rubies visited him. Recalling an order from a lady of Isfahan, he purchased a ring but insisted that he was really interested in larger stones. The merchant led him to believe that he had better goods to offer but not while the King's agent was present. In order to be alone with the merchant, Tavernier sent the agent on an errand, whereupon the merchant removed his headdress and extracted a small rag from his hair. Carefully unfolding the cloth, he revealed a sparkling diamond "...weighing 48.5 of our carats, of beautiful water and of cabuchon shape."

The merchant let Tavernier keep it until the following morning. They arranged to meet outside the town, where Tavernier could purchase the stone if he so desired. Tavernier kept the appointment and purchased the gem.

Three days later he had to leave town on short notice. When he presented himself before the Governor to take his leave, he was asked whether he spent all his money. When he replied that he still had in excess of £10,000, he was asked to show his purchases to the Governor.

Tavernier brought out all the gems he had bought and stated their prices, which tallied with the Governor's records. Even though the records did not show it, the Frenchman drew forth the 48.5-carat diamond and said, "Sir, this is not in the Banian's books, and there is no one in the town who knows that I have bought it, nor would you…had I not told you."

The Governor was so astonished at Tavernier's honesty that he immediately summoned the richest merchants of the town, ordering them to bring their finest gems. Tavernier was allowed to expend his remaining funds on these stones.

When the Governor instructed the merchants to present him with a souvenir, as they were dealing with an honest man, this they did. The gift was a small, beautiful diamond.

Tavernier also visited diamond mines seven days journey east of Golconda, which he called Cani, a term that literally means mine. These mines were actually alluvial deposits on a plain at the foot of some mountains. They produced many stones of ten to forty carats, and one—the "Great Mogul"—Tavernier estimates at 900 carats. However, the stones found here did not equal the quality of those found at Ramalakota.

According to Tavernier nearly 60,000 men, women and children worked the Cani mines, and in a manner quite different from Ramalakota. Here the mines were ten to fourteen feet deep. The residue removed from the diggings was washed several times. Then it was dried and winnowed in a basket to remove finer particles. The remaining coarse particles were then beaten with wooden pestles. What remained was sorted by hand for diamonds.

His next stop was at Isfahan towards the end of 1647. Presumably he was on his way home with the profits of his trading when something must have convinced him to return south. On

January 11th, 1648, he arrived at Vengurla on the West Coast of India, and on to Goa, where he remained for nearly two months. He made friends with the Portuguese Viceroy, the Archbishop and the Inquisitor-General. He returned to Vengurla in mid-March and boarded ship for Batavia in the Dutch East Indies.

Although Tavernier says only that he wished to visit this exotic land, he certainly had other reasons for making the voyage. While in Goa he had heard of an African port discovered by the Portuguese. This was information he knew he might exchange with the Dutch for commercial advantage. It is clear from his report of this voyage that he had transactions to carry out. They would lead to a contretemps with, and life-long distrust of, the Dutch authorities.

* * *

Having narrowly escaped shipwreck off the Malabar coast, Tavernier reached Batavia. According to Professor Ball's introduction to *Travels in India*, "On the following day he went to pay his respects to the General, Vanderling, and the Director-General, Caron, by whom he was at first well treated. However, he was subsequently involved in tedious investigations regarding his relations with M. Constant, the Dutch Commander at Bandar Abbas, for whom he had purchased diamonds at the mines."

The case of Monsieur Constant's diamonds, Tavernier's first clash with the Dutch, exemplifies his shrewd judgement.

He had carried out commissions from M. Constant to the satisfaction of them both. On this occasion, however, the Dutchman had left his post at Bandar Abbas and, via Batavia had returned to Holland before Tavernier could give him the diamonds he'd purchased on his behalf.

When Tavernier reached Bandar Abbas and found that Constant had departed, he arranged for the diamonds to be shipped to him in Holland. Upon his arrival in Batavia, Tavernier was confronted by the authorities, who somehow heard of the transaction. Since private business was forbidden to representatives of the Dutch East Indies Company, the authorities were intent on gaining evidence against Constant that could be used to strip him of his wealth.

At first they tried to loosen Tavernier's tongue by plying him with drink. But, in his usual forthright manner, he informed them "...that they need not have brought wine for that purpose...it is then I talk least."

With the failure of this and other not so subtle approaches, the authorities embarked on more direct methods to wring from Tavernier the information they sought. Early the following morning "...an officer of the Company handed me a summons to appear at 11 o'clock before the Town Council, where the Avocat Fiscal was present to take up the case on behalf of the Company." At first the proceedings were amicable enough and Tavernier admitted the transaction.

For him it was quite legal. He informed the authorities that he was no longer in possession of the diamonds. But when it was claimed that Constant could not have raised the funds, 8000 ecus (£1,800) without defrauding the Company, Tavernier became indignant. He told the President of the Council "...that if he had only carried off so much, it would have been a small matter...that there was scarcely a servant of the Company who had held M. Constant's offices, and...enjoyed the opportunity of trading...without fear of the Fiscal, who had not made at least 100,000 ecus (£22,500)." Since several of the Council members held posts similar to Constant's, an embarrassed silence followed, after which the meeting ended.

But the matter was far from closed. Three days later Tavernier was presented with pages of written charges, delving into all aspects of his relations with Constant. The enquiry dragged on for four or five weeks during which he "...gave always the same answer, that I knew nothing of M. Constant's affairs...."

Threatened with arrest, he boldly replied that "...I did not fear them, and...if they arrested me I had the honor to serve a Prince...Monseigneur le Duc d'Orleans, who would get me safely out of their hands, and would resent the affront they had done me." With those words Tavernier stalked from the chamber. They did not disturb him for fifteen days. Finally Tavernier was summoned.

The following day at the appointed hour Tavernier appeared before the Council and judges. The President asked "...if I would tell them something of what I had sent...M. Constant. I said...that I desired to give the account at full length, with which reply the President and Council told me they were quite content." Tavernier ingenuously launched into a detailed recital of Constant's every social activity, his exchange of gifts with local Indian officials in pursuit of duty, and his endless official functions.

Realizing they were being mocked, the Council then instructed him to describe the trade in which Constant had been engaged. "It was then I began to speak to them in a different way," Tavernier relates, "and told them I was not dependent on them and was not their spy; that if they wished to know so much they should have ascertained it when he was at Batavia, or they might write to him in Holland, and would thus be able to satisfy themselves." Taken aback, the councilors gave him four days to reconsider his answer.

When the four days had expired he was again summoned to the Council and threatened with jail. He stood his ground, writing, "...that I believed the gentlemen of the Council would think more than once before they carried (their threat) into execution...."

Once again the Council backed down, allowing a further eight days for his reply. Then "...seeing that the Council began to be annoyed, I thought that it was time to put an end to the affair."

The following morning he approached the Council President at his home and stated that he "...would conceal nothing that had come to my knowledge, even were it to the disadvantage of the General himself and many members of the Council, and of you yourself who urge me to speak." He then outlined the transactions he knew Constant to have carried out on behalf of the General, various members of the Council, and the President himself.

"Having given all this detail to the President, he appeared...alarmed, and besought me to make no noise about it, in which he did wisely...the principle part of the large sums which they had invested in diamonds having passed through my hands."

But Tavernier was now determined to play out the farce to the end. About noon he was on his way to the Town Hall to hear what the Avocat Fiscal, by now *au courant*, would have to say. He was met by the President.

"With a laughing face he asked me where I was going. I replied that I was going to Town Hall to reply to some of his questions."

"I beg you," he replied quickly, "let us leave that affair to go and have dinner together. I was presented yesterday with two cases, one of French wine and the other of Rhine wine, we shall see which is the best. All I ask from you is a word written with your own hand, that you have nothing belonging to M. Constant.

This I gave very willingly, and in this way the whole case came to an end."

Although this episode ended favorably for Tavernier, the Dutch authorities seemed intent on exacting revenge. While in Batavia he purchased a number of discounted pay-bills with a face value of 17,500 florins (about £3,500) that he intended to resell at par value in Holland.

Even though such transactions had been quite common, the Dutch authorities decided to prohibit them. They forced Tavernier to give up the pay-bills. In return, he received only a verbal promise that he would be recompensed in Holland. Much to his dismay, when he approached the company they disclaimed all knowledge of the pledge and refused to pay. It was after several years' negotiations that one of his brothers finally accepted 10,000 livres (£900) in full payment.

During his stay in Batavia, Tavernier made two trips to Bantam, a small kingdom on the western end of Java, to visit his brother Daniel and engage in trade with the King. Prior to his departure from Batavia his brother turned up in the city in extremely ill health that Tavernier claimed "...arose from the debauches he had indulged in with the King of Bantam."

Postponing his departure, Tavernier devoted himself to his brother. But he died a month later. Adding insult to the injury he already felt he'd received at the hands of the Dutch, he was forced to pay out £91 for his brother's burial. He resolved "...not to die in a country where it cost so much to be interred." He would later publish a tract, *The Conduct of the Dutch in Asia*, in which he laid out his grievances.

By the spring of 1649 Tavernier was back in Paris. For the next two years he occupied himself with selling the precious stones he had brought back from India, and in his negotiations with the Dutch East Indies Company over the pay-bills. In 1651, he departed from Paris on his fourth voyage. This time he was heading directly for the greatest profits—the mines of Golconda. However, owing to disturbances in the Levant, he did not reach the East Coast Indian port for Golconda, until the beginning of July 1652.

On the first of September he arrived at Gandicot. The King of Golconda's general, Mir Jumla, had recently captured it. Tavernier visited the general, as custom demanded, to show him the precious stones he proposed to sell to the King.

He succeeded in eliciting a letter of recommendation to the King. It would have been difficult gaining a royal audience without it. When he arrived in Golconda his jewels were, as was customary, pre-appraised by an official of the King's court. In this case it was a eunuch, who derided Tavernier's asking price. Insulted, the Frenchman immediately packed and departed.

When the King heard what had happened he sent messengers after Tavernier. But by the time they caught up with him he was in Mogul territory and refused to return to Golconda.

This turn of events proved more auspicious than Tavernier could have foreseen. Journeying on, he presented himself and his gems at the court of the governor, Shaista Khan. He realized a 200 percent profit of 41,000 livres (£3,075) on the sale of just five pear-shaped pearls to the governor. It set the stage for future dealings with this Mogul official.

In Kerman he purchased a large quantity of beautiful wool for transport to France, which he reached in the autumn of 1655. This time Tavernier remained in France little more than a year, departing for his fifth voyage in February 1657. No sooner had his ship left Marseilles than it was set upon by pirates and forced to take refuge in Toulon.

Tavernier was fearful that the pirates somehow knew of his jewels. He debarked and returned by land to Marseilles, while the ship proceeded with his heavier merchandise. He headed for Smyrna. There he sent his servants to Constantinople to purchase some pearls, which he knew were among the best items of trade.

In June 1657, he left Smyrna for Isfahan. He tarried there until the beginning of 1659 due to the unsettled state of India following Aurangzeb's usurpation of power from his father, Shah Jahan. By the end of that year he had reached Choupar in the Deccan, which Shaista Khan was besieging for Aurangzeb.

He brought many items specifically to sell to Shaista Khan, ordered on his previous visit to the general. He made 120,000 rupees (£13,500), and paid a visit to the Golconda mines before returning to Paris in 1662. It was yet another successful journey.

By this time Tavernier wished to settle down and enjoy his wealth. He had reached the age of fifty-six. Now a man of considerable means, he decided to marry. His wife was Madeleine Goisse, the daughter of a jeweler. But he could not long resist the call of the East and planned one last trip to round off his affairs.

He left Paris in November 1663, accompanied by his young nephew, Pierre, and four attendants of different professions, including a surgeon. He carried trade goods valued at 400,000 livres (£30,000). By early November of the following year he was in Tabriz when two of his followers died. Before proceeding further he entrusted the care of his nephew to the Superior of a Capuchin Convent and set off for Isfahan with his goods and a small party.

On his previous journey Tavernier sold jewels to the new Persian King, Shah Abbas II. The King was naturally curious to see what treasures he had brought this time and summoned the Frenchman to his palace. Knowing the value of the King's trade and good will, Tavernier presented him with fine presents.

Then he brought out his best jewels. The King paid a high price, reputedly in excess of £13,000. He was so pleased with the manner in which their business had been carried out that he granted Tavernier's nephew King's protection and granted duty-free trading privileges in Persia. In addition, he bestowed on Tavernier the fur-trimmed robe of honor and turban in which the merchant is most often depicted. To top it all off, the King gave him a commission for gold, enamel and precious stones.

In May 1665, he resumed his vendetta with the Dutch. Before boarding a Dutch ship at Bandar Abbas, the English agent in that city entrusted a packet of letters to him for delivery to the English Resident in Surat. The Dutch believed these letters to contain information about the outbreak of war in Europe between the English and Dutch, and stole them. The English were so incensed when they discovered the theft that they threatened Tavernier with assassination. Although he escaped this fate, he could never get the Dutch to admit their crime.

In Surat, Tavernier found that Shaista Khan, for whom he carried many exquisite gems, was no longer Governor. Moreover, the new Governor told him that the Mogul Emperor, Aurangzeb, desired to be the first to see his jewels.

Knowing the social value of beautiful gifts, he distributed many to the Emperor's chief retainers and officials. The most magnificent gifts, however, were reserved for the Emperor Aurangzeb. The first was a splendid gilded bronze shield originally made for Cardinal Richelieu. In addition, Aurangzeb received a gold inlaid, rock-crystal battle mace covered with rubies and emeralds; a Turkish saddle embroidered with small rubies, pearls and emeralds; and another saddle embroidered in gold and silver.

In all, these gifts were worth 23,187 livres (£1700), of which the Emperor's portion amounted to nearly half. Tavernier was not one to give away something for nothing but he knew that such lavish giving would be amply rewarded in trade with the Great Mogul and his noblemen.

It was during this visit that Tavernier became the first westerner to view the fabulous wealth of the Moguls. He was surprised at Aurangzeb's offer to let him see all his jewels. For a gem merchant such as Tavernier this was an offer that could not be refused. The Frenchman had already seen the fabulous Peacock Throne, and was intrigued to find what other fortunes lay hidden in the Great Mogul's Treasury.

He was brought to the Emperor's palace, where four eunuchs appeared with two large, gold-leafed wooden trays, at the command of the chief of the jewel treasury. Velvet cloths were swept aside to reveal a dazzling array of gems. The first diamond shown to him was the "Great Mogul," an enormous rose-cut of 280 carats which he valued at nearly £800,000!

When originally presented to Shah Jahan by Mir Jumla it weighed 787-carats in the rough. Tavernier reported that a Venetian, Hortensio Borgio, had cut it to its present size. Shah Jahan was enraged by the amount Borgio cut away. Instead of paying him he fined him 10,000 rupees. Borgio considered himself lucky that he had not lost his head.

Next came four more diamonds, three table-cut of 48 to 50.5 carats and one pear-shaped of 4.5 carats. Then a gorgeous jewel containing twelve 13-carat rose-cut diamonds encircling a heart-shaped rose-cut of approximately 35 carats. A further jewel contained seventeen diamonds clustered around another large diamond.

A series of beautiful pearls, ranging in weight from 12.5 to 52.5carats, were then given to Tavernier to inspect. These were followed by two chains, one of pearls and rubies with a 26.5-carat emerald, the other of pearls and emeralds with a perfect table amethyst of 35 carats in the middle.

Finally came a mixed series of gem stones, among them a 595-carat balas ruby cut *en cabuchon,* and a 210 carat oriental topaz. Although these gems were by no means the extent of the Great Mogul's gems, they must have been his very finest, and certainly impressed Tavernier.

At the time of Tavernier's visit Shah Jahan was still alive, although imprisoned in Delhi's Red Fort. Approximately £4 million worth of gems were added to Aurangzeb's Treasury upon his death. From this, and the accounts of a plunder carried off by Nadir Shah after he sacked Delhi, it is clear that Tavernier saw only a minute portion of the Great Mogul's jewel treasury, probably that kept close for his personal use.

Early in January 1666, Tavernier reached Dacca where Shaista Khan was now Governor. He visited the Wazir and "...presented him a mantle of gold brocade, with a grand golden lace of *point d'Espagne* round it...a fine scarf of gold and silver of the same *point*, and a jewel consisting of a very beautiful emerald."

In addition, he presented gifts to the Wazir's young son. There was a minor argument with Shaista Khan regarding the sale price of a large pearl. The Emperor's uncle, in a fit of spite at not having been able to buy the pearl, wrote Shaista Khan that it was overpriced by 10,000 rupees. The matter was resolved and the gems Tavernier brought especially for the Wazir were purchased at a price satisfactory to both.

Following the completion of this last transaction, Tavernier headed for home, stopping in Isfahan and Constantinople to carry out some business. He finally reached Paris in December 1668. At the age of sixty-eight he resolved to enjoy the riches he had acquired.

It was unthinkable that a man of Tavernier's exploits and fame would not come to the attention of Louis XIV. Anxious to meet such a renowned traveler, the King invited him to Versailles. A merchant first and foremost, Tavernier pursued his business. Upon presentation to the King in January, 1669, he sold him 1,167 diamonds, and other precious stones. The King was so taken with this intrepid traveler that he granted him letters of nobility.

In April 1670, Tavernier purchased the barony of Aubonne near Geneva and assumed the title "Seigneur Baron d'Aubonne." The following years were spent restoring and decorating the Castle of Aubonne as well as preparing his travel notes for publication. His first book, *Nouvelle Relation du Serrail du Grand Seigneur*, was published in 1675, followed by *Six Voyages* (later *Travels in India*). In 1679 another volume, the *Recueil de Plusieurs Relations* was published.

But Tavernier was not one, even in his seventies, to settle down. In 1684, at the remarkable age of seventy-nine, he was enticed by a new project. Frederick William, Elector of Brandenburg, summoned him to Berlin to advise on colonization and commercial projects in the East.

Attracted by the Elector's offer to make him ambassador to India, he threw himself wholeheartedly into the project. He had apparently lost little of his energy and enterprising spirit to age, undertaking to set up the company, arm and fit out three vessels, and visit various towns in Germany, France and Holland to drum up financial support.

It was at this stage that Tavernier's life-long luck began to desert him. Or was it that the malevolent powers of all the diamonds he handled through the years finally worked their treacherous intent?

His difficulties arose from the fact that he was a Protestant, against whom there was much prejudice in the period prior to the revocation of the Edict of Nantes. Someone named Tavernier was incarcerated in the Bastille. Whether or not this was Jean-Baptiste is uncertain but it may account for the gap in knowledge of his life at this time. In any case, the whole enterprise for the Elector of Brandenburg came to naught.

It was also at this time that Tavernier entrusted a valuable cargo for India to his nephew Pierre. Pierre absconded with this cargo, defrauding Tavernier of profits that should have amounted to nearly one million livres.

Rather than succumb to these misfortunes, the old man decided to set off to the East to recoup his losses. This time he proceeded by way of Scandinavia and then disappeared from the pages of history. It was nearly two centuries before historians succeeded in tracing his movements to Copenhagen in 1689.

Ball states that a Russian, M. T. Tokmakof "...described how, in the year 1876, when visiting an old Protestant cemetery near Moscow, he discovered the tomb of Tavernier...with the name still preserved in full, and a fragment of the obliterated date, 16—. Moreover, M. Tokmakof discovered documents proving that Tavernier, carrying with him the passport of the King of Sweden, arrived in Russia early in February 1689, and that instructions were sent to the frontier to facilitate the journey of the illustrious visitor to Moscow."

It is perhaps fitting that Tavernier should have met his end on a quest for the beautiful gems he so dearly loved, which provided him with such a full and adventurous life.

The Deadly Peacock Throne

Of all the fabled riches of the East, perhaps one object—the Peacock Throne—best symbolizes the unparalleled wealth of the Moguls and Persians, but also the depths to which man, noble and commoner alike, will stoop to acquire wealth. Worth millions, this throne witnessed the rise and hastened the fall of both empires.

It is tempting to believe the legend that this magnificent throne was built by Tamburlaine, perhaps from the spoils of his foray into northern India, but it is more likely that its construction was started early in the sixteenth century by his descendent, Babur. Babur was the founder and first emperor of the Mogul Empire.

It was not until 1635, that Shah Jahan, great-grandson of Babur and fourth Emperor of the Moguls, first sat on this glittering, sinister symbol of the immense wealth and power of the Moguls.

Jadunath Sarkar, a renowned historian of Mogul India, states that the throne was "…3.25 yards long, 2.5 yards broad, and 5 yards high." Apart from gems it contained, "3,255 pounds of pure gold."

The most complete description was given by Tavernier:

> Upon the four feet, which are very massive, and from 20
> to 25 inches high, are fixed the four bars which support

the base of the throne, and upon these bars arranged twelve columns, which sustain the canopy on three sides....Both the feet and the bars, which are more than eighteen inches long are covered with gold inlaid and enriched with numerous diamonds, rubies and emeralds. In the middle of each bar there is a large balas ruby, cut *en cabuchon*, with four emeralds round it, forming a square cross. Next in succession, from one side to the other along the length of the bars there are similar crosses, arranged so that in one the ruby is in the middle of four emeralds, and in another the emerald is in the middle and four balas rubies surround it.

The emeralds are table-cut, and the intervals between the rubies and emeralds are covered with diamonds, the largest of which do not exceed 10 or 12 carats in weight, all showy gems, but very flat. There are also in some parts pearls set in gold....

I counted the large balas rubies on the great throne, and there are about 108, all cabuchons, the least of which weighs 100 carats, but there are some which weigh apparently 200 and more. As for the emeralds, there are plenty of good color, but they have many flaws; the largest may weigh 60 carats, and the least 30 carats. I counted about 116....

The underside of the canopy is covered with diamonds and pearls, with a fringe of pearls all round, and above the canopy, which is a quadrangular-shaped dome, there is a peacock with elevated tail made of blue sapphires and other colored stones, the body of gold inlaid with precious stones, having a large ruby in front of the breast, whence hangs a pear-shaped pearl of fifty carats or thereabouts, and of a somewhat yellow water. On both sides of the peacock there is a large bouquet of the same height as the bird, consisting of many kinds of flowers made of gold inlaid with precious stones. On the side of the throne opposite the court there is a jewel consisting of a diamond of from 80 to 90 carats in weight, with rubies and emeralds round it, and when the Emperor is seated he has this jewel in full view.

But in my opinion the most costly point about this magnificent throne is that the twelve columns supporting the canopy are surrounded with beautiful rows of pearls, which are round and of fine water, and weigh from 6 to 10 carats each. At four feet distance from the throne two umbrellas are fixed, on either side, the sticks of which for 7 or 8 feet in height are covered with diamonds, rubies, and pearls.

Other contemporary travelers who saw this lavish masterpiece valued it at about £4,500,000. Without a professional examination of the gems and workmanship, it is difficult to fix the original value. What is clear is that, for all intents and purposes, the Peacock Throne was literally priceless. Who in the world could have afforded it save the Great Mogul?

The wealth that provided for it had been accumulating over the centuries. Even the orthodox and austere Muslim rulers of pre-Mogul northern India were not immune to the lure of the abundance available to them.

Muhammad of Ghor, founder of the Delhi Sultanate, ruled most of northern India prior to the Moguls. He was said to have left in his treasury 400 pounds, or more than 900,000 carats of diamonds! This treasure must have served as a powerful magnet for Tamburlaine's incursion into northern India, when he sacked Delhi in 1398. He massacred more than 100,000 prisoners during his raid, and made off with the Sultanate's wealth.

Tamburlaine then departed, satisfied with the booty of Delhi. But the remnants of the Delhi Sultanate haunted successive rulers, each intent upon replenishing its depleted treasury. The last of these rulers, Sultan Ibrihim of the Lodi Dynasty, had the misfortune to be opposed by Babur, who claimed descent from the great Tamburlaine and Genghis Khan, but only ruled over a poverty-stricken principality in the desolate interior of Afghanistan.

Babur was intent on finding a richer base upon which to build his power. He marched with a small force into northern India where he met and defeated the Sultan's army near Panipat in April 1526.

Unaccustomed as he was to riches that virtually fell into his lap, Babur embarked on an unprecedented spending spree. His memoirs, the *Baburnama*, record how he disposed of his windfall.

> On Saturday, May 12th, 1526, the examination and distribution of the treasure were begun. To Humayun (his son) were given 70 lakhs from the Treasury (one lakh equalling 100,000 rupees or £11,600) and, over and above this, a treasure house was bestowed on him just as it was, without ascertaining and writing down its contents. To some...10 lakhs were given, 8, 7, or 6 to others.
>
> Suitable money gifts were bestowed from the Treasury on the whole army, to every tribe there was, Afghan, Hazara, Arab, Biluch...to each according to its position. Every trader and student, indeed every man who had come with the army, took ample portion and share of bounteous gifts...17 lakhs to Kamran, 15 lakhs to Muhammad-i-zaman Mirza, while to Askari, Hindal and indeed to the whole various train of relations and younger children went masses of red and white (gold and silver), of plenishing, jewels and slaves....Valuable gifts were sent for the various relations in Samarkand and Khurasan, Kashgar and Iraq. To holy men belonging to Samarkand and Khurasan went offerings vowed to God; so too to Makka and Madina. We gave one shahrukhi (10d) for every soul in the country of Kabul and the valley-side of Varsak, man and woman, bond and free, of age or non-age.

No one would ever accuse Babur of being miserly.

But even he had his limits. Babur's conquests had to be consolidated and extended; that required extensive funds. By October 1528, the Treasury was exhausted. Orders were given that recipients of gifts "...should drop into the Diwan, thirty in every one hundred of his allowance, to be used for war material and appliances, for equipment, for powder, and for the pay of gunners and matchlockmen."

But even this step was not sufficient to sustain Babur's court and finance his military. Other sources of income were essential. To this end Babur issued decrees for revenues, decrees later expanded by his successors into a highly refined system designed to finance the Mogul court and administration.

There were the spoils of war: a ready, if somewhat unpredictable, source of income. A system of land revenues, or direct taxation on land and its produce was established as well. This last was the most important and reliable financial source for the Moguls as it guaranteed more or less fixed amounts of annual income.

Gifts poured in from newly subdued provinces, as did annual tribute from each province already under control. Sizeable gifts were received by the Grand Mogul from his nobles and officers as a matter of custom. These officials were keen on retaining their titles, which provided the means of building sizeable fortunes. They had to remain in the Emperor's good graces.

Since nobility and position were not necessarily hereditary, the estate of these nobles reverted to the Emperor after death. Nor was it unheard of for the Emperor to banish or sentence a noble to death in order to acquire his fortune.

Customs duties were levied on trade between provinces and on foreign commerce. Banking could only be carried on by superintendents of the treasuries, who also generated profits from the minting of coins and exchange.

The Emperor engaged in trade on his own account, which, naturally enough, produced no duties. Given his absolute authority, it's difficult to differentiate between personal and national revenue; the Emperor decided how all such revenue and income was to be disposed of.

* * *

The Mogul Empire nearly became a flash in the pan under Babur's son, Humayun. Babur had only been able to lay the foundation for his empire during the five short years of his reign (1526-30); it was up to Humayun to consolidate it. But, at the age of twenty-three Humayun was more interested in sampling the pleasures of life available through his inherited fortune.

Ensconced comfortably in his harem, smoking opium, he surrounded himself with the most exquisite luxuries his riches could obtain. He counted and recounted his growing treasure of fabulous gems. He was the first, but by no means the last, of the Mogul Emperors to show an inordinate interest in diamonds.

This interest is often credited as the source of bad luck that plagued his reign. From the time the notorious "Koh-i-Noor" diamond fell into his hands, misfortune dogged his footsteps. The barely pacified tribes and provinces his father had brought under the Mogul banner began to revolt. His incompetence led him from one military fiasco to the next until he was finally driven from India by Sher Shah, a former lieutenant of his father.

During Humayun's exile he was plagued by opportunists and petty chiefs. Under the pretext of loyalty to his cause, they were usually more intent on relieving him of the fortune in jewels that he managed to keep, even during his most desperate hours.

It was only after disposing of the "Koh-i-Noor" as a gift to the Shah Tehmasp of Persia for offering him asylum, that his fortunes took a temporary turn for the better. He was able to begin the long climb back to his throne. By 1555 he had recaptured Agra and Delhi and wrested power from Sher Shah's successors.

But his return to power was short-lived. He re-immersed himself in debauchery and began to assemble a new collection of jewels and precious stones. One day in 1556, having just counted his newly-formed treasure, he fell to his death—some say he was pushed—from the steps of his library, in an opium daze.

The nascent Mogul Empire was once again threatened with extinction. However, with a bit of luck, and perhaps his only real claim to fame, Humayun had sired Akbar, a son destined to become the greatest of all the Mogul Emperors.

* * *

Before Akbar there had not really been a Mogul Empire. But by his death that empire stretched from Kashmir in the north to the Deccan in the south. Although in many ways enlightened—he discouraged the practice of self-immolation of a Hindu's wife on his funeral pyre, and regularized the land revenue at one-third of a peasant's gross—Akbar was still an undisputed autocrat with the power of life and death over his subjects.

Only a man of single-minded and despotic authority could maintain control over so many disparate peoples. There were wild Pathan and Afghan tribesmen in the mountains of the north, fierce warriors from the Rajput as well as warlike Sikhs of the Punjab. It was up to Akbar to restore the fortunes, literally and figuratively, of the Moguls. This he did by surrounding himself with the ablest administrators and generals to be found in Persia.

It was their job to insure the expansion and submission of that domain as well as gather the revenue necessary to run it, all the while satisfying the whims and grandiose plans of its ruler. As was true of so many of history's leaders, Akbar felt the need to memorialize his power and prestige. Not with simple, transitory monuments but with concrete symbols that would live on after his death. The monuments Akbar visualized required funds that even today would be beyond alll but the wealthiest of nations.

The first monument was the city of Agra, destined to become the capital of the Mogul Empire. In 1565, less than ten years after Akbar's accession, it was little more than a mud-walled village with a ruined brick fort on the banks of the River Jumna.

Over the following sixteen years, five hundred masonry buildings were constructed to house Akbar's growing court and administration. Around them grew a city that was, in the terse words of an Englishman visiting Agra in 1585, "much greater than London." The London to which he referred was that of the richest English monarch until that time, Elizabeth I.

When the Emperor left the city to pursue his military campaigns, it nearly became a ghost town. All of the court and administration went with him. His entourage numbered 300,000 persons!

This vast caravan, comprised of soldiers, officials, servants, tradesmen and the imperial harem of more than five thousand women (three hundred for the Grand Mogul) streamed out before the Emperor in what must have seemed an endless stream of pomp and circumstance. Only unlimited wealth could have sustained such an entourage. The annual cost of the Imperial household alone exceeded three million pounds, an amount of almost incalculable proportions in those times.

This wealth "...was so enormous that all attempts at inventory would be given up after four hundred pairs of scales oscillated day and night for five months." Was it any wonder that Akbar needed more than one hundred Treasuries to account for all his riches?

But an even grander and more extensive monument was yet to come. Having begun one city, Akbar became convinced that ghosts overran the new Red Fort and were responsible for the deaths of his twin sons Hassan and Hussain. A more propitious site for his capital was needed. Akbar settled on Sikri, the home of the Muslim holy man, Salim Chisti, who had prophesied the birth of the male heir, Jahangir, in 1569.

Building began in 1571. The foremost artisans and craftsmen in India descended on Sikri. The city was created by those gifted in painting, stonework, design, marble inlay, precious gems in stone, and glorious tiles. Vast elaborate palaces, embellished with lace-like stone carving rose before the Emperor, his wives and the imperial princes.

There were grand reception halls, their echoes muted by fine silk, silver/gold-threaded carpets and tapestries. There were luxurious baths in which the eyes and nose were at once bathed in the scent of the most exotic spices wafting across shimmering pools set with intricately figured tiles and gems. All were lavishly decorated with sculpture, inlay and painting that only a ruler could afford. It was truly an imperial city, dominated by one man and his dreams of grandeur.

Although Akbar was responsible for establishing the wealth of the Moguls, he saw it as a means to an end rather than as personal treasure. He never became personally enamoured of this wealth, although he certainly was not austere in its use. His strongly built, five foot seven inch frame was clothed in the finest silks and muslins his empire could produce, set off by glittering jewelry and a gem-encrusted dagger. In view of the number of his enemies, it must not have been entirely ornamental.

Even though his wealth ensured his legacy, not even the richest man on earth could live forever. Akbar died of dysentery at Fatehpur Sikri in 1605. He left behind a well-ordered realm to his son, Jahangir, as well as two hundred million pounds in treasure and coin.

* * *

The reign of Jahangir lasted nearly twenty-three years (1605-27). But Jahangir was not the energetic, driven man his father had been. His proclivities were more those of his grandfather, Humayun. Although he assiduously maintained the court ritual expected of the Emperor, his life was occupied by pleasure. Running the empire was mostly in the hands of his Persian wife, Nur Jahan.

His attentions were devoted to the most beautiful women, the most talented singers, the tastiest wines and the most luxurious goods and jewels his power could demand or his money buy. It was during Jahangir's reign that the English and Dutch made their first attempts at setting up Indian trading empires. It was from these Europeans, and the Portuguese of the previous century, that we learn about the Moguls and their courts.

In 1616 Sir Thomas Roe, on an embassy from James I to establish trade ties between England and the Moguls, witnessed Jahangir's luxury. His departure from Ajmer, which Roe recorded, is retold by Hansen:

> Attendants rushed to buckle on Jahangir's sword and scabbard, encrusted with huge diamonds and rubies...each side of his turban blazed with rubies and diamonds the size of walnuts, while in the middle a huge emerald gleamed. The Emperor stood bedecked in jewels; a chain of pearls, rubies and diamonds covered his midriff; a three-strand pearl necklace vied in splendor with jewelled bracelets and armlets set with diamonds, and every finger boasted a ring....Two eunuchs carrying gold maces set with rubies ran along on either side of the Emperor's vehicle....Three palanquins trailed in Jahangir's wake, gold-plated and also adorned with precious stones; a footman carried a gem-encrusted footstool of gold.

Roe claimed that "[I]n jewels (which is one of his felicityes) hee is the treasury of the world, buyeing all that comes, and heaping rich stones as if hee would rather build than weare them."

Jahangir's jewelry, and that of the Moguls in general, was created less for its artistic form than for its ability to impress and bedazzle the onlooker. Colored stones were in great demand. But diamonds, for which Jahangir seemed to have a particular penchant, were also valued if exceptionally large and of good water. William Hawkins, another Englishman who visited India during Jahangir's reign, had this to say about the Emperor's collection.

> Hee is exceeding rich in Diamants...and usually weareth every day a faire Diamant of great price, and that which he wearest this day, till the time be come about to weare it againe, he weareth not the same; that is to say, all his faire jewels are divided into a certaine quantitie or proportion, to weare every day....Hee hath another Jewell that cometh roundabout his Turbant, full of faire Diamants and Rubies.

Nor was the Emperor the only person at the court to bedeck himself in jewels, although those who did so took care not to outshine him. His nobles adorned themselves with jeweled turbans, great gold necklaces and belts, and diamond encrusted dagger and sword scabbards. Sparkling gems glittered in their ears, nostrils and even between their teeth.

The women of the court were even more densely adorned. Gemmed tiaras, braids and brooches dangled tinkling gilded pendants. Precious stones, pearls and gems pierced their ears or left nostril, and were embedded in their foreheads. Long necklaces of gemmounted filigree extended below their navels. Jewelled girdles encircled their waists, often with chains reaching upward to their necks and downward to thigh bracelets. Armlets, anklets and even toe rings, rounded off this glittering display.

Jahangir drifted further into drug-addicted dissolution, debauchery and cruelty. After a revolt led by his son Khusrau, he ordered the boy's eyes stitched shut and bathed in a concoction of caustic leaf, relenting later, by which time Khusrau was blind in one eye.

Manipulations grew after the succession. The wife who had controlled the realm, Nur Jahan, connived at retaining her privileges and power following Jahangir's death. Meanwhile his sons vied with each other to establish their claim to the throne. War broke out and Shah Jahan emerged victorious. But he was not merciful in victory. In order to secure his claim, all his brothers were put to death on his coronation day, a decision he would live to regret.

* * *

Of all the Mogul emperors, Shah Jahan is probably the best known in the West, primarily for his conception of the Taj Mahal, that immortal memorial in shimmering white marble to his favorite wife,

The Eureka diamond, the first diamond found in South Africa, in 1866. 10.73 carats

Cecil Rhodes, 1853-1902, founder
of De Beers Consolidated Mines
Limited.

Sir Ernest Oppenheimer, 1880-1957, Chairman of De Beers Consolidated Mines Ltd. and founder of the Central Selling Organization, through which all major diamond producers sell their diamonds

Barney Barnato, 1852-1897, an early diamond magnate who, together with Cecil Rhodes, dominated the diamond fields of South Africa in the late 1800's

Harry Oppenheimer, Chairman of De Beers
Consolidated Mines following the death of his father, Sir
Ernest.

A diamond cutter at
work.

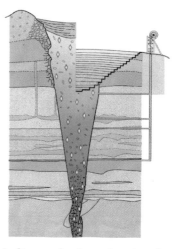

A diamond mine, showing the
"pipe" of blue ground in
which diamonds are found.

The Kimberly mine, perhaps the most famous diamond mine in the world.

A view of the Kimberly mine 1872-1877

The Lichtenberg diamond rush

Brilliant diamond cut

The Florentine Diamond. A great yellow diamond of 137.27 carats, possibly dating from prior to 1477.

A collection of polished diamonds

A collection of uncut diamonds

A brilliant pink diamond said to have been worn by the first Moghul
Emperor, Babar (1483-1530)

A replica of the 49-carat Pigot diamond, the only diamond known to have
been deliberately destroyed by its owner, Ali Pasha, ruler of Albania, in
1822.

A replica of the original uncut Cullinan
diamond and the cut diamonds made
from it.

The Regent, a 140.50-carat diamond, with a history dating back at least to the 17th century. Now in the Louvre.

The 55-carat Sancy diamond dates back to at least 1580. Probably still extent as the "Astor", the property of the Astor family in England.

The 56.71-carat Shah Jahan diamond, a gift to the
Empress Mumtaz, was believed to have been taken to
Persia after the sacking of Delhi and then given to
Empress Elizabeth of Russia in 1739.

A round, brilliant cut diamond

The Hope diamond. This supposedly jinxed, 44.50-carat blue, first appeared in London in 1830 but may have been part of the French Crown Jewels which were stolen in 1792.

Mumtaz Mahal. By the time of its completion twenty-four years after Mumtaz Mahal's death, he had poured more than 20 million pounds into its jewel and colored marble inlaid decoration and construction. Twenty thousand men worked on it daily amid the hammering of stone masons and artisans gathered from the far corners of the empire.

The Taj Mahal was only one of the many edifices Shah Jahan erected. He far exceeded Akbar's building spree and contributed to the drain on the imperial exchequer. Palaces rose for himself, his wives and children. Magnificent mosques, forts, royal buildings and gardens grew in Agra, Delhi, Lahore and countless other cities. All consisted of the highest artistic and architectural levels to be had.

Shah Jahan's love of the opulent exceeded that of any of his predecessors. The Red Fort at Delhi boasted a private audience chamber with a ceiling of beaten silver and marble walls embedded with precious stones. In addition to decorating his buildings, he expended stupendous amounts on satisfying his obsession with gems and jewelry.

The value of his personal gems was said to exceed ten million pounds, four million of which he wore constantly. Jadunath Sarkar states that, "[H]is rosary contained five rubies and thirty pearls, and was valued at eight lakhs" (800,000 rupees or nearly £100,000). This rosary, so Sarkar claims, contained only second-class gems!

He describes an aigrette Shah Jahan wore on his turban that contained five large rubies and twenty-four pearls, valued at 1,200,000 rupees. Even the fabulous but ill-fated "Koh-i-Noor" diamond, by this time back in India, graced his turban, set off by a plume of the Bird of Paradise.

The cost of maintaining the elaborate daily life of the palace must have been enough to drive any responsible paymaster to distraction. Meats and vegetables flavored with rare herbs, sweetmeats and exotic fruits, flowed from the kitchens on trays of silver and gold. Nor was such opulence restricted to the Emperor, although it may be wondered how anyone could match him.

No one was foolish enough to outshine him. Still, there was plenty of room for maneuver and the Emperor's officials vied with one another to see who could entertain him the most lavishly. One such occasion was recorded for posterity by a Portuguese friar, Sebastian

Manrique, on the occasion of a feast given for the Emperor and Crown Prince: "...the banquet hall was adorned with rich carpets of silken, silver and golden embroidery, which covered the floor so as to form tables on the ground."

Manrique's eyes popped at the sight of five-tiered stands covered with gold vessels, silver braziers and perfume holders; odors of ambergris, eagle-wood, and civet drifted up to him, and a seven-spouted hydra of silver spewed scented water into a trough.

"The meal lasted over four hours; dancing girls accompanied dessert, along with three great gold vessels filled with diamonds, rubies, and other gems.

The Emperor's love of gems was well known. On his coronation day his royal harem showered him with a cascade of precious gems from enormous gold platters. In the last year of his reign, gifts poured in from his nobles totaling over one million pounds

Shah Jahan was generous, in fact more so than any Mogul Emperor. By the tenth year of his reign, the Emperor's court historian reported that ninety-five million rupees (£10.8 million) in cash and kind had been given away, of which about five crores, or 50 million rupees, was in gems, jewels and precious accoutrements.

This largess was lavished in particular on Shah Jahan's children; over one million pounds in gems alone was distributed. Dara Shikoh received the lion's share. At the Emperor's sixty-sixth birthday celebration in 1655, the Crown Prince made his appearance in a gold-embroidered vest, covered with a prince's ransom in pearls and diamonds bestowed upon him by his father.

Then, Shah Jahan compounded the honor. He ceremoniously placed his own ruby and pearl studded turban on the Crown Prince's head, and announced that the prince would henceforth carry the title of Shah Buland Iqbal, which Jahangir had bestowed on Shah Jahan so many years ago. He bade Dara sit in a specially placed golden chair beside the Peacock Throne.

All this favoritism toward the Crown Prince stoked the fires of resentment among Dara's brothers, particularly Aurangzeb, third son of Shah Jahan and Mumtaz Mahal. That resentment was to hold dire consequences for all the brothers.

In September, 1657, Shah Jahan was taken seriously ill in Delhi.

To deflect revolt by his brothers, Dara Shikoh rushed to his father's side and banned all news of his condition and of court affairs. However, this only aggravated matters; the land became rife with rumors that the Emperor was dead.

In the Deccan where he had been sent as Viceroy in 1652, Aurangzeb bided his time and nursed his overwhelming hatred of his brother, Dara. Why should this apostate, this mocker of Muslim belief and tradition, be allowed to ascend to one of the greatest thrones in Islam?

Aurangzeb was crafty. First he encouraged his brother, Shuja, to advance against Dara from Bengal, where he had crowned himself head of state. While professing only to be interested in freeing Shah Jahan from Dara's clutches and purging the state of Dara's non-Muslim influences, Aurangzeb made an alliance with his younger brother, Murad.

He swore on the Koran to recognize Murad's claim to Mogul territory from the Punjab west, and began to march on Agra. Dara was forced to split his forces. One was defeated by Aurangzeb at Dharmat.

Before Dara's other army could return to help, he was forced to flee to Delhi by Aurangzeb's forces, leaving Shah Jahan almost defenseless in Agra's Red Fort. Aurangzeb drove Dara out of Delhi to wander through northern and western India until his capture and murder by Aurangzeb's slaves.

Aurangzeb now held the upper hand. Even the weak-willed, some say simple-minded, Murad knew Aurangzeb wouldn't honor his sacred pledge to acknowledge Murad's claim to the throne. He dreamed of sitting on the glorious Peacock Throne or at least on the golden seat he had zealously transported through two great battles. But the Peacock Throne was not destined for him. At a banquet in 1658, Aurangzeb took him prisoner and had him beheaded.

But Aurangzeb was not destined for the Peacock Throne either; for the time being at least. Even though he had forced his father to surrender the Red Fort by cutting off his water supply, he still did not dare to harm the old man nor openly usurp his symbols of power. Instead, he advanced on Delhi where he had himself crowned Emperor.

The remaining eight years of Shah Jahan's life were spent in total sequestration in the Red Fort, accompanied by a steadily diminishing group of servants, his harem, and his faithful daughter, Jahanara. Aurangzeb had not seen his father since departing for the Deccan in 1652. He maintained contact only through caustic notes that heaped petty insults and deprivations on his father in attempts to wrest from him the last perquisites of the Crown.

Although the ascetic Aurangzeb was apathetic to jewels, he became obsessed with depriving his father of them. He viewed them as symbols of the imperial dynasty that now rightly belonged to him. Aurangzeb claimed the Shah was an emperor in retirement leading a life of religious meditation, thus requiring no jewels.

One by one the jewels were removed; first, three million pounds worth Dara Shikoh left in the fort when he fled Agra. Then various items of Shah Jahan's personal jewelry, including a highly prized diamond thumb ring and a large diamond pendant. The ex-emperor drew the line when it came to his rosary of one hundred perfectly matched pearls, threatening to grind it into powder before relinquishing it.

Even the Peacock throne was finally removed. But not before Shah Jahan, hoping to retain some of his be-gemmed masterpiece, detached two diamond and ruby encrusted panels. However, even these were eventually forfeited.

* * *

Who was this Aurangzeb, this cunning and totally ruthless man who presided over the decline of the Mogul Empire? His religious zealotry dominated and defined all his actions.

He ruled himself and his empire by the Koran. His acts of religious intolerance toward the Hindu majority of his subjects did much damage to the tolerance and religious harmony attempted by his grandfather, Akbar. Even Shah Jahan had nurtured this enlightened view.

The new Mogul empire alienated many trustworthy Hindu nobles. Proclaiming himself "Grasper of the Universe," Aurangzeb managed to preserve, and even extend, his stolen empire for over fifty years. But only by means of crude oppression. He was a practicing ascetic, reading the Koran and praying incessantly, copying the holy book in his free time and giving the profits from these copies to the poor.

He observed all the precepts and prohibitions of the Muslim faith, abstaining from liquor, meat and frivolities of any sort. He banned music at court and even ordered the exquisitely carved figures on Akbar's tomb to be painted over.

In short, Aurangzeb's religious fanaticism made him a destroyer rather than a builder like his predecessors. Even though he did not squander wealth, his forebears had. This, combined with his constant warfare, emptied his treasuries by the time of his death.

Even such an austere ruler had to maintain the facade of imperial splendor. Tavernier recorded that, "Aurangzeb...has no great regard for jewels...." He did not wear them, due to Islamic law, but his court retained the outward glory of his ancestors.

Tavernier further relates that thirty lavishly caparisoned horses were kept ready for Aurangzeb's use. "The bridles are...enriched with diamonds, rubies, emeralds, and pearls...and suspended from the neck...a fine jewel, either a diamond, ruby, or an emerald." He goes on to describe the Emperor's normal throne at Delhi, "....In the middle of this hall...they place the throne when the Emperor comes to give audience and administer justice. It is a small bed of the size of our camp beds, with its four columns, the canopy, the back, a bolster, and counterpane; all of which are covered with diamonds."

Diamonds were in no short supply in Aurangzeb's India. Nine-tenths of the annual precious gem trade was in diamonds alone. Bernier, a traveler and contemporary of Tavernier, states that while serving the King of Golconda, Mir Jumla "...caused the diamond mines...to be wrought with extraordinary diligence, so that people discoursed of nothing but of the riches of Emir Jemla, and of the plenty of his diamonds...not reckoned but by sacks."

In Tavernier's time nearly all the diamonds in the world originated in the famed mines of Golconda, a name synonymous with wealth. These mines, some of which produced for more than two hundred years, were now in Aurangzeb's hands.

By the time Tavernier reached Aurangzeb's court he knew gifts would be necessary to gain the trade he sought. No favors could be expected except in return for those given. Upon being presented to the Emperor on September 12th 1665, he made the following gifts:

> Firstly, a shield of bronze in high relief thoroughly well gilt...the whole piece (costing) 4,378 livres...I also presented the Emperor with a battle mace of rock crystal, all the sides of which were covered with rubies and emeralds inlaid in gold in the crystal....Also a Turkish saddle embroidered with small rubies, pearls and emeralds...another horse's saddle with the housing the whole covered with an embroidery of gold and silver....The entire present which I made to the King amounted to 12,119 livres.

Presents were also necessary for high court officials and relatives of the Emperor.

The custom of the Emperor receiving gifts from his nobles on his birthday continued under Aurangzeb, but with a twist. Not content with the riches that would be literally heaped upon him that day, Aurangzeb devised an ingenious stratagem to accumulate even more.

Prior to his birthday his treasurers were instructed to sell jewels from his Treasury to the nobles, ensuring that he received their value twice over. Tavernier relates: "In diamonds, rubies, emeralds, pearls, gold and silver, as well as rich carpets, brocades of gold and silver...elephants, camels, and horses, the Emperor receives in presents on this day to the value of more than 30,000,000 livres."

Aurangzeb never sat comfortably on his throne; the combined influences of the Peacock Throne and the diamonds in the Mogul's Treasury dogged him throughout his fifty-year rule. He could never forget how he had acquired his throne.

He felt constantly threatened, not only by the alienated Hindus but by his own family. His eldest son had deserted to Shuja during the War of Succession, and was imprisoned until his death in 1676. His second son, Muazzam, had conspired with the kings of Bijapur and Golconda and was placed in confinement.

His third son, Azam, was extremely temperamental and lacking in self-restraint. Aurangzeb distrusted him. Akbar, the fourth son, rebelled against his father in 1681 and was driven into exile in Persia where he died in 1704.

The youngest, Kam Raksh, was a pampered, foolish and headstrong child of his father's old age. It was he and Azam who fought over the throne when Aurangzeb finally died in 1707. Although Azam initially proclaimed himself Emperor, within two years he was ousted by his brother. Like father, like son.

* * *

In the thirty years following Aurangzeb's death his descendants hastened the disintegration of the great Mogul Empire, in a witch's brew of uncontrolled expenditures, oppressive taxation and religious conflict. Governors stopped paying tribute and established themselves as independent monarchs in their provinces. Hindu rajahs rose up seeking revenge.

The British seized upon all the chaos to expand their influence. By 1739, little power remained to the ineffectual and degenerate Mohammad Shah outside of Delhi.

The plum was ripe for plucking. Nadir Shah, the ruthless but militarily talented ruler of Persia, decided to harvest it. He met and routed Mohammad Shah's army at Karnal, seventy miles north of Delhi, in February 1739, taking the unlucky Emperor prisoner in the process.

Intent on capturing the Mogul treasure, he proceeded to Delhi and began an orgy of looting and pillage. When a popular uprising in the city resulted in the deaths of several hundred Persian soldiers, he loosed the remainder of his army on a rampage of indiscriminate massacre, leaving, in the words of a contemporary chronicler, "the streets...strewn with corpses, as the walks of a garden with dead flowers and leaves."

The wealth from 213 years of Mogul rule was now Nadir Shah's for the taking. The French Abbe de Claustre described this booty.

> A hundred laborers were occupied for fifteen days in melting down and casting into ingots the gold and silver...not already in the form of coins....Two ingots, pierced through the middle and tied together with heavy cord, constituted one camel load; five thousand chests were filled with gold rupees and eight thousand with silver rupees. There was also an inconceivable number of ...chests filled with diamonds, pearls and...jewels. In a word, the value of the treasure...the King of Persia carried off from India can be estimated at three hundred carols of silver rupees: which

is the equivalent of five billion, four hundred millions of our silver.

Streeter, writing in 1882, estimated the value of this booty at thirty to sixty million pounds. Put in another, perhaps more understandable context, it was said that the loot from the sacking of Delhi exempted the people of Persia from all taxes for three years.

One item included in the loot, perhaps the most prized by Nadir Shah, was the Peacock Throne. However, as with many of the Moguls, Nadir Shah had little chance to use it. Its curse followed him, nevertheless.

Nadir suspected his eldest son of complicity in an attempt on his life in 1741 and had him blinded. Now, instead of the victories he'd always known, he was faced with setbacks. He took it out on his subjects with higher taxation and many executions. Exhausted by the constant campaigns, deaths and ravage, his subjects rose up in revolt. He was assassinated near Fathabad on June 19th, 1747.

* * *

We have already followed the course of the "Moon of Mountains" diamond. The histories of the "Koh-i-Noor", "Taj-i-Mah" and "Darya-i-Nur", all included in Nadir's booty, will be dealt with later.

What of the immense treasure Nadir Shah carried back from India? Like the Mogul rulers, Nadir transported his Treasury wherever he went, no doubt in part to protect it from unscrupulous officials. V. B. Meen and A. Tushingham write, "When the Shah left his capital, the Crown Jewels accompanied him, not only because they were his indispensable insignia of rank but because they were the portable treasury of his kingdom and could provide the means of winning allies and recruiting troops, buying off the enemy, or rewarding the loyal servant."

One diamond from this hoard, weighing 99.52 carats, the "Shah of Persia", was used in exactly that manner. It was presented to General V. D. Starosselky near the end of World War I for services rendered as commander of the Persian Army.

Another diamond, an oblong, yellowish one of 88.7 carats, known as "the Shah", figured in an act of international politics between Russia and Persia in 1829. Following the assassination of the Russian Ambassador in Teheran it was presented as a token of grief to Czar Nicholas I. It became part of the Russian crown jewels.

Many of the gems reputedly carried off by Nadir Shah may have disappeared from the Persian Treasury in the manner noted above. Others undoubtedly disappeared during the unsettled years following his assassination. This was the case with the "Moon of Mountains". Still, one of the most formidable collections still extant remained to form the backing for modern Persian currency.

Until the overthrow of Reza Pahlevi, part of this treasure could be seen on display in Teheran. Meen and Tushingham reported that one case "...contains a number of tiaras and thousands of cut but unset stones: scores are over twenty carats in weight and six exceed 100 carats. In fact, more than half of all the cut diamonds of this great size whose locations are known (or even reported in the literature) are in this collection."

* * *

But what happened to the Peacock Throne? No one knows for certain. Although succeeding kings of Persia claimed to sit on it, there is some doubt that the throne from which recent Persian dynasties have taken their name is really the same Nadir Shah carried off from Delhi. Lord Curzon inspected the throne in Teheran toward the end of the nineteenth century and categorically stated:

> The Takht-i-Taous (Peacock Throne) is not an Indian work at all....The original Peacock Throne of Nadir Shah was discovered in broken-down and piecemeal condition by Agha Mohammed Shah (1785-97) who extracted it, with many of the conqueror's jewels, by brutal torture from his (Nadir Shah's) blind grandson, Shah Rukh...then had the recovered portions of it made up into the throne of modern shape and style, which...stands in the palace in Teheran....In this chair, therefore, are to be found the sole remnants of the Great Mogul's Peacock Throne.

One need only review the history of its most recent possessor, Reza Pahlevi, ShahinShah of Persia, to realize that the throne, witness to some of the most momentous events in Indian and Persian history, has retained its malevolent powers.

The Age of Brilliance

*D*iamonds reached their zenith in the eighteenth century as the most exalted precious gem and the bearer of great misfortune. Neither before nor since, has it been used so lavishly. The dispersion of the English crown jewels by the Commonwealth was a trifling inconvenience compared with the sacking of Delhi or the destruction of the wealth of the French Crown during the Revolution.

The century began auspiciously enough with the discovery of the brilliant cut around 1700. Although its invention was attributed to a Venetian jeweler named Vincenzio Peruzzi, there is now doubt that he even existed. Be that as it may, the brilliant cut was far superior to those that preceded it.

Its fifty-eight facets—thirty-three above the girdle (crown) and twenty-five below (pavilion)—brought the diamond's scintillating light and colors to their full glory.

The diamond became the most sought-after and valuable gem. Candle-lit salons and courts, led by Versailles dominated the social activities of the rich. They were the perfect setting for the diamond's new fire and brilliance.

Nor did the diamond brook much competition from colored

stones. Light, airy forms dominated by diamonds replaced the ornate Baroque jewelry of the previous century. Settings now tended to be invisible or, as with silver settings, blended with the diamond's luster. Sparkle was coveted by eighteenth century fashion plates.

And sparkle they did. From men's shoe buckles to their waistcoat buttons. Louis XIV glittered in a grand coat displaying 171 diamond buttons! The breasts of European monarchs began to twinkle and glimmer like star-studded firmaments. Rings shimmered on the fingers of men and women; light flashed from women's coronets and brooches, set with diamonds dancing on the ends of gold coils that caught and reflected light with each movement.

The crowned heads of Europe were literally weighed down by masses of diamonds. Louis XIV, on the occasion of the Persian Ambassador's presentation at court, appeared in a gold-ornamented black suit embroidered with 12 million pounds worth of diamonds! At the coronation of George II and Queen Caroline in 1727 the Queen's dress was so burdened and stiff with £100,000 worth of jewels that she was unable to kneel. A system of pulleys was devised to control her skirts.

Although sumptuously rich, the French court by now had competition. The treasuries of the Holy Roman Empire are legendary. Austrian monarchs bedazzled onlookers with a fabulous Toison d'Or studded with diamonds. A diamond tiara containing the 44 5/8-carat, brilliant-cut "Frankfurt Solitaire" often graced the head of Maria Theresa while the so-called rose necklace, consisting of fourteen rose-shaped ornaments, each containing one large diamond surrounded by smaller ones glittered upon her bosom.

The pride of the Bavarian royal jewels was the 35.32-carat "Wittlesbach Blue". This beautiful brilliant was part of the bridal treasury of Princess Maria Amalia of Austria when she married Elector Charles Albert of Bavaria, who later became Emperor Charles VII of the Holy Roman Empire.

In 1722 it was valued at 240,000 florins. It was worn as a breast ornament by the Empress, then later by the Emperor as the centerpiece of a floral design containing 700 brilliants from which hung a Golden Fleece. When Bavaria became a kingdom, it was an integral part of the royal crown.

In 1701 Prussia came into existence as a kingdom. The Elector of Brandenburg assumed the title of King. Prussia under Frederick I, was by no means impoverished, as evidenced by the crown jewels. His crown contained 110 rose-cut diamonds, 8 brilliants, 8 drop pearls and 83 round pearls. The orb was of 18 carat gold and contained 50 diamonds, and 36 rubies and garnets. The scepter held 690 diamonds, 3 large oriental garnets as well as 332 smaller ones, and an oriental ruby.

That the King loved gems was clear. By his death in 1713 he acquired the aforementioned 34.5-carat "Little Sancy", the centerpiece of the Prussian crown jewels. He also acquired various gem-encrusted grand orders and 120 diamond-studded buttons, twenty-six of which weighed between 5.13 and 16.38 carats.

Frederick's successors continued to build the Prussian jewels to provide objects of readily convertible value in time of need. At the beginning of Frederick's reign they were valued at nearly 2 million reichs thalers, a suitable war chest to finance his expansionist wars.

Peter the Great, who reigned over Russia from 1696 to 1725, laid the foundation for what was to become "the most magnificent collection of personal jewelry in the world." Determined that his wife Catherine would succeed him as Empress, he had a crown designed for her that far exceeded in value and beauty any his predecessors had worn.

Topped by a large balass ruby "of greater size than a pigeon's egg," the crown was lavishly covered with diamonds—2,536 to be exact—and "oriental pearls all of equal water and extraordinary dimensions."

No less than seven monarchs reigned in the period between Peter's death in 1725 and the accession of Catherine the Great in 1762. But none had the power, political acumen or style to bring the Russian court to the heights of opulence which characterized her reign, especially when it came to diamonds. Never one to be outdone, Catherine decided that the coronation crown must outshine even that of the first Catherine.

Jeremie Posier, a Genevan artist Catherine commissioned to design her crown, states that he "...picked out the biggest stones, diamonds as well as colored gems, most suitable for mounting, and...thus obtained the richest object that ever existed in Europe." He well might make that boast for the finished product contained nearly 5,000 diamonds weighing over 2,800 carats!

However, the only colored gem that actually appeared on the crown was a great ruby-colored spinel said to have been purchased in Peking for a "load of gold ingots." What a spectacular sight Catherine must have made on her coronation day, crowned with this creation.

Catherine's collections are too numerous to note here; it has been estimated that she added over 10,000 carats in diamonds to the Russian crown jewels! The story of how she acquired the "Moon of Mountains" has already been related and the tale of the famed "Orloff", which crowns the Imperial Scepter, will be told.

Perhaps mention of one item of her jewelry will serve as an example of the sumptuous diamonds with which she surrounded herself. It was a beautiful necklace, the main part of which contained thirty-six perfect diamonds weighing a total of 475 carats, an average of thirteen carats per stone!

* * *

The court of the Hanoverian sovereigns of Great Britain was different from the rest of the courts of Europe as far as crown jewels were concerned. The legacy of the Commonwealth was still making itself felt. When the crown jewels were needed for ceremonies, they were set with gems hired for the occasion.

Anyone not aware of this might have marveled at the £375,000 worth of gems in the King's Crown and the £100,000 worth of jewels on Queen Caroline's petticoat at the coronation of George II. Here the diamond was the dominant gem. £375,600 worth were hired in for the coronation of George III and Queen Charlotte in 1761.

It is a wonder that jewelers were willing to hire out their gems. In a bill for the rental of these stones an item of £42 is noted to cover gratuities to persons finding and returning carelessly mounted jewels dislodged from the coronation regalia. During the actual coronation the Sword of State was forgotten, and the Sword of Justice lost at the coronation banquet because "the person carrying it had slipped away to a brandy shop".

Hire gems were used only for state occasions and then returned to their owners. However, the Hanoverian kings accumulated large collections of jewelry for their personal use. Queen Charlotte had several magnificent pearl necklaces as well as five splendid brilliants given her by the Nawab of Arcot, the largest of which weighed 38.7 carats. Two diamonds set as earrings weighed 23.6 and 33.7 carats. A particularly munificent gift worth several lakhs of rupees was made to George III in 1765 by Shah Alam, the Mogul Emperor. One lakh equaled £11,250. The gift consisted of:

> an exceeding fine string of pearls with an awbray studded with diamonds; a perfume box in the form of a casket on a tray, both objects...studded with diamonds; a dagger with a handle of jasper to fasten it to the girdle; a sword of gold mounted with diamonds, and with buckles of diamonds; a shield with four flowers of gold enameled with a belt and buckles set with diamonds.

The Lisbon court of the Portuguese monarchs had long been resplendent with wealth from the East. Many diamonds were purchased by Portuguese traders in Goa and sent to the mother country. But an event occurred in 1725 that would make Portugal one of the wealthiest nations in Europe and send tremors through its diamond markets.

For some years the Portuguese had been mining gold in the province of Minas Geraes in their Brazilian colony. Many miners had come across sparkling stones, but they weren't known to be valuable. One day a prospector named Bernardo Lobo, who'd seen uncut diamonds in the east, recognized the stones and the rush was on.

Gold seekers became diamond hunters overnight. At first it seemed one had hardly to exert oneself to find these highly valued gems. A five-carat stone was found sticking to the cabbage picked by a slave for his dinner. Even crops of fowls were diligently searched for diamonds that the birds may have swallowed.

Most of the mining in this disease-ridden area was carried out by slaves. As in India, finding a diamond over eighteen carats was rewarded with freedom. Smaller gems were rewarded with new clothes, a hat or a knife. But the punishment for attempting to steal a diamond was much more severe than in India.

The apprehended thief could expect a beating or an iron band fastened around his throat. None of it was enough to deter those willing to take the chance. It's estimated that nearly one third of diamonds found were surreptitiously withheld.

The poor inhabitants of the area seemed also to suffer their curse. One diarist observed it was "as if the genii, guardians of the treasure, were indignant at the presumption of man, and tried by every means to prevent the dispersion of the buried treasure." Drought and earthquake followed in the wake of the Brazilian discovery. But the greatest cruelty came from man himself. A greedy government drove the native inhabitants from their land, to remote and wild regions where they died of exposure and starvation.

For the twenty years following the discovery of the Minas Geraes fields annual production was estimated at 144,000 carats, of which the King of Portugal took a steadily increasing royalty. He also claimed any stone over twenty carats. It has been estimated that the King's income exceeded £100,000 a year from diamonds alone.

Such was the wealth that poured from Brazil. Ruby, topaz, garnet, amethyst and other precious stones were also mined there. When the Lisbon earthquake of 1765 destroyed much of the Portuguese crown treasure, it was soon replenished by the Brazilian mines.

* * *

The discovery of Brazilian diamonds had implications for the diamond market as a whole. A glutted market with sharply falling prices threatened the fortunes of those dependent on Indian diamonds for their livelihood. Panic ensued in the diamond centers of Europe, culminating in rumors spread by Dutch diamond merchants that the Brazilian stones were of inferior quality or, worse, not real.

These rumors gained such credence that the Portuguese were forced to first ship their gems to Goa from whence they were re-exported to Europe as Indian stones.

In actual fact, the increased influx of Brazilian diamonds to Europe came at an opportune moment, as the Indian mines were beginning to dry up. Ironically, the saturated market only stimulated demand. By now the steadily growing middle class desired and wore this irresistible gem. Once the market stabilized and prices began to rise again, the demand for diamonds had to be met in other ways.

Imitation seemed to be the answer. False diamonds were nothing new. People of wealth had been wearing quartz and rock crystal imitations for years. The first satisfactory substitute for the masses was called Paste or, as it's now known, paste. It was discovered by a German named Paste, who established himself in Paris about 1758 as a purveyor of imitation diamonds.

Others were soon to follow. So many that by 1767 a corporation of *joailliers-faussetiers* was established in Paris. In Switzerland, where it was forbidden to wear diamonds, marcasite or white iron pyrite became fashionable and ladies spent much care and expense on its setting.

* * *

Real diamonds, particularly the large stones preferred by royalty, never lost their allure. Nowhere was their use more notable than at the French court where eighteenth century fashions and standards of opulence were set. With the possible exception of Catherine the Great's, no other European court was as dazzling as that of Louis XIV.

The Duke of Orleans, regent for the child king Louis XV, forbade the wearing of pearls, fine stones and diamonds in 1720 in an attempt to quench the hemorrhage of funds and restore state finances to a sound footing. The attempt failed.

When Louis XV attained his majority in 1722, a crown was ordered for his use after the coronation. Twining described it as "the most splendid that ever existed." A complete description of this fabulous regalia would be too extensive to repeat here. But an indication of its sumptuousness is that it contained, among numerous diamonds, eight of the Mazarin table diamonds, the 140.5-carat 'Regent' and the 55-carat 'Sancy', with 15 diamonds set back to back and joined together by little ornaments to correspond with the 'Sancy'.

Louis XV had acquired a taste for diamonds at an early age and particularly loved the "Regent" and "Sancy". The young king wore both of these on several occasions before his coronation. At the reception of the Ottoman Ambassador he appeared in "'a flame-colored coat with diamond buttons and button holes of Louis XIV; the "Sancy" diamond in a large agraffe in his hat and the "Regent" diamond set in a knot of pearls and diamonds on a shoulder ornament."

Louis' consort, Marie Leczinska, also loved gems. For her marriage to the King on September 5th, 1725, a crown containing 138 diamonds, 40 rubies, sapphires, topazes and emeralds, as well as numerous fine pearls was constructed from gems taken out of the crown jewelry. The Queen was also especially fond of the "Sancy", often wearing it as a pendant.

The King lavished jewels on his Queen and various mistresses. The most famous of these were the Marquise de Pompadour and Madame du Barry, both of whom were often seen sporting crown jewels. While the ambitious Marquise used her position to advise and influence the King, du Barry was more interested in the material rewards she could gain from her liaison. It was her obsession with jewels, and particularly diamonds that ultimately led to her downfall and execution.

Du Barry was an obsessive spendthrift, constantly lavishing funds she did not have on jewels and badgering the King for even more. Having accumulated an extensive collection, she became a target for thieves. A large part of her collection was stolen. The missing gems consisted of 140 large and 700 smaller diamonds, 300 large pearls, 7 large emeralds and other gems worth, by du Barry's own estimate, 1,500,000 francs.

Many were state property. Such was the public outcry that nineteen years after the death of her lover, this episode figured in the decision of the Revolutionary Tribunal to sentence her to the guillotine.

Contrary to popular opinion, the reign of Louis XVI was not as prestigious as his predecessors'. This had more to do with Louis' disinterest in pomp and circumstance than the impoverishment of the court. The taste in jewelry was changed by Marie Antoinette's preference for lighter settings designed to set off great gems. The great crown diamonds, including the "Regent", the "Sancy" and the "Mazarins" were, according to Twining, "set negligently in an aigrette of heron's feathers, or as drops of water on garlands of flowers." Although her taste differed from her predecessors, there is no denying that Marie Antoinette preferred diamonds. The King, wishing only to be left to his own interests, showered her with beautiful diamond parures, earrings and jewels.

* * *

Of all the instances of intrigue, perfidy and avarice that have surrounded the diamond through the centuries, none has had a greater impact on the course of history than the notorious Affair of the Diamond Necklace. It has been called the spark that ignited the French Revolution and left its impervious brand on all, high-born and low, connected with it. Because of her known penchant for diamonds, it was not difficult to imagine Marie Antoinette's complicity in this fateful episode.

The axel upon which this wheel of misfortune spun was the Countess de la Motte-Valois. Born Jeanne de Saint Remy in 1756, she was the daughter of the last heir to the once illustrious name of Valois. She was made fatherless at five and abandoned by her ne'er-do-well mother at the tender age of eight. Jeanne had the fortune— or misfortune—to be taken into the protection of the Marquis and Marquise de Boulainvilliers who raised and educated her along with their three daughters.

However, Jeanne resented the treatment she received at school. It lacked the deference she felt her due as a Valois. In 1770 she complained to the Marquise who removed her from school and apprenticed her to a fashionable dressmaker in the capital, a step Jeanne viewed as further degradation.

The year 1770 also witnessed the arrival from Austria of Marie Antoinette. She was to become the catalyst for future calamities, and the particular nemesis of Jeanne de Saint Remy. Only a year older than Jeanne, Marie Antoinette came to wed the heir to the French throne. Unfortunately, her husband, the hulking but gentle, Louis XVI, was more interested in machinery and hunting than in his vivacious young consort. He left her to her own devices. She surrounded herself with courtiers who shared her love of gay and frivolous activities, fabulous balls, horse racing and especially all-night gambling for huge stakes.

But the most costly of her passions was diamonds, especially the lavish, elaborate creations of Bohmer and Bassange, the crown jewelers. Shortly after his accession to the throne, the king lavished more than 100,000 ecus' of diamonds on her but she was not satisfied. She paid 400,000 francs for a pair of girondele earrings, each composed of six perfectly matched, enormous white diamonds. She paid even more for a set of diamond bracelets.

But the diamonds that really took the Queen's fancy were those in an incomparable necklace originally intended as a gift from Louis XV to his mistress, Madame du Barry. Composed of 647 flawless white diamonds totaling 2,880 carats the necklace was the *piece de resistance* of the crown jewelers, who had spent years assembling it.

Unfortunately for them, that "...glorious ornament, fit only for the Sultana of the World," in Carlyle's words, was unfinished at the time of Louis XV's demise in 1774. Nor was there any written order that would have obliged the new king to pay for it.

For this, Louis XVI must have been grateful, the jewelers were asking 1,800,000 francs, an incredible amount even at that spendthrift court. The Queen, although coveting the necklace, could find no pretext to justify such an expenditure, which, she noted, was enough to supply another battleship to the French fleet.

The years 1770 to 1776 were eventful ones for Jeanne. She attracted the attentions of countless gentlemen, not the least of whom was her foster father, the Marquis de Boulainvilliers. She felt he could assist her in establishing her claim to the Valois name and fortunes.

In 1775 she finally gained royal recognition of her claim as well as a crown pension. But the minuscule pension came nowhere near covering the extravagant expenditures of the newly-named Countess. So the Countess schemed at being recognized by Marie Antoinette, by which means she hoped to recover the lands and fortunes she felt were rightfully hers. This led her even further into debt.

Many a noble family breathed a sigh of relief when the Countess married a dashing, but impoverished, cavalryman, thus preventing their male heirs' involvement with this charming seductress. But marriage did not deter the Countess' seduction of anyone who could help her gain a position in the court to which she felt her name entitled her.

A chance meeting in 1783 brought the Countess into contact with Prince Louis de Rohan, Cardinal of Strasbourg and Grand Almoner of France.

It was a meeting that held dire consequences for them both. Before long she learned of his desire to be recognized by Marie

Antoinette. To obtain this recognition, the Prince was willing to go to any ends. During his assignment as French Ambassador at the Austrian court he had gained the enmity of Empress Maria Theresa, Marie Antoinette's mother.

In 1785, claiming to be a confidant of the Queen, the Countess convinced the credulous Cardinal that he would be able to gain the Queen's good graces by acting as go-between for the purchase of the fabulous diamond necklace the queen so coveted.

In order to allay the Cardinal's doubts, she even arranged a midnight rendezvous in the palace gardens between him and a courtesan disguised as the Queen. By means of forged letters that guaranteed payment for the necklace, the Countess, acting as courier was able to obtain the necklace in the Cardinal's name from Bohmer. He asked no questions, only too glad to rid himself of this encumbrance.

Since the first payment was due months after the necklace had been turned over to the Countess, she had sufficient time to dismantle it and send her husband to England to dispose of the loose diamonds. However, as the time for the first payment drew near, the Cardinal became uneasy. He had neither received the official recognition promised by the Queen nor heard that she had worn the necklace. He had given his personal guarantee to the crown jewelers.

One is naturally led to wonder how the Countess expected to get away with such a scheme. She knew that sooner or later her machinations must come to light. It can only be guessed that she counted on the scandal and disgrace that would befall the Cardinal. She thought it would force him to secretly honor his guarantee to pay for the necklace, leaving her with the proceeds from its sale.

As is often the case, chance played its unpredictable hand. Impatient to receive the promised payment, Bohmer approached the Queen directly. Even this might not have led to exposure were it not for the Cardinal's arch enemy, the Secretary of State, Baron de Bretuil. He insisted that the Cardinal be publicly arrested and brought to trial. This was followed by the arrest of the Countess.

Many, whose only crime was their acquaintance with the accused, were thrown into the Bastille. Mademoiselle d'Oliva, the prostitute who impersonated the Queen; Retaux de Villette, the forger of the letters; hapless members of the de la Motte family; and, most notably, one Count Cagliostro and his wife were put away. Only Count de la Motte, who was still in England, escaped.

On May 31st, 1786, judgement was pronounced. Villette was banished for life from France; Mademoiselle d'Oliva was acquitted for lack of sufficient evidence but died, destitute, shortly thereafter. Count de la Motte was condemned in absentia to be flogged, branded and to serve a life sentence in the King's galleys. Of all the conspirators, he was to suffer the least. A Revolutionary court overturned his conviction and he died peacefully in 1831.

The severest sentences were reserved for the Countess and the Cardinal. Jeanne was "condemned to be flogged and beaten, naked, with rods by the public executioner; to be branded upon both shoulders with a hot iron with the letter V (for voleuse, or *thief*); to be imprisoned in the female house of correction of the Salpetriere for life; all of the goods of the said Jeanne de Valois de Saint Remy, Countess de la Motte, to be forfeit to the King."

The Prosecutor General's recommendation stated further:

> That the Cardinal Prince de Rohan be sentenced to appear eight days hence in the Great Hall of the Palais de Justice to make public statement to the effect that he has been guilty of criminal temerity, of disrespect to the sacred persons of the sovereigns, in betaking himself to the Grove of Venus in the belief that he was there to meet Her Majesty the Queen of France; and to the effect that he has contributed to the deception of the jewel merchants by allowing them to believe that the Queen had knowledge of the necklace transaction; that the Cardinal Prince de Rohan be sentenced to express his repentance publicly, and publicly to seek the pardon of the King and Queen; that he be condemned to divest himself of all his offices, to make a special contribution of alms to the poor, to be exiled for life from all the royal residences and to be held in prison until execution of said sentence.

The Countess' sentence was readily approved by the Parliament of Paris. But the Cardinal was a different story. In the days preceding the French Revolution the royal family was in public disfavor. The sensational publicity surrounding the trial only heightened the belief that the Cardinal was being used as a scapegoat for the Queen.

This was reinforced by the fact that for the rest of her life the Countess would never retract her claim that the Queen devised the whole scheme. In the shadow of scandal, wishing to establish their independence of the King, the Parliament of Paris voted, twenty-six to twenty-three, to acquit the Cardinal of all charges.

The curse of the diamonds should have ended at this point. But that was not to be the case. In what could only have been contrived by someone on high, the Countess managed to escape from prison and make her way to England, From there she issued a steady stream of written denunciations and attempts at self-vindication. These lurid missiles were hurled with deadly effect at the Queen, adding fuel to the pyre of lies and rumor that were to consume her.

Neither did the Cardinal get off as easily as it seemed. The King held enormous powers and used them to force the Cardinal to resign as Grand Almoner and take up exile at the Abbey of Chaise-Dieu. The French Revolution, which might have provided restoration to a man so maligned by the King, was not even beneficial to him.

When offered the chance by the Revolutionary government to remain in France if he denounced his allegiance to the Church he chose to flee the country. Although far from destitute, the Cardinal's fall from power must have been particularly humiliating to a man of such pride. He died in Germany in 1803.

The Countess de la Motte-Valois remained at large, sowing her seeds of deceit. Her husband absconded with the remains of the funds raised from the diamonds, the Countess was left to survive on her own, admittedly prodigious, wits.

Making use of her feminine wiles, she found a place among the French exile community in England, which provided for her until she could publish her memoirs. This exposé was an immediate sensation in England and France but its profits were claimed by the Countess' many creditors. They hounded her every footstep. In June 1791, she jumped from a second story room to the pavement below in an attempt to escape them. Although mortally injured, she languished in excruciating pain for over two months before dying.

Even the queen was not destined to escape the diamonds' curse. In 1793, she was found guilty of crimes against the state by the Revolutionary Tribunal and guillotined.

* * *

The Diamond did not restrict its bane to French royalty; the new Revolutionary government was also affected.

For hundreds of years the monks of the Abbey of St. Denis kept the priceless French coronation regalia. Although the regalia suffered damage, it still contained items that attested to the sanctity of the French Crown. Wishing to eradicate all symbols of the royal house, the Commissioners of the Directory of Paris removed the royal ornaments from the Abbey.

The Crown of Charlemagne, the *Sainte Couronne* and the Crown of Jeanne d'Evreux, symbols of regal authority, were thrown into the melting pot to provide funds for the Revolutionary government, while *Joyeuse*, the coronation sword, was sold in 1798.

"On July 31st, 1793," Twining records, "Barrere proposed the destruction of all the "frightful souvenirs of the former kings in the Abbey of St. Denis." This led to the destruction of a country's royal heritage seldom equaled. A commission oversaw the destruction of fifty-one tombs. Two months later a revolutionary mob venting its fury against the crown entered the crypt and desecrated fifty-seven royal coffins, many of which held priceless funeral regalia.

But the most sacred article, the *Sainte Ampoule* containing the consecrated chrism used to anoint French kings at their coronation, was still held by the Church of Rheims. A representative of the National Convention was sent there in October, 1793 with orders to locate and destroy this most holy of all the coronation regalia.

Although half-hearted plans were made for a substitution, the *Sainte Ampoule* was seized. At two o'clock on October 7th, 1793, it was carried to Rheims' Place Nationale, placed on the base of Louis XV's statue and smashed with a hammer.

By these wanton acts of destruction the Revolution hoped to eliminate all regalia that could be used in restoration attempts. But, as history would show, men are not so easily thwarted.

Another treasure consisting of the crown jewels and personal jewelry of the King and Queen, was assembled and placed on public display in the *Garde Meuble*. The theft of this treasure-trove, and the tracking down of its perpetrators is surely one of the most fantastic episodes of the Revolution and of diamond's checkered history.

The Robbery of the Garde Meuble

*P*aris in mid-September, 1792, was in the throes of anarchy brought on by a violent and tempestuous revolution. France's armies suffered a series of defeats. The way to Paris stood clear for the invading army of the Prussian Duke of Brunswick. On July 25th he called for the liberation of Louis XVI and threatened to destroy Paris if the King should be harmed.

Enraged at this presumption to dictate their affairs, the Paris mob stormed the Tuilleries, imprisoning the royal family. This was followed by mass arrests of royalist sympathizers until more than 2800 prisoners crowded the makeshift prisons of the capital.

Inflation was rampant. Counterfeit paper money (*assignats*) flowed from the loosely controlled prisons. Brunswick was drawing nearer and chaos ruled the streets. Military units and able-bodied men lined the outskirts of the city in its defense. Fear of the royalists incarcerated in the city's jails became endemic, leading to mob attacks on institutions between the 2nd and 7th of September.

Almost 1400 prisoners were massacred, only about a quarter of whom were actually political prisoners. Surviving prisoners, mostly riffraff or petty thieves, were free to roam the streets looking for prey among the now defenseless citizens.

It was in these circumstances that possibly the largest jewel robbery in history took place. The French crown jewels had been placed in the *Garde Meuble*, or royal furniture repository, near the Tuilleries. The public was able to view these hated symbols of their deposed monarchy.

Included were the crown, scepter and coronation regalia, as well as precious objects such as a rich collection of fine tapestries, Cardinal Richelieu's church plate, the arms of various French kings and, most important, the crown jewels. These jewels, mostly diamonds, included the "Regent", "Sancy", "Guise", "Blue Diamond of the Crown" and nearly 7500 others valued at 30 million francs.

Any Parisian that ventured out did so at his own risk. Armed bands posing as revolutionary militia roamed the city relieving anyone they saw fit of valuables "in the name of the revolution."

Even before these bands proliferated there had been concern for the safety of the items stored in the Garde Meuble. Protection of the two entrances was slipshod at best. The number of guards varied daily. If their relief did not appear, they might desert their posts leaving the Garde Meuble completely unprotected.

Jean Marie Roland, the Minister of the Interior, foresaw trouble, and requested a permanent armed guard, but his warnings went unheeded.

Such was the state of the Garde Meuble's protection that its curator, Thierry de Ville d'Avray, removed all the diamonds in June and placed them in a cupboard in his own quarters. Had he left them there, they might have been saved. But in August he returned them to the repository.

During the September massacres Thierry was killed. Rumor had it by his replacement, one M. Restout.

Restout also complained about the lax security, requesting twenty armed men for each entrance. He was told there was nothing to fear since the doors were locked at night. The next night the head guard told Restout either to guard the gates himself or lock them. Restout locked the gates.

On Monday, September 17th at ten o'clock in the morning Roland sent a message to a sitting of the legislative assembly that the Garde Meuble had been robbed. Two thieves were arrested, but all the diamonds and most of the other valuables had disappeared. The crown jewels alone were valued at nearly 30 million francs, all that remained were a few stones worth 5,500!

Who had planned this audacious theft? Accusations flew. Roland accused M. Danton, under whose jurisdiction the Garde Meuble came. The Public Prosecutor of the Revolutionary Tribunal accused Marie Antoinette. Even the aristocracy was accused. All these accusations were wild guesses, politcally motivated. The truth was much simpler.

On the days when the Garde Meuble was open to the public there had been one regular visitor. His name was Paul Miette. At thirty-five, Paul already had a long criminal record. He was now planning the crime of the century. But before his plans were completed he was arrested on another charge and thrown into La Force prison.

While there he met an old friend named Deslandes and related his plan. He knew it was no more difficult to break into the Garde Meuble than into a private house. The two men then took other prisoners into their confidence and a sizeable band gathered.

Then fate lent a hand. The attack on the prisons set most of them free. In the final plan, even more men were included. One of the original La Force plotters named Cadet Guillot went to Rouen and brought back four partners unknown to the others: Bernard Salles, Fleury-Dumoutier, Francois-Auguste and Gobert. Another plotter named Letort helped a friend of his named Bazile escape from a prison in Brest to join the group.

At 11:00 on the night of September 12th the conspirators gathered in the Place de la Concord. The Pont de la Concorde and three narrow streets, the Rue Royale, the Avenue des Tuilleries and the Champs Elysees accessed it. The Champs Elysees was nothing more than an infectious sewer then. It was the haunt of Paris's most desperate criminals. North of the square stood the Hotel Crillon and the Garde Meuble.

The Garde Meuble had two entrances, one on the square and the other on the Rue Saint Florentine. While some of the thieves stood watch disguised as citizens' patrol, another group began to break into the repository. Using the rope of a street lamp they climbed onto the roofs of neighboring lodges, tore the shutters off the Garde Meuble's window and cut a hole in the glass. Once again luck was on their side; the heavy iron bars meant to secure the window were not in place.

The thieves were now inside, behind secured doors. They placed iron bars on the inside so if they were heard, the guards would have to force their way in. Two thieves, Gallois and Badarel, held lighted candles and the rest went to work.

From his many visits to the Garde Meuble Paul Miette knew exactly where to go and what to take. In a room on the first floor was a maquetry chest of eight drawers with a heavy copper lock. The first of these drawers contained the "Regent", the "Sancy", pearl jewelry and precious gems. The other drawers contained diamonds set in wax trays, the greatest part of the treasure. There was also a coffer banded with copper that held the King's decorations and begemmed buttons.

Miette headed for the maquetry chest with a man named Francisque (rumored to be the nephew of the Bishop of Nice and related to the Foreign Minister of Sardinia). After breaking the lock they began to load their pockets. In addition to some of the mounted jewelry the gang took necklets, the King's shoe buckles, a pearl in a golden box, the sword of Louis XVI and two diamond-chain watches.

When they had all they could carry they went out the way they had come. In the square everybody divided the spoils and left immediately for Rouen.

The next night the thieves rested. But they could not forget about what still lay in the Garde Meuble. So they returned. Finding the window *still* open, they went inside. This time they made off with most of the loose diamonds. It was probably on this night that the "Regent" and "Sancy" were stolen.

On September 15th and 16th they came back a third time—in somewhat augmented numbers. This time they did not bother to leave a patrol. They even brought wine and food to dine amid the remaining armor, tapestries and art works, toasting the success of the most audacious robbery of modern times.

Since so many had taken part in this night's theft, they had to meet the following evening to divide the loot. They gathered on the banks of the Seine near the Palais Bourbon.

Two men, Le Blond and Le Feu, were passing by. They came closer to investigate the commotion, and were offered a chance to buy a box containing three diamonds and seven pearls. Le Blond bought it and added a few pearls he found laying on the ground. Le Feu wished to buy the box from Le Blond but they decided to first consult a goldsmith about its value.

In the meanwhile, the other thieves went to a local tavern for a share-out but ended up quarreling. They decided there was more where that came from and decided to go back the following evening.

The next morning found Le Blond and Le Feu at a goldsmith, who told them they should inform the Committee of Public Safety about how they had obtained the box of jewels. But at the Town Hall no one would receive them.

They went to the Superintendent of Police for the Pont Neuf area. He sealed the box, and had them take him to where they had bought it. There they found two rubies on the ground. They all went to the Garde Meuble but as the gates' seals were intact, they decided the gems had not come from there.

They went back to the Town Hall. This time they were received. A jeweler was called in but he refused to comment on the contents of a sealed box. He suggested that they all visit the curator of the Garde Meuble. When they found him he insisted, without actually investigating the display rooms, that the guards had been there day and night, that the gems could not have come from the Garde Meuble and had probably been stolen from the Tuilleries.

The police superintendent was skeptical, but he had no authority over the curator. He posted a notice stating that pearls and diamonds of great value possibly from the Tuilleries or the Garde Meuble had been found. Any goldsmith or jeweler who might have gems brought to him was to keep them and detain their sellers until the police arrived.

By this time word of the theft had spread through the Paris underworld. On the nights of September 16th and 17th, about fifty persons gathered in the Place de la Concorde. Some were dressed in the uniform of the National Guard. Others arrived singing the *Carmagnole*, a revolutionary song. The sentry guarding the gates to the Garde Meuble took them for good patriots and let them pass.

After that, he later confessed, he had gone off duty due to the cold.

Part of the group in the square entered the Garde Meuble, leaving the remainder on guard. A few objects, like Cardinal Richelieu's gold plate, remained. Everything else was pillaged. Stones were pried from their gold settings and the gold broken into more manageable pieces. When an object proved too large to fit in their pockets, the thieves threw it from the gallery to their compatriots in the square below. There had been violent struggles over the loot. The strongest made off with the best pieces.

By 11:00 PM almost nothing of value remained in the Garde Meuble. It was as if it had been picked clean by vultures. Everyone left except for two avaricious thieves searching for anything that might have been overlooked.

In the square the thieves who'd emerged were surrounded by those who stood watch. They demanded a sharing of the booty. They made so much noise that a National Guard patrol from the St. Honore appeared. Seeing the riotous crowd, they fixed their bayonets. But everybody managed to slip away.

The National Guard divided into two groups. One went to the Rue Saint Florentine and the other to the Rue Royale. One of the two thieves who'd stayed inside the Grade Meuble caught their eye when he passed before the glow of a street lamp. The patrol rushed to the spot and captured him while descending the wall, followed a moment later by his accomplice.

The commander of the patrol went for the keeper of the Garde Meuble. They all went to the repository and found the guards sound asleep. The two prisoners were entrusted to the guards' somewhat questionable care.

In the meantime, M. Camus, the archivist of the Garde Meuble, was stopping coaches in the square and questioning their occupants. In one, was a policeman named Collette sent to investigate the turmoil. Camus, the policeman, and his two assistants entered the building and looked in the display rooms. At the entrance they discovered that the rooms were still sealed. This made Camus suspicious of the policeman's orders. He ordered the man and his assistants taken into custody along with the two thieves caught descending the wall.

Camus returned to the spot where the two thieves had been caught. He climbed onto the gallery and found a massive gold vase the city of Paris had presented to Louis XV. A quick search revealed the broken shutters and the window through which the thieves had entered the building.

He found the display rooms a shambles. Small, loose diamonds, a superb pearl and an ivory box, along with various tools for breaking and entering were strewn across the floor. Camus began to question the prisoners but no one was talking.

While this was happening, the remaining thieves fled. When they were out of sight they demanded an immediate division of the spoils. Moving to the banks of the Seine near the Pont Concorde, they again quarreled over the booty. Sixteen men surrounded Francisque, handkerchiefs spread to receive the handfuls of diamonds he distributed.

Under the protection of darkness some more dexterous than others stole stones from the box and even from Francisque's pockets, spilling them on the ground in the process. Twice they were interrupted, first by a man carrying a lantern then by an old woman. At the last interruption Francisque advised them to separate and meet the following morning at Laconte's tavern.

Carrying a huge amount of loot, Badarel and Gallois separated from the other thieves when they left the square. They soon found they had too much to carry; and had in fact been losing jewels along the way. They stopped for a few minutes to hide some under stones and then went to Badarel's room to split the remainder.

Among their inventory was some of Richelieu's gold church plate, which they broke up to remove the gems and sell the gold in pieces. They were so rushed, they left some on the floor. This would later be found by police.

The next morning they buried another batch of jewels in the Allee des Veuves.

Others of the thieves took their haul and left Paris before the final share-out, realizing that once the theft had been discovered, there would be no place to hide. Some went to the provinces while others fled to England where they easily disposed of their ill-gotten gains.

The evidence against the two found leaving the Garde Meuble was damning. In addition to being caught at the scene of the crime, they were armed with a knife, dagger and burglary tools, and were carrying loose diamonds in their pockets.

One, Chabert, carried jewels worth 10,000 livres that had been given to the King by Tipoo Sahib, the Maharajah of Mysore. He also had a statue—a golden *Bacchus* (god of wine) astride an agate barrel, and an emerald/topaz-encrusted cross.

The other thief, Douligny, was found with a golden ship weighing over three pounds, decorated with "ten shining pink stones and twelve rubies," a crown decorated with rubies and table-cut diamonds, and a 24,000 livre golden diamond-covered bauble that Catherine the Great had given to Louis XVI.

It's difficult to imagine how the thieves could hope to explain their presence at the Garde Meuble, considering their new wealth. When Judge Fantin questioned them, Douligny claimed he had not known he was climbing into the Garde Meuble—he said he thought he was at a girlfriend's bedchamber. When he arrived on the balustrade people put the jewels in his hands and pockets and he had been too drunk to realize what was happening.

Chabert's alibi was equally weak; he claimed that a gang of armed robbers forced him to help carry things from the building to the middle of the square and it was then that he had been caught. It was discovered that Douligny gave a false address, and Roland halted the interrogation and held the men for trial.

The investigation was placed in the hands of Jean Marie Roland, Minister of the Interior, and Petion, the mayor of Paris.

Luck played into Roland's hands almost immediately. A forger by the name of Lamy-Evette had been released by the September massacres. He had a mistress named Corbin, a regular visitor to the *Jacobin* club. Roland was a regular there too.

Corbin approached Roland at a soiree, with the proposition that Lamy-Evette would provide information about the Garde Meuble theft in return for a pardon of his unfinished sentence. Roland agreed. Armed with a written warrant from the Interior Minister, Lamy-Evette visited criminal hang-outs. At one he met one of the thieves named Cottet and offered to buy some of his loot. Cottet agreed and a rendezvous was arranged. Cottet was met by a policeman instead, and was arrested with the jewels in his pocket.

Now Roland had his first breakthrough. Because of the number and value of the jewels Cottet had, Roland realized that he must have been one of the ringleaders. He offered Cottet protection if he would lead him to the rest. Cottet had little choice but to cooperate. But even with names and addresses, the authorities made little headway.

Some of the robbers had fled to England. Cottet was furious that the authorities waited so long before sending him out, giving the thieves time to escape. But there was little he could do about it.

Roland's only other break was minor. A gendarme observed a M. Anselme Lion buying some stolen jewels and arrested him. But the seller escaped. With so little to show for his efforts, Roland decided to at least hold on to what he had and ordered the arrest of Cottet and Lamy-Evette, despite his promise of immunity.

Some positive action was now required. The public and his political opponents were already using Roland's lack of progress to attack him. The 21st of September was set as the date for trial for the few arrested in connection with the robbery. When they came before the Tribunal they were charged with trying to overthrow the government.

The argument was that the proceeds from the theft were to be used for this purpose. This premise was supported by Douligny's Italian origin and the fact that Jean Jacques Chabert had been a valet to a member of the aristocratic Rohan family. The judge repeatedly tried to get them to admit that the nobility was behind the theft. But the accused maintained they were innocent dupes.

Finally Douligny broke down and agreed to take the authorities to a cafe on the Rue d'Angivilliers where some of the principles could be found. Several arrests were made.

Even so, Douligny and Chabert were sentenced to death. Faced with the end, the two thieves broke down completely, denouncing many fellow conspirators in hopes of mercy. When he heard their sentence Badarel, one of the two who took more than they could carry, also appealed to the court's mercy. His and Gallois' gold scraps had been found in their room. His only chance was to confess to the jewels were hidden in the Allee des Veuves.

A small treasure trove was discovered there. It included a piece of silver gilt decorated with nine large pearls; six small loose pearls; nine emeralds and rubies; an "agonthonis" representing the holy face mounted in gold; a golden figure ornamented with enamel; fifteen large set diamonds threaded on silken cords; eighty diamonds in settings on cords in two rows; and thirteen diamonds, nine of them rose cut. Because of this discovery, and in the hopes that Chambon and Douligny might have yet further revelations to make, their execution was stayed.

The pieces of the robbery began to fall into place. Each arrest led to new accusations and the recovery of more of the plundered items. In addition to the actual thieves, a large number of fences surfaced. Like a row of falling dominoes, each thief took another with him, offering incriminating evidence in the hopes of a lesser sentence.

Louis Lyre, another prisoner freed by prison riots, was accused of selling eighty fine pearls and twenty-four other stones taken from the Garde Meuble. He implicated his mistress, a cousin and another receiver. Although from surviving police records it's obvious that all were guilty, Lyre was the only one condemned to death. A few minutes before his execution, he named Lyon Rouef and several others as accomplices.

Rouef was arrested. He in turn named Fontaine as the receiver of a large quantity of diamonds, Israel of having bought pearls and large diamonds, and a man named Soloman of buying diamonds for one million five hundred thousand livres. Rouef's wife was accused of helping him sell a massive gold pot and a large number of silver gilt watch plates. Although Rouef had the greatest number of jewels from the Garde Meuble, both he and his wife were acquitted.

Francisque, the distributor of diamonds after the robbery, was accused of taking the "Regent" and the "Sancy". Badarel was accused of taking a large number of jewels later found in the Avenue Montaigne. They were both condemned to die, but Badarel was granted a postponement when he confessed.

As he mounted the scaffold Francisque asked for a stay of execution, promising to show where more diamonds were hidden. He led the authorities to the attic of his house and turned over diamonds valued at one million, two hundred thousand livres. Included was a 24.75 -carat pear-shaped stone and a pink diamond called the seventh "Mazarin", now on display in the Louvre.

As the trials continued into October and November, more was uncovered. Gallois, Cottet, Manger and a fourteen-year-old jockey named Alexandre were tried. The first three were sentenced to death, but not before they had named many. Alexandre was acquitted due to his age. Ashamed and depressed by what his son had done, Manger's father killed his wife and then poisoned himself.

On November 20th Paul Miette, the ringleader, came before the Tribunal. He had bought a house at Belleville for 15,000 livres with the proceeds from his theft. When the arrests began he went to his old house on the Rue Bossu, sold his furniture, and disappeared. He was apprehended at his new home but no incriminating evidence was found, despite Douligny's insistance that Miette had taken jewelry worth well over two million livres.

Meanwhile Miette's wife could not satisfactorily explain where she had obtained the 3,000 livres found on her. Miette's wife was acquitted but Miette was sentenced to hang.

During these early trials seventeen persons were brought before the Tribunal for the robbery of the Garde Meuble. Of these, five were acquitted. The remaining twelve were to be executed. But only five actually were.

The remaining seven sentences were reduced on appeal. These included Douligny, Chambert, Badarel, Francisque, Gallois and Manger. They were retried at Beauvais during May/June 1793. Miette also appealed and was acquitted, probably due to some connection on high.

Several well-known jewelers were retained by the government to determine what had been stolen and whether the recovered gems came from the Garde Meuble. Luckily, an inventory of the crown jewels had been completed less than a month before the robbery.

In drawers that held twenty million livres of unmounted diamonds only 192 carats in 81 stones remained. The drawer containing mounted jewelry had only a few diamond and pearl pieces of no great value and a poor quality sapphire. The part of the inventory listing the art objects and other valuable items showed clearly what was missing. With the exception of pieces of Cardinal Richelieu's plate recovered from the Allee des Veuves, everything was gone!

On December 10th, 1793, an announcement was made to the Convention that the "Regent", at 12 million livres the most valuable item stolen, was recovered and the thief and receiver arrested.

Three months later, the "Sancy", the "Guise" and some others worth several million livres were found in the house of a notorious thief and murderer named Tavenal. The following year one of the Rouen thieves was arrested for forgery and in the course of his interrogation his role in the robbery came out. The man, Dumoutier, claimed that the Rouen thieves had sold part of their loot for 8,000 gold louis, which they had divided among themselves.

His friends still held jewels worth over one million livres. He offered to turn these over to the authorities if he was allowed to return to Rouen. The request was denied and of the spoils carried off by the Rouennais, only the sword of Louis XVI was recovered. The rest probably found its way to England in the hands of Cadet Guillot.

In the inventory of 1792 was a magnificent Toison d'Or (Golden Fleece) valued at 3,394,000 livres. In its center was the famous "Blue Diamond of the Crown" that Louis XIV had bought from Tavernier. This diamond accounted for three million livres of the total worth of the jewel. The Golden Fleece itself was held in the jaws of a dragon cut from the famous ruby, the "Cote de Bretagne".

In 1796 a Hamburg painter named Brard reported to the Minister of Police that an émigré named Lancry had arrived in Altona with a ruby called the "Dragon". According to Brard, Cadet Guillot escaped to London with the bulk of the Rouennais' booty and gave the "Cote de Bretagne" to Lancry in return for debts owed.

Brard negotiated with Lancry for the sale of the ruby to the French government. He was assisted by M. Reinhardt, the French Minister Plenipotentiary in Hamburg. To force Lancry to sell, Reinhardt had him arrested. But he was released the next day, probably by the influence of the Prince of Wurtemberg who also wanted it. The Russian and Austrian courts were after it as well.

Although the French government offered 50,000 livres for this stone, it wasn't taken seriously since the French themselves valued it at 100,000. Finally Reinhardt was forced to admit that Lancry no longer had the ruby and it was being offered to the Pretender (later Louis XVIII) by the Royalist General Danican. The ruby can be seen today in the Louvre but how and when it finally returned to France is unknown.

What happened to the fabulous "Blue Diamond of the Crown"? No one is certain although there is evidence that it was removed from the jewel and cut, resurfacing as the "Hope" diamond.

Over the years many of the articles stolen from the Garde Meuble were recovered by the French government. But this jewel robbery was the most bizarre, before or since, in the history of diamonds.

Fatal Fascinations

The "Sancy"

No diamond had a more direct and bloody effect on European affairs than the "Sancy". Exactly when and where it was found is unknown. It turned up as one of the first diamonds cut by Louis van Berquem for the fifteenth century Duke of Burgundy, Charles the Bold.

It was claimed that Charles wore it in battle as a symbol of invincibility. If so, it certainly did not exert its powers in his favor. A Swiss soldier plucked it from his dead body in the Battle of Nancy, January 5th, 1477.

Not realizing the value of the gem, the soldier sold it for one gulden to a clergyman, who in turn sold it for 5,000 ducats to a dealer in Lucerne. From there it passed into the hands of King Manuel I of Portugal in 1495 and then, through one of his successors, to Nicholas Harley, Seigneur de Sancy.

The "Sancy's" story, up to this point is generally discounted, because it has too many similarities to the history of another famous diamond, the "Florentine". Also the "Sancy" is faceted top and bottom, a method of cutting unique to India.

What seems certain is that the Seigneur de Sancy did come into possession of this stone sometime between 1570 and 1580 while serving as French Ambassador in Constantinople. When he returned to France his diamond helped him maintain his position at the court of the mad king, Henry III. Sometimes Sancy loaned the diamond to the King or used it to raise money for the King's constantly depleted coffers.

Sancy raised funds on the diamond that helped secure the throne of Henry IV. One Sancy legend is that in order to finance the King's activities, he gave the diamond to Metz as security for a loan from that city's bankers. Enemies of the King heard of the transaction and managed to waylay the unfortunate messenger entrusted with the diamond's safe delivery. But the thieves could neither find the stone nor force Sancy's servant to tell what he had done with it.

They murdered him and buried the body. When news of what had happened reached Sancy he sent out a party of men to find the unfortunate servant's remains. The spot was found, the body exhumed and cut open. Sure enough, the faithful servant had protected his trust to the last. In his stomach lay the bloodstained, but intact, diamond.

During his reign Henry IV purchased gems whenever he could afford them. So it was not unusual that Sancy should offer his diamond. Henry considered it but thought 60,000 ecus too high. In 1604 Sancy finally found a buyer willing to meet his price in the person of James I of England, at whose court he served as Henry's ambassador.

With this sale, the story of the "Sancy", as it was now commonly known, took two paths. One version claimed that the wife of Charles I of England, took the "Sancy" with her when she fled to France. There she used the diamond as loan security.

She borrowed 427,566 livres from the Duke de Epernon to finance Charles' attempt to regain his throne. With the failure of Charles' cause, she authorized the Duke to keep the diamond in partial repayment of the loan. He later sold it to the acquisitive Cardinal Mazarin, who included it in a formidable collection known as the "Mazarin Diamonds". He eventually bequeathed them to the French Crown.

The second version of the "Sancy's" history maintains that the diamond stayed in England and was given to the Earl of Worcester for safekeeping. This version is substantiated by a letter from Henrietta

Maria in which she "...caused to be handed to our dear and well-beloved cousin, Edward Somerset, Count and Earl of Worcester, a ruby necklace containing ten large rubies and 160 pearls...strung together in gold. Among the(m)...are also two large diamonds, called the 'Sanci' and the 'Portugal'...." Following the restoration of Charles II in 1660, the Earl of Worcester returned the "Sancy" to the Crown.

But the diamond seemed destined to return to France. When James II fled to that country in 1688 he took the "Sancy" with him. Louis XIV grew tired of supporting his demanding and uninvited guest. James was thrown back on his own resources. He sold the 'Sancy' in 1695 to the French king for £25,000.

By whatever means it came into the possession of the French Crown, the "Sancy", along with the 'Regent', was set in the beautiful crown worn by Louis XV at his 1722 coronation. Although outshone by the much larger "Regent", the "Sancy" was a favorite decoration of French royalty when not fulfilling its fund-raising role for the perennially overspent French exchequer.

Whether hanging brilliant and aloof from a black velvet band around the neck of Marie Leczinska, complimenting a shoulder knot of pearls for her husband, Louis XV, or enhancing the beauty of Marie Antoinette, the "Sancy" was a truly royal gem.

The mystery of the "Sancy" was compounded when it was noted in the 1791 inventory of the French Crown Jewels. Valued at one million francs, it was listed at only 33.75 carats. Its actual weight was 53.75 carats (55 metric carats). Perhaps the turmoil in revolutionary France contributed to a less than exact inventory. Whatever the case, its whereabouts in the years following the robbery of the Garde Meuble remain unclear.

Many believe it was one of the gems recovered after the robbery. A 53.75 carat diamond, considered by many experts to be the 1691 "Sancy" was pledged by the French Directory to the Spanish Marquise of Iranda for a loan in 1795. The loan may have been instrumental in propping up demoralized forces taken over by Napoleon Bonaparte in 1796. He led a series of successes against the Austrians in Italy and Sardinia, which firmly established his power.

When the loan was redeemed the stone was supposedly bought by the Spanish Prince Godoy in 1809—doubtful since the Prince had fallen from power by that time—passed into the hands of the Spanish Bourbons or was given by the Queen of Spain to her lover, Godoy. Whoever possessed it, a stone reputed to be the "Sancy" was sold to the Russian house of Demidoff in 1828 by a French merchant, for £35,000.

In 1865 it turned up for sale once again, this time in its land of origin. It was purchased for £20,000 by a Bombay merchant, Sir Jamsetjee Jeejeebhoy. He did not keep it long, for in 1867 it was shown at the Paris Exhibition, and listed as the property of the famous French jeweler, G. Bapst. It was valued at one million francs.

As if the history of the "Sancy" wasn't confusing enough, another claimant entered the melee. During a tour of India in 1875 the Prince of Wales was shown a diamond that its owner, the Maharajah of Patiala, called the 'Sancy'.

For many years there was considerable confusion between this stone and another so-called "Sancy" purchased by William Waldorf Astor in 1906 for his son's bride, later Lady Astor. Although similar in coloring, at 60.4 metric carats the Patiala diamond is somewhat larger than the historic "Sancy". It is now generally agreed that the diamond now in possession of the Astor family is the true "Sancy".

* * *

The "Regent"
Like so many Indian diamonds, the story of the "Regent" is fraught with tales of deceit, robbery, political intrigue and murder. Sometime in 1701 a 410-carat rough, the largest diamond found until then, was unearthed by a slave in the Partial mine on the Kistna River about 150 miles from Golconda.

The slave was determined to reap the full benefit from such a rare find. Instead of turning it over, he wounded his own leg and wrapped this giant gem in the bandages. He managed to escape from the mine and make his way to the seacoast.

Aware that if caught he would be severely punished or put to death, the slave was anxious to find a buyer and purchase his escape to freedom. He was overjoyed to meet an English sea captain whose ship was about to depart for Madras. The captain agreed to take him on board in return for one half of the value of the stone when sold.

But the captain soon came under the diamond's deadly spell.

140

Why should a poor, ignorant native reap such a windfall when the stone was his for the taking? As soon as the ship was at sea he arranged an "accident." The slave was lost overboard and the captain pocketed the diamond.

Upon reaching Madras, the captain headed for the bazaar to dispose of his ill-gotten treasure. He soon found a buyer in Jamchund, the largest diamond merchant in India. Jamchund knew better than to ask about the genesis of this unmatchable stone and could hardly conceal his delight at being able to purchase it for only £1,000.

The captain quickly accepted Jamchund's offer and headed for the brothels and pubs of this port city to squander his wealth. But the diamond's spell followed. He could not forget the poor native he had so rapaciously robbed and murdered. The more he gave himself up to debauchery the greater his remorse. When all was spent, he hanged himself.

Jamchund was faced with the problem of reaping the profit he knew lay in his newest acquisition. This was not as easy as it might seem, for few had the wealth to purchase such a large diamond and those who did might ask awkward questions about its origins. So Jamchund waited. In 1702 he finally found him.

By the beginning of the eighteenth century the British East India Company was firmly established with three presidencies at Calcutta, Bombay and Madras. The Governor of Fort St. George at Madras was Thomas Pitt, an ambitious Englishman in India to make his fortune. Pitt had made some minor purchases from Jamchund in the past.

The Indian merchant now approached him with an offer to sell the diamond for 200,000 pagodas, about £85,000. Pitt considered this price exorbitant but continued bargaining. Negotiations went on for several months until a price of £20,400 was finally agreed.

Pitt then sent the stone to England by boat, insuring it for only £3000 to avoid attracting attention. The stone lay idle in England until Pitt returned in 1710. Pitt decided to have it cut and polished. This was a long and tedious process since the cutting technique of that time called for the use of a fine wire impregnated with diamond dust.

The process took two years, reducing the 11/6 inch rough to a cushion-shaped, 140.5-carat brilliant of the finest quality. The cutting cost £5000 but this was more than recouped by the sale of the dust and several small rose-cuts made from the cleavage pieces. They went to Peter the Great for £45,000.

The cutting neither diminished nor ended the diamond's pernicious history. After Pitt returned to England envious gossip that he had acquired the stone by unfair means haunted his every step.

This publicity, and the possession of the gem so worried him that he took to travelling in disguise. He never spent two nights in a row sleeping in the same bed while he possessed the diamond. He published a denial of the rumor in *European Magazine* of October, 1710. Seventeen years after his death his family republished his denial in the *Daily Post*, to counter the resurrection of this gossip by politically motivated opponents.

In 1717, Pitt was finally able to rid himself of what he now considered a bane. For some time he had been trying to sell the diamond that now carried his name. To this end he provided a model of the cut gem to one John Law, an Englishman who acted as his agent at the court of the Duke of Orleans, Regent of France.

To sell such a gem, based only on a model, must surely be one of the greatest feats of salesmanship ever recorded. But succeed he did, obtaining £135,000 for the diamond. His commission was £5000. The sale of the diamond not only removed a great weight from the shoulders of Thomas Pitt, but permanently established the fortunes of the Pitt family. It was to produce one of England's greatest statesmen, William Pitt, Prime Minister under George III.

Pitt's diamond might never have come to France were it not for the self-proclaimed efforts of a member of the regency council, the Duc de Saint-Simon. In his *Memoirs*, a questionable record, Saint-Simon claims that it was he who persuaded Philippe of Orleans, Regent for the boy-king Louis XV, to buy the diamond. Although admitting that Philippe felt the country could ill afford such a luxury, Saint-Simon writes:

> I applauded this sentiment but added that one could not
> think of treating the greatest monarch in Europe as one
> might an ordinary commoner, and that he was obliged to
> consider the honor of the Crown and could ill afford to miss

this unique chance to provide it with a priceless diamond which would excel all the rest of Europe.

Philippe could no more resist such pandering to his vanity than his predecessors and agreed to the purchase. The price of two million livres was to be paid in installments, with other gems used as security until the final payment was made. The diamond became known as the "Regent" after this sale, a name it carries to the present day.

The "Regent" first appeared in public in France on March 21st, 1721, when it was worn by Louis XV while receiving the Turkish Ambassador. Never had such an immense diamond appeared in the West before.

Not only was its size unparalleled but its dazzling beauty was nearly flawless. Its only imperfection was hidden by expert cutters. From the time of its use as the premier gem on Louis XV's coronation crown until the fall of the unfortunate Louis XVI it was never far from French royalty. Marie Leczinska had it removed from the crown to wear it in her hair. Marie Antoinette set it on a large black velvet hat where it dazzled her subjects.

In the 1791 inventory of the French crown jewels, the "Regent" was valued at twelve million francs, or approximately £480,000. It disappeared from the Garde Meuble in 1792 along with the crown jewels but was recovered some months later.

The "Regent" was used as security for a loan of four million francs from the Berlin banker, Treskow, in 1797 to prop up the financially shaky Directory. Redeemed, it was used immediately to secure another loan from a Dutchman named Van den Burg. He displayed it at parties and receptions. It was only after Napoleon redeemed it in 1802 that Van den Burg admitted he had exhibited a copy. His wife had worn the diamond around her neck, under her bodice, the whole time.

Once Napoleon brought the "Regent" back to France it was never to leave the country again. Napoleon had it set in the hilt of his coronation sword when he crowned himself Emperor in 1804.

Following his final exile it was taken by Marie Louise to her chateau at Blois. Her father, the Austrian Emperor Francis I, convinced her to return it to the French government. Charles X wore it at his coronation in 1825 and Napoleon III had it set in a Greek diadem for the Empress Eugenie. In fact, Eugenie was wearing it when Orsini and Peiri tried to assassinate her husband at the Opera in the rue Louvois.

Because of its historic significance and great value, the "Regent" was placed in the Louvre where it could be viewed by the public. It remained there until the approach of the German invaders in 1940. Smuggled from the museum, it was hidden from the reach of the grasping Nazis in the Chateau Chambord for the remainder of the war years.

Once more the "Regent" glitters cold and enticing from its display case in the Louvre. Should anyone be foolish or bold enough to consider stealing it, the entire glass case is automatically lowered into a vault each night.

* * *

The "Orloff"

It was a summer night in the mid-1760s. Heavy monsoon winds and rain from the Bay of Bengal lashed the temple courtyard as a dark figure made its furtive way across. The man was well known to the monks guarding the gates and had no difficulty crossing the previous six courtyards. He slipped past the monks guarding the last gate into the innermost holy of holies and stood, breathless, before the lofty blue statue of Vishnu.

Had the guards guessed the man's intentions he would never have made it past the first gate. But he had laid his plans carefully. After deserting the Carnatic Wars some years earlier, the ex-grenadier repaired to the island temple at Srirangam on the Coloroon River. Once there, he disguised himself as a native, professed Hinduism and slowly but surely worked his way into the confidence of the monks who guarded the temple. As a devout worshipper, he was admitted to the inner shrine. At last, his years of planning were about to come to fruition.

The Frenchman's body shook with excitement, his eyes drawn to two enormous diamonds glimmering in the head of the Hindu deity inside the shadowy temple. He shook off their mesmerizing effect and approached the statue. Clambering onto one of the god's four

144

outstretched arms, he reached up and began to pry the largest gem from its socket.

After fondling it for a moment he dropped it into his pocket. Then, whether startled by sound or simply too nerve-wracked to continue, he dropped back to the ground and hurried through the seven walls. By the time the monks discovered the theft he was deep in the jungle, heading for the coast. Some time later he turned up in Madras where he sold the diamond to an English sea captain for £2000.

One story has it that the "Orloff" was, in fact, the "Great Mogul" seen by Tavernier at Aurangzeb's court. Such was the story related by Dutins, a French traveler writing about precious stones in 1783. It explains how the "Orloff" came into Western hands but it is one many legends that grew up around this fabulous gem.

This story has been thoroughly discounted by Streeter, who argues that although the diamonds were both shaped like half an egg and similar in cut, the "Great Mogul", as described by Tavernier, weighed nearly 100 carats more than the 189.6-carat "Orloff".

Nor has anyone been able to explain how the diamond, if it was the "Great Mogul", ended up in the temple at Srirangam.

In any case, the diamond was carried to England by its purchaser and sold to an Armenian. At this point the story of the "Orloff" becomes confused with that of the 'Moon of Mountains'. Both diamonds were in Amsterdam in the hands of Armenian merchants at about the same time, and both ended up in Russia.

At this time the man for whom the "Orloff" was named also appeared in Amsterdam. Count Grigori Grigorievich Orloff was the grandson of Ivan Orel, who had served in the *Strelitzes* (Archers) under Peter the Great. This elite group fell into Peter's disfavor and were ordered beheaded, with Peter himself wielding the axe. When Ivan's time came, so the story goes, he was led to the beheading block to receive the fatal blow and found the head of the man just executed resting on the beam.

Kicking the head nonchalantly away, he remarked, "If this is my place, it ought to be clear." Peter was so impressed that he spared his life and placed him in a line regiment. His bravery in battle won him an officer's appointment and ennoblement.

Grigori must have inherited much of his grandfather's ruthless daring. By the age of twenty-four he was already a seasoned artillery officer. It was in 1758 after he had been wounded three times in the Seven Year's war that he was sent to escort Count Schwerin, a Prussian officer captured in the battle, to St. Petersburg. He was a dashing young officer who graced the most fashionable balls. At one he met the Grand Duke Peter and his wife Catherine, a meeting that would drastically affect his life as well as the history of Russia.

Catherine was immediately drawn to Grigori. He became her lover and she bore their illegitimate son, Count Brobinski. When her husband became Czar Peter III in January, 1762, Grigori and his brother Aleksei hatched a plot to depose him and raise Catherine to the throne. In June they murdered Catherine's husband. All was ready for Grigori's next step—marrying the Empress.

But Catherine kept putting him off. Grigori feverishly tried to prove his worth, and became one of her most astute advisors. When the Empress sent him to Moscow in 1771 to deal with an outbreak of disturbances he earned high marks. Later that year he was her premier representative at the Russo-Turkish peace conference at Focsani. But all these activities removed him from the center of power and from his Empress and lover.

Grigori had powerful opponents, most notably in the person of Nikita Panin, Catherine's political mentor. Although Catherine created him a count and made him adjutant general, director-general of engineers and general-in-chief, she denied him his ultimate goal. When Catherine took Alexander Vasilchikov, and later Potemkin, as her lovers in 1775, Orloff left Russia to nurse his wounds.

It was during this self-imposed exile that he made his way to Amsterdam. There he heard of the wondrous diamond for sale. This, he told himself, was the means by which he could win his way back into Catherine's favor. Not even an Empress could resist a lover bearing such a sumptuous gift.

One story was that Orloff met another Russian in Amsterdam who purchased a half-share of the diamond and in turn sold it to Orloff for 400,000 rubles. However, the most generally accepted story is that Orloff bought it directly from the Armenian merchant for £90,000, with a £4000 annuity.

Elated, he hurried back to Russia. On Catherine's saint's day in 1776 Orloff arrived at the palace with her other well-wishers. He bided his time until he was certain that all attention was focused on the Empress and approached the throne. Instead of the traditional bouquet of flowers, he extended a small box. Catherine's eyes must have danced when she saw the gorgeous gem, for she loved nothing more than diamonds. Orloff waited expectantly for some positive sign but the empress only thanked him politely and received the next visitor.

Orloff waited in St. Petersburg for days, caught between his high expectations and the nagging fear that it had all been for nothing. Still, his hopes remained high. Although she had returned many other valuable gifts, Catherine kept the diamond. But nothing happened. Weeks passed without a word. He left the capital a broken man.

As so often happens in unrequited love, Orloff turned to another woman. In 1777 he married his cousin, and embarked on another tour of Europe. But his mind still dwelt on the past and on what might have been. When his new wife died in Lausanne in 1782 it was more than he could bear. He returned to his estate near Moscow and died, insane, on April, 24th, 1783.

Although Catherine kept the diamond, she did not wear it. Instead, she had it set in the Imperial Scepter beneath the Russian double eagle, a fitting setting in the symbol for the world's largest nation, for it was then the western world's largest cut diamond.

Even in this grand setting the "Orloff's" mystique continued to grow. According to Russian legend, when Napoleon approached Moscow in 1812 the "Orloff" was hidden in a priest's tomb in the Kremlin. Napoleon ordered that the diamond be found and brought to the Kremlin as his own.

When the tomb was opened the diamond lay for all to see. One of the bodyguards reached out to pick it up. At that moment the ghost of the dead priest rose up and placed a curse on the invaders. Such a story illustrates the awe in which diamonds of the East were held, and the fear of tampering with them.

Perhaps that is why the government of the Soviet Union, to whom symbols of the deposed Russian monarchy were anathema, never tempted fate by selling, or even removing from the Imperial Scepter this ominous stone.

The Phoenix Stone

The diamond's prospects in the France of 1800 did not seem good. The country most responsible for raising the diamond to unprecedented heights was impoverished by the Revolution. Its diamond-filled collections of Coronation, crown and royal jewelry had been decimated by thievery and the armies of the Revolution.

Fortunes in diamond jewelry had been smuggled out of the country by Royalist émigrés. The few jewelers who managed to survive couldn't find a market for their wares since jewelry was frowned on by the country's austere masters. The diamond seemed to be dying, at least in France.

But the effects of the Revolution were short-lived. In a few years the diamond rose like a phoenix from the ashes of the country's poverty to prosper as never before. The coronation of Napoleon I in December 1804 marked the diamond's resurgence and heralded a new era of sumptuous display.

Although the Emperor reconstituted the French crown jewel collection, he only wore a few at his coronation, most notably on the hilt of his sword. Empress Josephine, and the rest of the royal entourage knew of his wish that the French court should eclipse all those before it. They were only too happy to oblige.

Jacques-Louis David's famous painting, "The Coronation of Napoleon," in which the female guests in diamond-encrusted parures nearly overshadow the Emperor, shows how dramatically diamonds regained eminence.

Napoleon was not usually surpassed. A favorite item of official dress was his sword, the guard of which was set with the 140.5-carat "Regent". According to L. Giltay-Nijssen:

> At the wedding of Prince Jerome and the Princess of Wurtemburg, Napoleon wore a fabulous chain with a diamond star of the Legion of Honor, valued at 188,221 francs and a jewel of double this value in his hat. In the center of this sparkled a diamond of more than 25 carats...bought for 180,000.

During the following years, Napoleon continued building the French jewel treasury, showering Josephine, and later Marie Louise, with magnificent diamond gifts. Among the most valuable was a great diamond parure, costing 1,654,460 francs. It was composed of a crown, necklace, comb, a pair of earrings, a pair of bracelets, and a belt. It contained two diamonds, each, exceeding 24 carats in weight!

Napoleon I amassed a diamond collection superior to that of the Bourbons. It brought him and his consorts no better luck than it had their predecessors. In 1809, after thirteen years of marriage, he cast Josephine off in favor of a more politically propitious marriage to the daughter of Emperor Francis I of Austria.

Josephine died in seclusion in 1814. Although his second wife, Marie Louise, survived him by twenty-six years, she lived them out as a duchess, and an inept one at that.

Napoleon retained his love of diamonds to the end. When leaving for exile on St. Helena his stepdaughter Hortense, Queen of Holland, sewed her diamond necklace into his waistcoat for security. Napoleon kept this gift as a symbol of the splendor that had once been his. He bequeathed it on his death-bed to his valet.

* * *

The diamond retained its place of importance in other European courts, even during the tumultuous Napoleonic Wars. In

England burgeoning wealth from the Industrial Revolution fueled the demand for gems, not only at court but among the newly rich middle classes. No longer was the diamond to be solely a prerogative of the aristocracy.

At the same time, the Brazilian mines were at peak productivity, providing an inconceivable wealth to the Portuguese treasury. (It's estimated that more than 1,300,000 carats were produced in the period 1772-1818.) When the Portuguese King, John VI, whose personal collection was worth more than £3,000,000, needed funds to finance his war with Spain and France he pledged the output of the Brazilian mines and raised 12,000,000 florins.

Production was so prolific that in the early 1830s, Dom Pedro, Emperor of Brazil, repaid the interest on the state debt to England in diamonds rather than cash, causing a glut on the diamond market and a temporary fifty percent reduction in their value.

The "Braganza" was the largest, most famous and certainly most enigmatic of the stones delivered by the Brazilian mines. Discovered around 1800 by three criminals exiled to the interior of Brazil, it weighed in excess of 1600 carats.

The stone was taken first to a priest who advised the three men to present it to the governor of the province. This they did, hoping that by offering up this stupendous stone their sentences would be commuted. Hardly believing what he saw, the governor called in experts who declared it a genuine diamond. He then suspended the sentences of the criminals and forwarded the stone to Lisbon. John VI was so taken by it that he wore it, uncut, suspended from a chain around his neck.

After a time the stone disappeared from public view, to be held in the Portuguese Treasury. Supposedly, it resides there still. Because no one has been permitted to examine it since then, it is conjectured that this enormous gem, once valued higher than £5,500,000, is actually an aquamarine or colorless topaz.

Many European treasures suffered drastically from Napoleon and his forces. Under the terms of the Treaty of Tolentino, the Papal Treasury, like many churches', was stripped of its wealth to support Bonaparte's armies in Italy. In 1806 all the silver and gold plate of the Prussian royal family was melted to support Frederick William

III's forces against Napoleon. The Prussian crown jewels were saved only because the chaos of the time had devalued them.

The bulk of the rebuilt French treasury fell into the hands of Louis XVIII during the Bourbon Restoration. After the escape of Napoleon from Elba, Louis fled to Ghent, taking the jewels with him. By his second restoration they were somewhat depleted, having financed the King's forces and been used as gifted allied generals for their services. Among these recipients was the Duke of Wellington who received 10 diamonds set in the Star and Badge of the Order of St. Esprit.

Charles X, who ascended the throne in 1825, wore a splendid diamond crown for his coronation, originally created for Louis XVIII. When his popularity began to diminish he ordered the crown jewels sent to him in Rambouillet, where he was ensconced. By August 5th, 1830 the Paris mob had again overthrown the government.

In an act reminiscent of the storming of Louis XVI's palace at Versailles, they converged on Rambouillet in a crowd of fifty to sixty thousand armed citizens intent on destroying the royal family. To save his own skin, Charles abdicated and agreed to return the crown jewels.

The mob marched triumphantly back to Paris with the jewels. They were stored in the Central Treasury of the Finance Ministry, locked by five keys held by three officials. In 1832 they were moved again to the vaults of the Civil List in the Louvre. By this time the crown jewels contained 64,812 diamonds valued at £836,000.

Following Charles X's abdication, Louis Philippe, Duke of Orleans, was elected King of the French. During his reign little use was made of either the crown jewels or the Royals' personal jewelry, all of which had been moved to the Tuilleries. However, Louis Philippe could no more escape the diamond's bane than his forebears could. Lord Twining recounts the opera bouffe events that ensued:

> On February 29th, 1848 when a new insurrection broke out and Louis Philippe abdicated, a mob entered the Tuilleries, but they were interested in finding wine rather than the crown jewels. In the cellars of the Commandant of the National Guard they found 10,000 bottles, upon

which they fell, as a result of which orgy twelve bodies were found next morning on the floor of the cellar...littered with broken bottles and swimming in wine.

Owing to the presence of mind of a laborer named No a detachment of the National Guard, under a sergeant, was procured and a scheme was devised to carry the crown jewels to safety on a stretcher and the valuables of the royal family were so removed. On February 26th the three key-holders appeared...it was decided, owing to the deteriorating situation, to remove the crown jewels to the headquarters of the National Guard. The safe was opened...no time to check the inventory, they stuffed some of the jewels in their pockets. General Courtais, carrying the crown with the Regent at its summit, ordered the party to follow. They proceeded through a subterranean passage to the Chief-of-Staff's office where the jewels were placed in a corner and covered with a tablecloth. Later in the day the jewel cases were...escorted by a detachment of the National Guard...to the Ministry of Finance where the bags were sealed. On March 12th a verification of the inventory was made and it was found that a box containing a hat button in brilliants and two rose diamond pendants valued at 300,000 francs were missing. Despite a widespread search they were not recovered.

During the period of the Second Republic (1848-52) the crown jewels remained in the Treasury, unused. The advent of the Second Empire under Napoleon III brought them once more to the fore.

For his marriage to the beautiful and vivacious Eugenie in January, 1853, the Emperor ordered all the old crown jewels to be dismantled and reset, a task that employed many jewelers. A new Imperial Crown and decorations for the Emperor, as well as numerous jewels and parures for the Empress incorporated the remaining "Mazarins" and the 'Regent'. Once again the French court dazzled the eyes of Europe. But only until Napoleon III's 1870 defeat and capture by the canny Bismarck at Sedan.

Napoleon III was deposed by a bloodless coup in Paris in 1871.

When Bismarck was released him he went into exile in England, accompanied by his wife. But for her foresight, his remaining years and the forty-three she survived him, might have been spent on a level far inferior to that which they were accustomed.

At the time of his arrival in England, Napoleon III was reputed to have only £60,000, but Eugenie retained her extensive Spanish properties and brought most of her large collection of jewels from Paris. One item, a beautiful diamond necklace, reached England and safety in the boot cupboard of the Princess Metternich. Many articles of the Empress' jewelry were auctioned at Christies in 1872. One, a ring containing a pink diamond surrounded by brilliants, realized 400 guineas.

Not all Eugenie's jewels were disposed of during her lifetime. At the time of her death a strange gift was made to her godchild and favorite granddaughter, Ena, Queen of Spain. Eugenie bequeathed her a simple china box. The box was opened to reveal a gorgeous tiara of emeralds and diamonds.

Following Napoleon III's defeat at Sedan the French crown jewels were packed off to the Public Treasury, then to Brest, where they were placed aboard a ship with instructions to sail for Saigon at the first sign of danger. The ship rested from 1870 until 1872, when the jewels were returned to Paris and placed in the cellars of the Ministry of Finance.

On June 7th, 1878, one Benjamin Raspail, a deputy with a grudge against Napoleon III, tabled a motion in the Chamber of Deputies to sell the crown jewels. It was not until June 20th, 1882, that the motion was carried. But not everyone agreed to what purpose the proceeds of the sale should be put.

A revised bill was agreed upon in December 1886. According to Twining, "[U]nder this enactment certain objects of historical, artistic or scientific merit were to be preserved in the Louvre, the Natural History Museum and the School of Mines. The imperial crown and the swords of Louis XVIII and the Dauphin were to be destroyed and the remainder...sold by public auction, the proceeds to be converted into government stocks."

Among the items retained were the most famous diamonds, like the "Regent," said to represent two-thirds of the value of the crown jewels. Another was the 20-carat "Hortense Diamond" supposedly brought back from India by Tavernier. Also notable were a broach containing two 21-carat pink diamonds as well as 93 brilliants weighing over 143 carats, and Charles X's coronation sword encrusted with 1,570 brilliants weighing 330.75 carats.

The sale attracted buyers from around the world, including representatives of many of Europe's remaining crowned heads. The sale yielded 7,220,360 francs profit. It was a sad ending to one of the most fabulous collections of crown jewels ever assembled.

* * *

Another set of crown jewels had a nineteenth century history nearly as bizarre. They belonged to the Electorate of Hanover. With the marriage of Elector Ernest Augustus to Sophia, granddaughter of James I of England, the Electorate of Hanover's fortunes became inextricably entwined with those of England. In 1714 Elector Augustus' son and successor, George Louis, became George I of Great Britain and Ireland.

The union of the Hanoverian and British royal houses posed many problems with the Hanoverian crown jewels. Although George II scrupulously separated the jewels of each country, his successors—particularly William IV—were not so meticulous. Following William's death many of the jewels claimed by the Hanoverians remained in Great Britain. All the Hanoverians' attempts to regain what was rightfully theirs were brushed off.

Twenty years elapsed before the British government decided to resolve the impasse. It was creating considerable ill will, especially in Hanover. A settlement was reached in 1858 and most of the jewels were handed over. Among them was a diamond crown, profusely set with brilliants and four large pendaloque diamonds.

The Hanoverian royal family had little chance to enjoy their newly returned jewels. In 1866 Prussia issued them a two-hour ultimatum to join it against Austria. The ultimatum was rejected and Hanover was immediately occupied by 80,000 Prussian troops. As there had been no time to prepare, all the crown and royal family's private jewelry and plate, were in the royal castle when the Prussian soldiers occupied it.

For once the Prussians did not live up to their vaunted methodi-

155

cal reputation. They failed to take possession of the Hanoverian treasure. The Hanoverian royal officials were not so hesitant. Gathering a large troop of retainers, they managed to remove a few of the crown jewels, as well as a gold and silver dinner service for 2,000, to the castle cellars under the noses of the Prussian guard.

From there, by means of a nearly forgotten subterranean passage, the treasure was smuggled to a deserted church.

Piece by piece the bulky treasure—some dinner service pieces measured four feet—was packed in wine casks and gradually shipped to Vienna and England. Even though the Prussians offered a reward not one of the many involved betrayed the secret.

The Lord Chamberlain and his mother managed to smuggle out some of the crown jewels along with the Queen's private jewelry, which they buried in a corner of their garden. They soon decided that this spot was not secure enough. Also, the crowns of the King and Queen, the coronation regalia and various jeweled orders and swords, were still hidden throughout the castle. A safer hiding place for all the jewels had to be found.

One dark night the Chamberlain and two servants dug up the buried treasure, concealed it in the linings of their winter capes and transported it to the ducal vaults beneath the Royal Chapel. Their plan was to secret the jewels in the dusty sarcophagi in the vaults.

A large tomb belonging to an infant held all the jewels that night, but the crown jewels remained in the castle. In the next few nights these were removed and the journey repeated. Astute observers might have wondered at the stiff-legged gait of the men as they made their way through the castle, swords concealed in their trouser legs.

For several years the jewels lay hidden in the tombs, their whereabouts known only to the King, the Lord Chamberlain and his two trusted servants. But times were troubled. The claim of Prince Leopold of Hohenzollern to the Spanish Throne meant the threat of war was near. The King decided the jewels had to be removed to England for safety. To accomplish this would require daring and ingenuity.

Once again the royal household was rallied. On a glorious summer day in 1869 a boisterous party issued forth from the gates of the castle, past bemused Prussian guards. On what was ostensibly a hunting party and picnic, this happy throng was led by the

Chamberlain and his servants in a large coach full of picnic baskets packed with jewelry and gun cases concealing jeweled swords.

The coach wound its way deep into the woods and stopped at a forester's cottage where the hampers and gun cases were unloaded. One by one six ladies of the court disappeared into the cottage to have items of jewelry secreted about their bodies under the voluminous clothing of the day. At last everything was hidden. Everything except the diamond crown. It was proving almost impossible to camouflage.

Finally, the eighty-year-old Countess Kielmansegge removed her frilly lace bonnet, set the crown firmly on her head and fastened the bonnet back in place. Literally weighed down under their massive loads, the Countess and five ladies departed by train for Vienna, to be followed later by the swords.

The tribulation of the nineteenth century certainly did not inhibit the growth of the fabulous jewel treasury of the Romanovs. Forty percent of that 25,300-carat diamond hoard of the Russian Tsars was acquired during this century. The court at St. Petersburg rivaled even that of Versailles in its displays of wealth. The German-born wife of Nicholas I was so enamored of this profusion of jewels that she attempted to take the whole of them, plus her private collection, wherever she traveled. This security nightmare was overcome by reproducing the whole thing in paste replicas.

***

The coronation of Queen Victoria in 1838 was relatively austere. Only £1000 was spent on resetting existing stones into a new imperial crown, and for repairing other regalia. This did not mean that the new Queen disdained jewelry; on the contrary. At her birthday reception she appeared in a dress with "stripes of diamonds down it and fastened at the bottom with a large double row of diamonds."

At one stage she even wore "...diamond earrings so wide they had to be suspended from the tips of (her) ears...." This love of jewelry and diamonds existed before the death of Prince Albert. When he died she reverted to the somber dress in which she is commonly portrayed.

The growth in value and importance of the British crown jewels and of the famous diamonds in that collection, stems from Victoria's reign. As we will see, many diamonds came into the crown collection from India. The acquisition of the most famous—the "Koh-i-Noor"—will be discussed later. The most important gains came from the newly discovered African mines. Just as Brazilian diamond mines were discovered as those of India were exhausted, so too were diamonds discovered in Africa just as the Brazilian mines dried up. This discovery changed the view of diamonds as none before it had.

Of all the diamonds found in Africa, the largest and most famous is the "Cullinan". Unlike its sister Indian stones it has no history of evil or violence attached to it. Nevertheless, its story is wondrous.

On January 26th, 1905, Captain M. F. Wells was making an inspection tour of the Premier Mine, some twenty miles northwest of Pretoria. It had opened just two years earlier. During the inspection he spotted something glistening in a rock wall. It turned out to be an enormous diamond the likes of which had never been seen before.

Captain Wells could hardly believe his eyes when the stone was removed from the wall for it turned out, at 3,106 carats, to be the largest diamond ever found. Not only that, but it seemed to be part of an even larger stone, probably twice as large as the fragment discovered!

It was colorless, transparent and nearly unflawed. This diamond, which weighed over a pound, was turned over to the mining company, which named it "Cullinan" after its chairman. Wells received £2000 as a reward for his discovery.

But what could be done with such a stone? Potential purchasers were certainly limited. The new government of the Union of South Africa solved this problem. By a resolution passed by the Transvaal Legislative Assembly in August, 1907, the diamond was purchased for £150,000 as a present to King Edward VII to show the Assembly's appreciation for the granting autonomous government.

One might expect such a gift to be enthusiastically accepted. Such was not the case. The passing of the resolution to buy the "Cullinan" had not been unanimous. Legislators of English origin resented that the resolution came from the Boers. The British government balked at accepting the gift and dropped the decision in the lap of Edward VII. The King decided to accept the gift.

Such a gem was not easy to transport. As might be imagined, many a thief had his eye on it and waited for the slightest opportunity to steal the most priceless object known to man. (Although insured for only £250,000 when shipped, it was sometimes valued as high as £15,000,000.) In the end it was decided that the safest method was to send it in a wooden box wrapped in plain paper by ordinary parcel post. The diamond arrived in England without incident and was officially presented to the King on his sixty-sixth birthday, November, 9th, 1907.

Now came the daunting task of cutting the stone. The renowned firm of I. J. Asscher of Amsterdam was given the nod. Joseph and Lodewijk Asscher, the oldest of five brothers who owned the firm, had met with the King to discuss how the stone should be handled. Its unprecedented size required special cutting tools. Needless to say, the tension was great, and for no one more than Joseph Asscher who would make that vital cut.

If the calculations were wrong, or if the cutting knife was not placed precisely, a literally priceless diamond could, in one instant, be reduced to worthless rubble. Joseph raised a metal rod high above the stone, then dropped the rod lightly on the cutting blade. The blade fell to pieces.

There was a moment's stunned silence. Asscher calmly placed a new blade in the *kerf*, a notch in the stone in which the cutting blade is set. Once again his arm rose and fell. This time the stone split exactly as predicted. Many stories maintain that Joseph Asscher then fainted, but his descendants have denied these rumors.

The major portion of the "Cullinan" became the 516.5-carat "Star of Africa", the world's largest cut diamond. It's now set in the royal scepter. A second stone of more than 309 carats graces the Imperial State Crown. For their work, the Asschers received the, clippings, except for a small portion allotted to the men who supervised the operation.

From these "clippings" were produced seven full gemstones and 96 brilliants. King Edward purchased one, an 11.75-carat marquise, as a gift for Queen Alexandra. The remaining stones and brilliants were purchased by the Union of South Africa and presented to Queen Mary on behalf of the government of South Africa.

The discovery of the South African fields opened a new world for diamonds. The African discoveries corresponded with the growth of the middle classes, especially in Great Britain and America. Increased availability made diamonds more attainable.

Their popularity grew, influenced by lower prices, the decline of other gems, but mostly because of widespread use of electric light, which enhanced their beauty.

By the late 1800s France had again regained its role as arbiter of jewelry fashion. Naturalism was the key word in forms such as fruit, flowers, plants, animals and insects executed entirely in gems. Diamonds glittered in "invisible" settings designed to show them to their best advantage.

Englishwomen, in particular, were bedecked in diamonds from the seemingly inexhaustible mines of Africa, that put to shame all previous records for weight and splendor. Alexandra, wife of the Prince of Wales and later of Edward VII, set the standards by which all fashion-conscious Englishwomen of the era were judged.

It was a difficult standard to uphold, not only because of the jewels' ready availability to her, but because of her willowy beauty. One of Edward VII's first acts on ascending the throne was to purchase a lovely diamond parure for Alexandra that accentuated that beauty.

The onset of the Great War of 1914 and the subsequent demise of the British Empire brought about a shift in the diamond market. America, with its new wealth, became the premier marketplace. The first diamond sent to America for sale was a solitaire that arrived by ship in New York in 1764.

Dolly Madison, wife of the fourth President of the United States, wore a diamond crescent in her turban. Diamonds were generally little valued and worn by early Americans, perhaps due to their association with European nobility, a status despised by Americans of the time. However, they regained their popularity in the 1840's during the presidency of John Tyler.

About 1850 Charles Lewis Tiffany set up shop in New York and began to produce jewelry for what would become an unquenchable thirst for diamonds. His designs included a unique diamond setting that carries his name. It won him many admirers and clients, from Sarah Bernhardt to President Lincoln.

The South African diamond boom started a rush to find this most valuable of gems in America. In 1871 two prospectors turned up in San Francisco claiming to have found extensive deposits in Wyoming. Gullible financiers paid them $600,000 for their claim only to find that it had been salted with $25,000 worth of rough diamonds. Although some diamonds have been found near Murfreesboro, Arkansas, they have never been in commercially exploitable quantities.

In February, 1866, the *New Harper's Monthly* reported it "…doubtful whether there is any diamond in the United States over twelve carats." As the great wealth of America began to be tapped, the demand for diamonds grew. By the late 1800s no self-respecting lady of fashion would be seen in public without her quota of diamonds.

One eccentric Boston socialite, Mrs. Jack Gardner, set two enormous Indian diamonds, the "Light of India" and the "Rajah", from Tiffany's, into a springing hair ornament that waved like sparkling antennae with her every movement.

Ostentation was the theme among the American nouveau riche. Since social etiquette decreed it improper to wear diamonds during the day, the great displays took place at evening social gatherings— the American equivalent of the great state balls of Europe.

Foremost among these were grand operas performed in the New York Metropolitan Opera House, with its aptly named "Diamond Horseshoe." This was a tier of parterre boxes filled with patrons wearing diamond tiaras, necklaces, rings and anything else that might carry this aristocrat of gems. They shimmered and shone nightly throughout the opera season.

This orgy reached its height with a ball given by Mr. and Mrs. Bradley-Martin on February 10th, 1897, at the Waldorf Astoria Hotel. A local newspaper reported:

> …there were gowns that spoke of Paris ransacked…diamonds enough for an emperor's ransom and to spare; there were enough diamond crowns to fit out all the crowned heads of Europe and have some left over for Asia and Africa; there were necklaces worth $100,000 apiece on several throats. It was a delirium of wealth and an idyll of luxury and magnificence.

But the idyll was short-lived. There was a storm of criticism over this vulgar display by a population struggling through a major depression. The Bradley-Martins hurriedly left for England.

* * *

Male attire in this era was quite somber. A diamond cufflink or stickpin twinkled now and again. One exception was James Buchanan, "Diamond Jim" Brady. Evidence of the American Dream, Brady progressed from hotel porter and messenger boy to supplier for the rapidly expanding railroad. His passion for diamonds has probably never been equaled by another American. His collection of thirty complete sets of jewelry was estimated at the time to be more than $1,000,000.

The nature of some of these sets was bizarre. Joan Dickenson describes:

> His most famous was his bizarre transportation set studded with a total of 2,548 diamonds. Each piece was a different railroad car: a tank car, a coal car, a caboose, etc. It was freight cars [that] made him rich....His racetrack set he wore only on days he was going to the races; his Napoleon set—made only of jewels once worn by Napoleon—he wore only on grand occasions. It was believed he owned more than 20,000 diamonds all told, (and) that sometimes he wore as many as $250,000 worth on a single day....

Brady was renowned for the way he used his diamonds in business. A favorite ploy was to invite a prospective client, and wife, to dinner. Dinner was elaborate, and the wine freely flowing but all this took second place to Brady's own diamond-studded attire. Few women could resist expressing admiration for it. If the business discussion showed promise, he would nonchalantly remove a diamond cufflink or stickpin and present it to her. Such tactics clinched any business deal.

***

Many of the fine cut diamonds in the world's markets during the thirties found their way from Soviet Russia. The Romanov's diamond

162

collection grew during the late 1800s until it was one of the most formidable collections in existence.

We know this because of the complete cataloguing of the imperial jewels carried out by Agathon Faberge. He was a scion of the house of Faberge—court jewelers to the last three Tsars, famous in the West for their exquisite bejeweled Easter eggs.

Agathon suggested the overhaul and re-cataloguing of all the crown jewels in 1913 and began this almost impossible task early the following year. He was just preparing to begin on the crowns when the threat of war caused the crown jewels to be locked in the Kremlin for safekeeping. They remained there, untouched, until after the war.

After being arrested during the Russian Revolution, Faberge was invited by Trotsky to sit on a commission organized by the Soviets to place values on the regalia and crown jewels. Twice Agathon refused, but Soviet soldiers delivered a third invitation at 3 AM This was an invitation Faberge thought it prudent not to refuse. He began work in the autumn of 1921, photographing and weighing each stone. This monumental task was completed in the spring of 1923.

The Soviet government was badly in need of foreign currency to make purchases on the international market. After putting the jewels on public display in 1926, a catalogue in four languages was prepared for a sale that would have eclipsed even that of the French crown jewels. For some reason there was a change of heart and the catalogue was withdrawn. A syndicate bought some items and put them up for sale at Christies's. The bulk of the crown jewels were retained by the Soviets and are now a part of the Diamond Fund.

Although most of the Russian crown jewels remain in modern Russia, many notable gems were smuggled out by émigrés who sold them off, one by one, to support themselves. This was particularly true during the war period in Paris. For many years a debonair gentleman with a pronounced Eastern European accent appeared annually in the shop of a New York diamond merchant, peddling another valuable diamond.

Jewelers and diamond merchants had to be cautious in such dealings. They could never be certain whether the gems were fake, stolen or smuggled. Ingenius ruses were used. One of the most common was to pass off inferior off-color diamonds as more valuable whites by treating their edges with blue pigment. They were placed in a setting which covered the telltale coloring.

A. Monnickendam, who relates an endless collection of diamond stories and anecdotes, knows of one such instance. Using £3000 worth of off-color diamonds tinted to appear white, one unscrupulous English merchant prepared a beautiful necklace. A female accomplice posing as a society matron approached a reputable jeweler with an offer to sell. While the jeweler was examining the necklace he was informed that a familiar diamond merchant was calling to inquire whether he had anything for sale.

Sensing a quick profit, the jeweler hurried the merchant into his office where he showed him the necklace. Under the pretence of examining the necklace he'd actually made, the merchant offered £13,000 for it. The jeweler said he would relay the merchant's offer to the lady and invited him back that afternoon to hear the result

After the merchant left the jeweler returned to his customer and offered her £11,000 for the necklace. Playing her role to the hilt, the lady said she expected much more and would have to consult her husband. She returned an hour later with an acceptance of his offer. However, as she was in urgent need of the money, would the jeweler be so kind as to pay her by bank draft? He readily agreed and then sat back to await the diamond merchant and reap his £2000 profit.

He had a long wait for the merchant was never seen again.

Monnickendam also tells about how two Indian diamond merchants in Antwerp proudly showed him a pair of 10.5-carat green brilliants they recently bought. After examining the gems carefully he asked the merchants how much they paid for them. When informed that the gems had cost £5,300 he told them the diamonds were not worth more than £400. They were, in fact, inferior quality yellow diamonds treated with radium to turn them green.

***

For almost as long as there have been diamonds, there have been fakes. Since there has never been a shortage of gullible people it is not surprising that some, even those who should know better, are taken in.

One such case occurred when Henri Lemoine, a Frenchman, approached the head of one of England's most prestigious diamond import and export houses with an offer to produce diamonds synthetically. Although skeptical, the diamond merchant agreed to visit Lemoine's Paris laboratory to witness an experiment. Two experiments produced genuine diamonds.

Based on this, the merchant agreed to finance a large-scale production of diamonds to the tune of £80,000. In return, Lemoine deposited a sealed envelope containing the secret formula for the process in a London bank. If he should die the formula would become the property of the merchant.

Three years transpired; no diamonds were produced. Finally, the merchant sued. The envelope with the secret formula was opened. Needless to say, it was worthless. In the meantime Lemoine had disappeared with the merchant's funds. Lemoine had simply concealed real gems in the furnace before the demonstrations and then produced them as proof.

***

The twentieth century has been a harrowing time for many large diamond collections, and often their owners. One need only remember the Austrian crown jewels. Many disappeared, probably in South America, at the hands of an unscrupulous court official after the fall of the Habsburgs.

Or the Saxon Diamonds. That collection, which includes the "Dresden Green, White and Yellow", contained more than 7,000 carats and was valued at nearly £1,000,000 in 1938. The Russians confiscated this treasure at the end of World War II, although they have since returned it. It is now on display in the Green Vaults of the Dresden Historical Museum.

The remaining French crown jewels were hurriedly removed from Paris before the Germans entered the city in 1940. They were hidden in various spots around the country. Although such treasures enticed the Nazis—Marshall Goering was a notorious "collector" of beautiful jewelry throughout occupied Europe—their primary interest was in the industrial diamonds essential to their war effort. The diamond centers of Amsterdam and Antwerp were prime targets.

The Whitsun weekend in 1940 was a tragic one for the Dutch. Because of the holiday, shops closed on the evening of Friday May 10th, not to reopen until the following Tuesday. As usual, the diamond cutters and merchants deposited their cut and rough diamonds, valued at more than £500,000, in the vault of the Amsterdamsche Bank Friday evening. They watched as the manager closed the heavy steel door.

At three o'clock the following morning Hitler's Blitzkrieg rolled into The Netherlands. Diamond merchants and bank officials rushed to the bank. But the manager was not among them. A director of the bank tried to open the vault door. Time after time he set the numbers and tugged. Nothing happened. Perhaps the bombs had disturbed the tumblers, the anxiously pacing dealers told one another.

The manager had probably set the timing device for the following Tuesday morning. Experts and professional thieves were called in with dynamite and carbon drills. But the door resisted them all. Even when the lock had been destroyed it refused to budge.

By now Nazis were swarming through Amsterdam. Blast after blast reverberated through the bank's corridors. Suddenly the door swung open and the dealers rushed in to gather their stones. But advancing Germans trapped them. They dashed out of the bank, dodging gunfire and made their way to a nearby canal.

To this day what became of these men and their priceless packages is unknown.

***

Since the war diamonds have once again become popular. But the ostentatious display of previous times is a thing of the past. Except, possibly, for huge engagement rings, the rich keep their jewelry locked safely away in vaults. That is, most of them do.

One diamond, a 33-carat citron gem known as the "Carlotta" or "Maximilian II", was bought by a New York jeweler in 1946 for a reputed $120,000. Instead of keeping it locked away, he kept it at home. One night in 1961, suspecting burglars, a member of the jeweler's family took the gem and hid it in a dustbin. The next day the refuse had been collected and the diamond with it. It has never been seen since.

Today diamonds are seldom seen in excess except in museum displays or at occasional charity balls, such as the one attended by Elizabeth Taylor in Monaco, November 1969. She wore a 62.42-carat pear-shaped diamond Richard Burton bought her for more than

£1,000,000. Today, such possessions are viewed as investments rather than adornments. The awe engendered by such gems is now much dissipated, particularly since magnificent fakes are readily available.

Crown jewelry can still be seen as it was originally worn during court functions attended by the British royal family. One cannot help but wonder whether the gems are real. While little is made public about the jewelry acquisitions of the royal family they are still the recipients of fine gifts. During her tour of the Persian Gulf states in 1979 Queen Elizabeth II received lavish gifts of diamond-studded watches, gold, and huge pearls thought to be worth well over a million pounds, from her Arab hosts.

Non-royal owners of fine jewelry do not advertise their wealth. Who wants to attract the attention of the tax authorities? Nor does it pay to alert thieves to easily disguised and portable sources of wealth. Criminal methods haven't changed much over the centuries as witnessed by the following article in the *London Daily Telegraph*, May 10th, 1980:

> The jewels theft suspect was the quietest man police in the Swedish town of Norrkoping had ever encountered, they said yesterday. After his silent arrest he listened to the officers' questions but said nothing. In fact, he did not say a word for more than an hour and then one of the policemen took a closer look at him and found the reason—in his mouth, police said, he had a case containing six diamonds.

Diamonds:
Famous and Fatal

*O*ver the centuries thousands of diamonds have made their appearance on history's stage. Some attained a degree of fame that ensured them a permanent place in the pantheon of the stars. Many have already been chronicled in these pages. Others played only bit parts or made their marks and passed into oblivion.

Great diamonds did not have to be large; many were actually relatively small. But they were famous because of their beauty or their effect on the events of their day. For great diamonds have always been recorded.

Sometimes the stories were clearly untrue, such as Alexander's and Sindbad's; allegorical, as in the case of the "Diamond Throne"; or a combination of these as in the stories of the "Shamir" and the diamond of the Jewish High Priest's Breastplate.

Some diamonds, such as the "Mahomet IV", spent long centuries in the Imperial Treasury of the Sultans of Turkey. According to tradition, this 24-carat gem, was found on a rubbish heap by a poor Turk during Mahomet's Reign (1648-87).

A few diamonds may have been nothing more than some storyteller's imagination. One, the "Emperor Justinian", was supposed to have been lost from that Emperor's crown in 548 AD during a ceremonial entry into Constantinople. Centuries later, a child supposedly found it in his playground. Another, the "Regale of France", was offered at the shrine of Thomas á Becket in England by the French king, Louis IX, who came disguised as a pilgrim.

Neither diamond has been heard of since. But on some cold, blustery mid-winter's night in the Middle Ages their beguiling tales may have given enjoyment to impoverished listeners, forgetting for a moment the wretchedness of their lives.

The most modern, and perhaps strangest, story of a diamond is that of the "Arabian Death". "This gem was bequeathed by (the last) Earl Lytton to Madame la Comtess Greffuhle, who showed it to a learned Indian Prince...in Paris....After reading the mysterious Arab words (engraved on it) the Prince told the Comtess that it was a stone of death, and advised her not to keep it. The lady, desiring to end the stone's power for mischief, threw it into the River Seine from the Pont Neuf."

It may seem strange that diamonds appear so briefly in history, only to disappear without a trace. This is not so surprising when one considers that such stones were an irresistible lure for every thief, brigand and marauder, easily disguised through recutting and bought for the right price with few questions.

Many of these diamonds owe their only mention to Jean-Baptiste Tavernier. He reported on the 103-carat rough at Raulconda that now carries the name of that mine. Then the "Throne", a 90-carat gem he saw gracing the Peacock Throne, and the 54.75-carat "Pear". None has been reported again.

Perhaps they went the way of the 250-carat "Great Table", a sketch of which appeared in one of Tavernier's books. It, among others he glimpsed, disappeared into Nadir Shah's voracious clutches. Although they never reappeared in their original form, it is believed that at least the "Great Table", was recut into the "Darya-i-Nur" and the "Nur-ul-Ain".

Possibly the most enigmatic diamond Tavernier mentioned was the "Great Mogul". It's much better documented than many of the stones that came to the French gem merchant's attention. It was discovered about 1650 in the Gani mine in India and presented to Shah Jahan.

When Aurangzeb showed this gem to Tavernier in 1665, it had been cut to 280 from its original 787.5 carats. It was valued by Tavernier at more than 11,700,000 livres! Also looted by Nadir Shah in 1739, it has since been identified with the "Orloff", the "Darya-i-Nur" and the "Koh-i-Noor". However, experts agree it had no relationship to these. It may well have been recut after Nadir Shah's death to escape detection.

Tavernier bought and sold many famous diamonds. Among these were the 48.5-carat, rose-cut "Banian" and the "Bazu", a 104-carat rough he sold to Dutch merchants. Louis XIV purchased diamonds from him in 1669, the most notable of which was the 112.5-carat "Blue Diamond of the Crown". It was recut four years later into a 67.13-carat heart shape. This diamond disappeared in the robbery of the Garde Meuble and was probably the progenitor of the infamous "Hope".

Tavernier reported on diamonds wherever he heard of them. His inquisitiveness was responsible for the only mention of two stones, the 57 and the 67.5-carat "Mascarenhas" I & II, belonging to the Portuguese Viceroy of Goa, Dom Philip de Mascarenha. This was also the case with the "Savoy", a 54-carat diamond he saw among the crown jewels of the House of Savoy.

Several diamonds owe their only historical mention to that famed goldsmith, raconteur and self-promoter, Benvenuto Cellini. Two, the "Cellini Peach" and the "Cellini Green", took their names from their vivid color descriptions in his *Treatise on Goldsmithing*. Cellini reported on a stone, the "Pope Paul III", which was given to the Pope by the Holy Roman Emperor, Charles V, in 1536. Cellini received 12,000 crowns to set this diamond in a ring for the Pope. Nothing more is known about any of these diamonds.

Some were mere flashes in the pan. Philip II of Spain presented the "Antwerp" to his third wife, Elizabeth, as a wedding gift. Cardinal Mazarin bequeathed the "Rose d'Angleterre" to Anne of Austria. The "Russian Table" is only known for its inclusion in the nineteenth-century Russian crown jewels, and the "Napoleon", which Bonaparte bought to have mounted on the sword he wore at his wedding to Josephine was then lost at Waterloo.

Others enjoyed greater fame. The pyramid-shaped "Charles the

Bold" is one of several diamonds that the Duke of Burgundy reputedly lost, along with his life, in his Swiss campaigns in the 1470s. Eighty years later it was bought by Henry VIII and, passed through his daughter, the notorious Bloody Mary, into the hands of her husband, Philip II of Spain.

The "Great Harry" was another stone of vague origin and bad luck. It turned up first among the jewels of Francis I of France, whose reign was marked by spending and the loss of France's foreign territory and possessions. Sometime after her marriage to the Dauphin, later Francis II of France, Mary Queen of Scots came into the possession of the diamond.

Mary willed the "Great Harry" to her son, James I of England, who was responsible for events that led ultimately to the English Civil War. After James had it set in a jewel called "The Mirror of Great Britain", it disappeared.

The "Guise" was a diamond with a relatively long history. Its first owner was Henri de Lorraine, third duc de Guise, who helped plan the infamous Saint Bartholomew's Day Massacre of the Huguenots in 1572. He was assassinated, at Henry III's order, in 1588. The diamond passed from the Guise family when Marie of Lorraine sold it to her cousin, Louis XIV.

It is mentioned in chronicles of the succeeding years as a favorite gem of French royalty, enhancing the beauty of the king's mistresses. The "Guise" was listed in the 1691 inventory of the French crown jewels as 33 carats, but by 1774 had been cut to 28.39 carats. Last reported in 1888 when it was sold, the "Guise" is now nothing more than a brilliant memory.

Two point-cut diamonds of unknown weight figured prominently in sixteenth-century French history. The first of these, the "Pointe de Bretagne", appears first in the possession of Anne of Brittany. It passed into the first official French crown jewels when Francis I gave it to his Queen, Eleanor of Acquitaine.

Francis II married Mary Queen of Scots in 1559. The "Pointe de Bretagne", along with the second diamond, the "Pointe de Milan", was set in a carcanet by Francis' mother, Catherine de Medici, and presented to Mary. The "Pointe de Milan" had been part of Catherine's dowry from her uncle, Pope Clement III, when she married the future King Henry II of France in 1533. The two-diamond carcanet disappeared from history with Mary's fall.

The "Mirror of Portugal" was a 25.38-carat diamond of Indian origin. It played a prominent role in European events. After laying idle among the crown jewels of Portugal, it was taken from that country by Dom Antonio, the illegitimate son of the Cardinal King Henry, and claimant to the Portuguese throne.

Sometime after his defeat by Philip II of Spain it was used as collateral to secure funds for his struggle. As mentioned earlier, Elizabeth kept the diamond even though Dom Antonio failed. Becoming part of the English crown jewels, the "Mirror of Portugal" was used again, by Henrietta Maria, to raise funds, this time in support of Charles I's attempts to hold onto his crown. Charles was unsuccessful, so the diamond came into the possession of the Duke of Epernon and later Cardinal Mazarin, who included it in the "Mazarin Diamonds".

The 'Mazarins' was a collection of 18 diamonds totaling nearly 372 carats, ranging from 8.75 to 53.75. This collection included the "Mirror of Portugal", the "Sancy" and the 21-carat "Grand Mazarin". On his deathbed in 1661 he bequeathed the whole collection to the French Crown and tried to guarantee his legacy by ordering them named the "Mazarin Diamonds" in perpetuity.

This was not to be the case. By the time the 1791 inventory of the French crown jewels was made, only one diamond had the same weight as those recorded in the 1691 inventory. Most had either been recut or replaced by other diamonds. Although fifteen so-called "Mazarins" were noted on the auction list for an 1887 sale, only five could be positively identified with any of those in previous inventories. With the sale of these five to jewelers, the "Mazarins", as a group, passed into oblivion.

The most famous of all vanishing diamonds is undoubtedly the "Florentine". Its legend begins with Charles the Bold of Burgundy who, according to his contemporary, Philippe de Comines, lost "…his great diamond…one of the largest in Christendom," along with "all his large jewels" and baggage at the battle of Nancy in January 1477. Other accounts claim the diamond was lost at either the battles of Morat or Granson.

Wherever it was lost, the tale goes that a Swiss soldier discovered the stone on the ground, pocketed it and sold it later to a clergyman for one florin. The clergyman in turn sold it for three francs to the authorities of Berne. A wealthy Berne merchant named Bartholomew May bought the stone for 5,000 florins and resold it, at a small profit, to a Genoese dealer who, in turn, sold it to the Regent of Milan, Ludovico Sforza, for 10,000 ducats.

It was later purchased by Pope Julius II for 20,000 ducats. This version claims that the diamond was acquired from Sforza by the famous merchant house of Fuggers and came into the Medici family. The Fuggers themselves claimed it was bought directly from the Bernese authorities. It was then sold to Henry VIII of England, and remained there until Queen Mary presented it to her husband, Philip II of Spain, in 1554.

Edward Streeter discounts all these stories, pointing out discrepancies, the most damning of which was that the description of Charles the Bold's stone did not fit the actual shape and cut of the "Florentine". He theorized that the diamond went to Italy and became the possession of the Medici family.

It is not surprising that the Medicis should have acquired this magnificent diamond for they were one of the wealthiest and most powerful families of Renaissance Italy.

In any case, the "Florentine" was clearly in their possession in 1657 when the Duke of Tuscany showed it to Tavernier who wrote, "…it weights 139.5 carats, is pure and of fine form, cut on all sides in facets, and of a citron tint…should be worth 2,608,335 livres." Tavernier could not help but be impressed, for the "Florentine" was the largest diamond in Europe. Its cut was remarkable, a "double rose-cut of 126 facets with an irregular nine-sided outline."

The "Florentine" remained in the possession of the Medicis until 1743. When the last male Medici died without heirs in 1737 the title of Duke of Tuscany was offered to Francis Stephan, Duke of Lorraine. But he did not immediately gain the "Florentine"; it remained in the possession of Anna Maria Medici until her death in 1743.

In 1736 Francis had married Maria Theresa, heiress to all the Hapsburg lands. When Maria acceded to her inheritance it was contested in the War of the Austrian Succession. By the Treaty of

Dresden, Francis was recognized as the successor to the Holy Roman Emperor, Charles VII, and moved his court, and his "Florentine", to Vienna. There he had the diamond placed in the Crown of the House of Austria for his coronation and in this manner the 'Florentine' became part of the Austrian crown jewels.

For the following 175 years the 'Florentine' passed from one Austrian monarch to the next, making regular appearances from brooch to hat ornament, or in regalia.

At the beginning of the twentieth century the Austrian Crown could not resist the changing fortunes of time. At the fall of the Austro-Hungarian Empire, the Imperial jewels, property of the royal family not of the state, were carried off by Empress Zita. What became of the "Florentine" is unclear.

One story reports, erroneously, that the Nazis removed it after the Anschluss, but it was restored to Vienna after the war by America.

Another claims that an unfaithful royal retainer fled with it and other crown jewels, to South America in the 1920s. From there it supposedly entered the United States where it was recut and sold. Probably no one will ever know what became of this magnificent diamond.

At least one diamond, the 101-carat "Hastings", was involved in political scandal. In 1784 the diamond's owner and first Governor General of British India, Warren Hastings, returned to England where he was charged with crimes that took place during his administration.

Although he had been an able civil servant, and the charges against him were dubious, his problems were compounded by presenting the diamond to King George III, as a gift from the Nizam of Deccan. This was seen as bribery and Hastings was impeached the following year.

The "King Charles I Seal" was a semi-legendary diamond that moved uncharacteristically from West to East. Although it must have originated in India, this diamond was engraved with the English royal arms. It's first recorded in the possession of Charles I. At the time of his execution in 1649 he gave it to an attendant as he mounted the scaffold, with instructions to get it to his son. Charles II sold it to Tavernier in order to raise funds during his exile in France, and Tavernier later resold it in Persia.

With the exception of the "Florentine", all the previous diamonds were Indian stones that disappeared more than one hundred years ago. But other important stones of Brazilian or South African origin have disappeared in recent times.

In 1906 a 600-carat rough known as the "Goyaz" was found near a town of that name on the Verissimo River in Brazil. All that is known of this diamond is that when cut, its largest stone was 80 carats. Again, between 1934 and 1940 four very large stones, ranging from 180 to 400.5 carats, known as the "Coromandels I–IV," were found in the Minas Gerais province of Brazil. What is remarkable about all these Brazilian diamonds is that stones of such size could disappear without trace.

Many sizeable South African diamonds have disappeared. For example, the 106.75-carat "Star of Egypt", 250 carats in the rough, belonged to the Viceroy of Egypt. It was last seen in 1939 when it appeared on the London market. There was the brilliant-cut, 123-carat "Stewart", found in 1872. Originally weighing 296 carats rough, the stone was sold for £9,000, and cut. It, too has disappeared.

Another stone, the "Kruger", has a more interesting background. This 200-carat rough belonged to several native chieftains before the last one was taken captive by Paul Kruger, President of the Transvaal from 1883 to 1900. When Kruger freed him, the chief presented the diamond in thanks. Since then its whereabouts is unknown.

Theft has played a role in the disappearance of many of the diamonds mentioned, most notably those stolen from the Garde Meuble. Along with the "Florentine", two diamonds, the 30-carat "Baden Solitaire" and the "Frankfurt Solitaire" of 44.62 carats, were stolen from the deposed Austrian royal family in the twenties. The "Colenso", a yellowish 133-carat rough of fine quality presented to the British Museum in 1887, was stolen from there in 1965.

America has also had its thefts of notable diamonds. A family heirloom, the 31-carat "Amati" belonged to the former wife of the famous short story writer, Damon Runyon. It was stolen from her in 1949.

One of the largest diamonds found in America was the "Eagle", a 15.37-carat alluvial rough discovered near Eagle, Wisconsin in 1876. The farm wife who found it mistook it for a topaz and sold it for one dollar. It was later sold to the famous American financier and industrialist, J.P. Morgan, who donated the stone to the American Museum of Natural History in New York. It, too, was stolen from the Museum in 1964.

Museums proved to be lucrative targets for American diamond thieves. In 1961 the Witte Memorial Museum in San Antonio was robbed of a star attraction, the 49.4-carat "McFarlin" diamond, followed the next year by the theft of an 84-carat rough from the Harvard University Museum.

Jewelers and diamond dealers were ready targets for thieves. In 1947 Jensen and Co. in New York put a primrose yellow, heart-shaped, 28.5-carat diamond on sale. This Indian diamond had supposedly been given to the famous French actress, Gaby Delys by a maharajah.

A Latin con man approached the jewelers and, under the pretext of having it appraised, disappeared with this beautiful diamond. More direct methods were used with Miami gem dealer, Jack M. Werst. In 1958 armed robbers deprived him of three diamonds, the "Major Bowles" and the "River Styx I & II", which weighed a total of 80 carats.

While many diamonds have disappeared from the records, it's possible they still exist, perhaps unrecognized or in recut versions. But it is certain that one famous diamond was deliberately destroyed. This was the "Pigott", weighing anywhere from 47.5 to 82.5 carats. It was probably nearer the 49 carats ascribed to it by Mawe, who valued it at £40,000.

The diamond took its name from George Pigot, an eighteenth-century governor of Madras. Pigot claimed to have received the diamond as a gift in 1763. But he was not one to make the moral distinction between gifts and bribes, of which he received many from neighboring rajahs attempting to dissuade him from their territories.

He brought the diamond to England in 1775 at which time he also purchased an Irish baronetcy. He did not live long enough to enjoy it. In August 1776, shortly after returning to India, he was arrested by colleagues over a dispute. He died the following year in confinement. But not before willing his diamond to his two brothers and a sister.

177

In 1801 the diamond was put into a lottery where it raised £30,000. The young man who acquired it wanted ready cash and sold it for a low price. In the ensuing years it passed through the hands of Napoleon's mother, among others. By 1818 it belonged to London jewelers, Messrs. Rundell and Bridge who sold it for £30,000 to Ali Pasha, the infamous "Lion of Janina", Vizier of Albania.

Ali Pasha was one of those anomalies, a cultured tyrant, who appeared throughout history. By 1818 he had already been governor of Janina more than thirty years. He ruled with a brutal hand. His wild but cultured court was renowned throughout Europe and vividly described by Byron in *Childe Harold*.

His passion for jewels, especially diamonds, was also well known. One traveler who visited his court in 1812 tells of "...brilliants that actually covered the walls of his apartments." But only a trusted few were permitted to view his most prized possession, the "Pigott". He carried it in a green purse beneath his garments.

After so many years of unlimited power Ali Pasha should have been content to sit back and enjoy his gains. But for such a man ambition never dies. In 1822 the Sultan of Turkey, alarmed by Ali's continually growing power, sent emissary Raschid Pasha to bring Ali to Istanbul. Ali, nearly eighty years old, had been warned of the Sultan's plans. When Raschid confronted the old man with the Sultan's order to surrender himself, Ali fired at him. The shot missed and the "Lion of Janina" was tamed. Mortally wounded, he requested to die in peace, whereupon Raschid and his men gallantly retired.

Even at the gates of death Ali Pasha was determined to deny the Sultan his most cherished possessions. Calling for a French soldier of fortune, Captain d'Anglas, he drew out the green pouch containing the "Pigott" and instructed the captain to destroy it, and his favorite wife, Vasilikee.

The captain found a hammer and crushed the diamond described as "among the finest in Europe." Luckily for Vasilikee, the old man succumbed to his wounds before d'Anglas could carry out the second part of Ali's dying wish.

It's tempting to think that the tale of the "Pigott's" destruction was only Ali's last crafty scheme to confound the Sultan. Instead of throwing away the hammered diamond he gave it to Vasilikee, who lived for many years in luxury on its proceeds.

Fortunately, some historically famous diamonds have survived the centuries to beguile man. The British crown jewels, with their wealth of diamonds, are housed in London's Tower and open to the general public. Similarly, the Louvre offers a view of the remaining French crown jewels, including the "Regent" and the "Hortensia", a 20-carat, peach-colored diamond named after Napoleon's step-daughter, Hortense de Beauharnais, Queen of Holland.

Another museum, the Musee Conde in Chantilly, holds a light pink, pear-shaped diamond known as the "Conde" or "Chantilly Pink". This 50-carat beauty was awarded to Louis, Prince of Conde and Duke of Bourbon, by Louis XIII in 1647 for his service during the Thirty Years War. The diamond actually survived 250 years in the Conde family until it was bequeathed to the French nation in 1892, with the stipulation that it must always remain on the family estate at Chantilly.

The "Little" or "Beau Sancy", a 34-carat, rounded, pear-shaped brilliant left France sometime after the death of its first owner, Nicholas de Sancy, in 1627. The Prince of Orange bought it and left it to his grandson, Frederick I of Prussia. He, in turn, placed it among the Prussian crown jewels where it remained until the fall of the Hohenzollerns following the First World War. It may now be seen in the Royal Prussian House in Bremen, Germany.

In Istanbul, the Topkapi Museum displays an 84-carat, pear-shaped diamond set in a frame with 49 smaller diamonds. This gem, the "Spoonmaker", acquired its name from the legend that it was dis-covered by a Turkish fisherman in a refuse heap and sold to a spoon-maker for three spoons.

Not all diamonds on display are as accessible as those men-tioned. The Green Vaults of the Dresden Museum in the former East Germany house a treasure trove of beautiful diamonds. The twenty-five largest weigh nearly 600 carats. These gems are known collec-tively as the "Saxon Diamonds", the remainder of a collection begun in the seventeenth century by Augustus the Strong of Saxony.

Over the years, the collection was increased by Augustus' suc-cessors until, by 1938, it contained more than 7,000 carats. It's val-ued at nearly one million pounds sterling.

The Russians confiscated the gems, which are in dazzling settings, at the end of the Second World War but later returned them to the museum. The largest of the diamonds is a square-cut, white stone of 49.71 carats known as the "Dresden White". This is one of the original purchases of Augustus the Strong and, at a price of between £150,000 and £200,000, it may have cost the most per carat of any diamond ever bought. At least until Richard Burton purchased the 62.42-carat "Cartier" for a price in excess of $1,010,000 in 1969.

This record has now been exceeded. On November 22nd, 1980, the 40-carat "Polar Star" was placed on auction at Christie's in Geneva. Once described as the brightest diamond ever seen, the "Polar Star" had belonged to Napoleon's oldest brother, Louis Bonaparte; to the Russian Princess Tatiana Youssoupoff, whose collection once rivaled the Tsar's; and most recently to the late Lady Deterding, widow of Royal Dutch Shell's founder, Sir Henri Deterding.

The diamond was sold to a Sri Lankan dealer for £1,960,828, over £49,000 per carat! More than three times the previous record for a single stone!

In Russia, the vast wealth of the Kremlin's Diamond Fund is hidden from public view. Among its countless diamonds are the "Orloff" and the "Shah", one of the few engraved diamonds in existence.

The history of the "Shah" is lengthy. In his discourse on the treasures of Auranzeb's court, Tavernier describes "...a diamond of 80 to 90 carats weight" that dangled before the Great Mogul's eyes as he sat on the Peacock Throne. This stone is believed to have been the "Shah." How it came into the Mogul's possession can only be guessed.

The first engraving on the gem is "*Bourhan-Nizam-Shah II, in the year 1000.*" The year 1000 in the Muslim calendar corresponds to 1591 AD, when Bourhan was ruler of the province of Ahmednegar. He was defeated by Akbar the Great, losing not only his province but in all probability this flawless 88.7-carat diamond.

The second engraving states "*Son of Jehangir-Shah-Jehan, Shah 1051*" (1642 AD) and places the diamond in the possession of Shah Jehan, Aurangzeb's immediate successor.

The next clue to the "Shah's" history is the third engraving. It records "*Kadjar-Fatkh-Ali-Shah, Sultan*" who ruled Persia from 1797 to 1834. Most likely the "Shah" entered the Persian Treasury along with the other booty removed from Delhi by Nadir Shah in 1739.

A remarkable ruler, renowned for his fantastic jewels, Fatkh Ali must have been loath to part with such a priceless gem. Yet in 1829 he did. Following a disastrous war, he lost the Caucasus to Russia.

The Persians hated the new Russian ambassador, Alexander Griboyedov. A few months after his arrival in Teheran a mob stormed a Russian Embassy and Griboyadof was killed. Fearing reprisals, or even a new war, the Persian Prince was dispatched to Moscow where he presented the "Shah" to the Tsar as a token of grief for the murder.

Following the execution of Tsar Nicholas II in 1918 the "Shah", along with all the other Romanov wealth, became state property and was placed in the Diamond Fund.

Many diamonds of historical note have now passed into private hands, a large number through the New York City gem dealer, Harry Winston. One such diamond is the "Nepal", a pear-shaped white of 79.41 carats, which passed from one ruler to another in India until bought by Winston.

The "Shah of Persia" passed through Winston's hands before being sold to a private buyer in 1965. Such was Winston's fame that one diamond has even been named for him. The "Winston" is 154.5 carats in the rough. It was bought for $230,000 by the New York dealer in 1953, a year after its discovery in South Africa. He had it cut into a heart-shape of 62.5 carats, and sold it to a Saudi Arabian prince, probably King Saud.

Some months later the King sold it back to Winston in partial payment of a $2 million jewelry debt. The story is that the King claimed he really needed four identical diamonds, one for each of his four wives. Winston later sold the diamond to a private Canadian buyer.

Another diamond with possibly the longest record, also ended up with Winston. This is the "Briolette of India", a 90.38-carat gem first recorded in the possession of Eleanor of Aquitaine. She may have acquired it in Asia Minor while on the Second Crusade (1146-49). From Eleanor the diamond passed to her son, Richard the

Lionhearted, who probably relinquished it to Henry IV of Austria as part of his ransom for his imprisonment after the Third Crusade.

It also figured among the many gems bestowed on Diane de Poitiers by her lover, Henry II of France. The stone then disappeared for four centuries until an Indian maharajah sold it to Winston in 1950. Although Winston sold the diamond to Mrs. I. W. Killan, he reacquired it following her death and exhibited it after that.

On some forgotten date a 90-carat stone was offered to the shrine of the goddess Shiva at Nassak on the Upper Godavary River by an Indian prince. The stone was placed in the eye of the goddess' statue where it remained until 1818. In that year the British East India Company conquered the region and claimed the gem. It was brought to England by Warren Hastings where it was recut to a triangular 80.59 carats. The gem was known as the 'Nassak', for its place of discovery.

The Marquess of Westminster purchased it and it remained in her family for a century. In the 1940s Harry Winston bought the "Nassak" and had it recut to its present 43.38 carats. He sold it to Mrs. W. B. Leeds in 1944. In 1970 it was auctioned again, this time for $500,000, to a private buyer in Connecticut.

Two other diamonds are reputed to have come from the eyes of statues. The "Black Orloff", named for its gunmetal color and the fact that it was owned by the Russian Princess Vygin-Orloff, came from a shrine near Pondicherry, India. In the 1970s, its owner Charles F. Winson of New York displayed it at exhibitions.

The "Idol's Eye," a blue-white gem of 70.2 carats, supposedly came from the eye of a sacred idol in an Indian temple when it was claimed by the East India Company in 1607 as part of the debt owed by an Indian prince. It then disappeared for 300 years, reappearing as the eye of a temple god in Benghazi, Libya. The diamond belonged to Sultan Abdul Jamid II who sold it to a Spanish nobleman not long after the beginning of the twentieth century.

But the sale did not take place after the courier hired to take his jewels to Paris faked a robbery, shooting himself to prove the story. In 1949 it was sold to May Bonfils Stanton for $675,000. In 1962 it was auctioned to Chicago jeweler, Harry Levinson, for $375,000.

Although privately owned, some famous diamonds still make

periodic public appearances. One is the 25.95-carat "Moon of Baroda" whose history goes back at least to Nadir Shah's sacking of Delhi. From 1787 to 1939 it was in the possession of the Gaekwars of Baroda. It was borrowed from Detroit's Meyer Jewelry Company's Treasure Chest Collection for the film *Gentlemen Prefer Blondes*. One need only watch this classic to appreciate its beauty enhanced by Marilyn Monroe's in the number *Diamonds Are A Girl's Best Friend.*

A diamond seldom worn as an ornament but seen by over 25 million people is the famous "Tiffany". At 128.51 carats it is the largest known golden diamond. Mined at the Kimberly Mine in South Africa in 1878, it was bought the following year by Tiffany & Co. and cut to its present shape from 287.42 carats.

Since then it has been displayed either at Tiffany's, New York, or at expositions across America. It was worn as an ornament for the first time at a charity ball in 1957. Valued at more than $2 million, one can understand its owner's reluctance to allow it to be worn.

The number of historically significant diamonds known today is too extensive to list. The stories of a few will suffice. Many belong to private owners who seldom, if ever, exhibit them. Occasionally seen is the "Taylor Heart". It was purchased for $50,000 in February, 1972 by Richard Burton for Elizabeth Taylor's fortieth birthday. This heart-shaped pendant is engraved with the name of another beauty, Mumtaz Mahal.

A queenly diamond called the "Swan", was sold by Queen Isabella to finance Columbus' voyages. It was worn later by the Queens of France, Holland, Belgium, Bavaria and Portugal, and the Empress of Austria.

The rare blue "Wittlesbach" brilliant turns up in history as a gift from Philip IV of Spain to his daughter on her marriage in 1664 to Leopold I of Austria. The Bavarian Wittlesbachs gained possession of it in 1722 when Maria Amalia was betrothed to Charles Albert of Bavaria. The Wittlesbachs unsuccessfully offered the diamond for sale in 1931 after which it disappeared. It resurfaced in Belgium in 1961. In 1964 it was sold to a private collector.

The "Maximilian I", one of two diamonds named for the ill-fated Archduke Maximilian of Austria and Emperor of Mexico, is a 42-carat light blue cushion-cut stone that hung in a bag around Maximilian's neck while he was executed in Mexico, 1867. It was later returned to his widow, the Empress Carlotta. From 1919 until his death in 1946 it was owned by a Chicago gem dealer, Ferdinand Hotz, from whom it passed to a private owner in Florida.

Possibly the greatest single hoard of diamonds resides in the Iranian crown jewel collection. Unfortunately, they have never been catalogued. These diamonds have accumulated over centuries, but most notably since Nadir Shah acquired them as the spoils of pillaging Delhi.

Since then many have been added. So numerous are they—literally in basketfuls—that when Drs. V. B. Meen and A. D Tushingham, were granted permission to study them in 1966 they could only weigh and describe the largest. Among them is the "Nur-ul-Ain", or "Light of the Eye". At 60 carats it is the largest known rose-pink, brilliant-cut diamond. Harry Winston set this stone in the tiara he designed for Empress Farah at her wedding to the Shah of Persia in 1959.

The "Nur-ul-Ain" is reputed by scholars to have been cut from the "Great Table" Tavernier saw at Aurangzeb's court. According to Meen and Tushingham, the remaining portion of it may be the famous "Darya-i-Nur", or "Sea of Light". Although its exact weight could not be determined due to its setting, it is estimated between 175 and 195 carats.

In 1791 an English traveler saw it set in one of the two arm-bands worn by the Persian King, Lutf Ali Khan Zand. Since then it has been seen on Persian monarchs, the most recent of whom was the Shah of Iran at his 1967 coronation.

At only 115.06 carats by no means the largest Iranian crown jewel diamond, the "Taj-i-Mah", or "Crown of the Moon", is most famous, with the bloodiest history. This flawless white diamond is of Indian origin and probably arrived in Persia with Nadir Shah following his Indian incursions. As we have seen, Nadir was assassinated in 1747 and his treasures widely scattered.

The "Taj-i-Mah", however, came into the possession of one of his successors, Shah Rukh, who soon fell prey to a usurper, Aga Mohammad. Aga Mohammad was determined to have Nadir Shah's treasure and Shah Rukh was as equally determined to hold onto it.

But Aga Mohammad used his power ruthlessly. According to Streeter, Shah Rukh:

> endured with the constancy of a martyr the cruel treatment and horrible tortures to which the usurper subjected him. Exposed alternately to the pains of hunger and thirst, heat and cold, racked, torn with red hot pincers, and at last deprived of his eyes by the usual Persian process of cold steel, his firmness gradually gave way, and he yielded up the costly gems one by one, with each successive application of the rack or pincers, of burning heat and biting cold....

Ultimately, the magnificent "Taj-i-Mah" was given to Aga Mohammad. Aga Mohammad was assassinated soon after.

The "Taj-i-Mah" was set for many years in an armband matched with a "Darya-i-Nur" armband. It was not unusual for Oriental potentates to wear matching jewels. According to Kunz, this practice stemmed from the belief that otherwise "...one member should become jealous of the other, thus disturbing the equilibrium of the whole organism."

The founder of the Pahlevi dynasty, Reza Khan, was forced to abdicate in 1941 and died in exile in 1944. His son, Muhammed Reza Shah Pahlevi, ruled until 1978 when he, in turn, was overthrown. He died in exile in 1980. The "Taj-i-Mah," is still part of the Iranian crown jewels.

Queen of Diamonds:
The Koh-i-Noor

*A*ccording to the epic Hindu poem, the *Mahabharata*, Kama, a legendary hero king, went into battle some five thousand years ago wearing a diamond called the "Samantik Mani", or "Prince and Leader Among Diamonds". Legend further has it that this stone is actually that most famous of diamonds, the "Koh-i-Noor".

Its antecedents have been traced through Vikramaditya, the rajah of Ujain about 56 BC, to his successors, the rajahs of Malwa. They ruled vast areas of northern India for one thousand years before the advent of the Moguls. Whether one believes these legends or not, there is no doubt that the "Koh-i-Noor" has the longest, and most violent, history of any diamond known.

Its first verifiable mention is in the *Baburnama*, the memoirs of the first Mogul Emperor, Babur. In his May 4th, 1526 entry, Babur writes:

> Bikermajit, a Hindoo (sic), who was Rajah of Gwalior, had governed that country for upwards of one hundred years. In the battle in which Ibrahim was defeated, Bikermajit was sent to hell. Bikermajit's family, and the heads of his clan

were at this moment in Agra. When Humaiun (sic) arrived, Bikermajit's people attempted to escape, but were taken by the parties which Humaiun had placed...and placed in custody. Humaiun did not permit them to be plundered. Of their own free will they presented to Humaiun a "peshkesh" (tribute), consisting of a quantity of jewels and precious stones. Among these was one famous diamond, which had been acquired by Sultan Ala-ed-din. It is so valuable that a judge of diamonds valued it at half the daily expenses of the whole world. It is about eight mishkels. On my arrival, Humaiun presented it to me as a peshkesh, and I gave it back to him as a present.

Why should one assume that the "famous diamond" referred to was the "Koh-i-Noor"? Streeter pointed out that eight mishkels is a bit more than 187 carats and it is known that the "Koh-i-Noor" weighed 186 1/16 carats before its final cutting.

Babur also mentions that the diamond was acquired by "Sultan Ala-ed-din," one of the most illustrious of the Sultans of Delhi. This dates the "Koh-i-Noor" 200 years before Babur's time. Again Streeter states that "Ala-ed-din had obtained possession in the year 1304 when he defeated the Rajah of Malwa, in whose family it had been as an heirloom from time out of mind."

Another source claims that the King of Malwa, when "...besieged by the Sultan of Delhi in 1306, had made a golden replica of himself and sent it with a gold chain of submission to the Sultan's commanders with a message, '[I]f precious stones, gems and pearls are demanded....I have a stock of them such as the eyes of the mountains have not seen and the ears of fish have not heard. All these will be scattered in the path of the Imperial officers.'" Among these was the "Koh-i-Noor".

Regardless of when the Moguls obtained it, the fact is the "Koh-i-Noor" was their's from the beginning of their Empire. But it did not rest quietly. During Babur's reign, his son and heir apparent, Humayun, became seriously ill. Babur loved this son as no other and was grief-stricken when the doctors informed him there was no cure.

A holy man told him that when the efforts of man had failed, an offering of the sufferer's most cherished possession must be made to Allah. If the offering was accepted the patient would then recover. The wise men recommended selling the "Koh-i-Noor" and its proceeds used for charitable causes.

Babur interjected that nothing could be dearer to his son than his father. He circled Humayun's sickbed three times, each time praying that his son's sickness should be laid upon him. According to the story, Humayun soon recovered while Babur became ill and died soon thereafter.

As we have seen, Humayun was an ineffectual ruler, forced to flee India. But he did not flee empty-handed; in his baggage train was as much of the Mogul's treasury as he could carry, including the "Koh-i-Noor". In 1544 he arrived in Persia and was received by Shah Tahmasp. As thanks for his reception and help that the Shah had promised in regaining his throne, Humayun gave a gift of 250 rubies and the "Koh-i-Noor". According to Humayun's chronicler, Abu Fazl, "the value of these presents repaid the total expenditure of the reception and hospitality accorded him from beginning to end more than four times over."

While gratified by the size of Humayun's gift, Shah Tahmasp set no particular store by the "Koh-i-Noor" and, in 1547, sent it to Burhan Nizam, Shah of Ahmednagar, in the Deccan. Exactly how the "Koh-i-Noor" returned to the Moguls is not known. One theory is that the stone in the Imperial Treasury was taken by Akbar when he conquered Ahmednagar in 1600.

Once regained, the "Koh-i-Noor" disappeared from view. Recent theories state it may have been one of the eyes of the peacock in the Peacock Throne.

In 1739 the "Koh-i-Noor" again appeared, in a story unparalleled for its avarice. It fell into the hands of Nadir Shah following his pillage of Delhi in 1739, and received the name by which it is now known. Following the defeat of Mohammed Shah, all of the Mogul's jewels, except the "Koh-i-Noor", were given to the conqueror.

But Nadir Shah was not content with this wealth, desiring to possess the gem whose owner, legend claimed, would rule the world. For a long time he searched among the treasure. Finally a woman from Mohammed's harem told him it was concealed in the Mogul's turban. As Nadir Shah had by that time concluded a treaty with Mohammed Shah, he felt he could not again resort to force to obtain the wondrous diamond. So he formed an ingenious scheme by which he could acquire the gem without going back on his word to Mohammed Shah.

To celebrate the conclusion of their treaty Nadir Shah ordered a lavish feast at which Mohammed Shah was to be the guest of honor. During the feast Nadir took advantage of a time-honored Oriental custom. To seal their treaty and friendship, he proposed that he and Mohammed Shah exchange head-dresses.

Before Mohammed could refuse, Nadir took off his own begemmed headdress and handed it to Mohammed, at the same time removing the Mogul's turban. So outwardly calm was Mohammed that Nadir began to fear he'd been misinformed and hurriedly brought the feast to a close.

Rushing back to his tent, he began to unwind Mohammed's turban, hands trembling with excitement. Suddenly the gem fell glittering onto the carpet. Nadir picked up the diamond and, in a moment of rapture, dubbed it "Koh-i-Noor" or "Mountain of Light."

Nadir Shah did not live long to enjoy his ill-gotten gain. In 1747 Ali Kuli Khan, who, according to Sir William Jones, was "...eager to possess the treasures of his uncle and panting for the delights of a throne," assassinated Nadir Shah. Ali Kuli Khan was deposed and blinded shortly thereafter. The "Koh-i-Noor" came into the possession of his successor, and Nadir Shah's grandson, Shah Rukh.

The tales of duplicity and torture that follow the "Koh-i-Noor" are endless. Shah Rukh sat feebly and temporarily on the Peacock Throne. He was overthrown and blinded, in turn, by Aga Mohammed. For some reason Shah Rukh was allowed to retire to the city of Meshed as its governor following his overthrow, taking Nadir Shah's treasure and the "Koh-i-Noor" with him.

Aga Mohammed was just as greedy as his predecessors and decided to gain possession of this renowned treasure. Under the pretext of visiting a sacred shrine in Meshed, he occupied the city and demanded that Shah Rukh deliver up his fortune. At first Shah Rukh refused, but under torture disclosed the hiding place of most of the gems. He was so infatuated with the "Koh-i-Noor" and an

"...immense ruby known to have been in the crown of Aurangzeb" that he still refused to forfeit them.

At the end of his patience, Aga Mohammed resorted to the most horrendous of tortures to accomplish his purpose. According to Streeter, "He ordered his victim's head to be closely shaved and encircled with a diadem of paste, and boiling oil to be poured into the receptacle this formed...the frightful agony of this torture could only induce the victim to surrender the ruby."

Aga Mohammed gave up, certain that Shah Rukh would never recover from his injuries. But he was wrong. In 1751 Ahmad Shah Durani, an Afghan prince, came to Shah Rukh's aid as vengeance against Aga Mohammed. Soon after, Ahmad Shah routed Aga Mohammed's forces and put him to death. In gratitude, Shah Rukh bestowed the "Koh-i-Noor" on Ahmad Shah.

At first the "Koh-i-Noor" resided peacefully with the Afghans, perhaps because it had been given willingly rather than taken by force. The gem passed from Ahmad Shah to his son Taimur, who died in 1793. Then the diamond's nefarious influence re-surfaced.

From Taimur it descended to his eldest son, Shah Zaman, who was deposed and blinded by his brother, Shah Shuja. Although tortured and imprisoned Zaman refused to relinquish the "Koh-i-Noor". Were it not for an improbable twist of fate, the history of the "Koh-i-Noor" might have ended here, its hiding place carried to Zaman's grave.

On a visit to his royal captive, an officer of Shah Shuja's scratched his hand on something in Zaman's cell wall. The officer saw a flash and soon uncovered the diamond. Zaman had embedded it in the plaster but time had worked some of the plaster away, exposing the point.

Shah Shuja was now its possessor.

Not long after Shuja acquired it he was also overthrown and blinded by his brother, Shah Mahmud. Such was the power of the diamond that those who possessed it were ever more loath to relinquish it, no matter the horror.

Shah Shuja, although blind and incarcerated, held tightly to it. In a literal case of the blind leading the blind, Shuja managed to escape with Zaman, the brother he had himself deposed and blinded to gain possession of the "Koh-i-Noor". He sent his family to Lahore where they were placed in the protective custody of Ranjit Singh, "Lion of the Punjab."

Shuja's troubles were far from over for he was captured by a third party, Jahandad Khan, and imprisoned in Kashmir. Shuja's wife, Wafa Begum, pleaded with Ranjit Singh to rescue him, promising the "Koh-i-Noor" as reward. The lure was more than he could resist and he determined to have it.

Ranjit managed to free Shuja and bring him to Lahore, certain that the "Koh-i-Noor" would now be his. But Shuja couldn't bring himself to part with the gem for which he had suffered so much. He and his wife lied that the diamond had been pawned in Kandahar, which was outside Ranjit's power.

Ranjit did not believe them and offered to buy it for £30,000 and an annuity of £5000 per year. Hoping to satisfy him without releasing the diamond, the Begum offered Ranjit an assortment of very valuable gems, among which was an exceptional ruby. Ranjit thought that the ruby was the stone he sought. He called in an expert. When asked whether the famous diamond was among the gems laid before him the man replied that they were of little value compared to the great diamond, which was not there at all.

Incensed at his guests' duplicity, Ranjit kept all the gems. Ranjit ordered troops to Shah Shuja's quarters and separated him from his wife. He cut off their food and drink for two days.

Realizing that Ranjit would stop at nothing to obtain the "Koh-i-Noor", Shuja agreed to give up the gem. On the first of June 1813, Ranjit arrived at Shuja's lodgings and was led to the royal audience chamber. He seated himself cross-legged opposite Shah Shuja, exchanged a few pleasantries, and awaited the transaction. But nothing happened. Shah Shuja could still not bring himself to part with his most cherished possession.

After an hour in which the two silently faced each other, Ranjit's patience came to an end. He called a retainer to his side and told him to remind Shuja of the purpose of his visit. At this, Shuja motioned casually to a slave, still maintaining his silence. The slave returned a few minutes later with a package, which he placed on the carpet between the two princes.

Silence again. Finally Ranjit could stand it no longer and unwrapped the packet. A glittering, unusually shaped gem of great size was revealed. Having once been tricked, Ranjit called on his expert who without hesitation, identified the stone as the "Koh-i-Noor". Ranjit was overjoyed and left with his long-coveted treasure.

Being relieved of the stone's onerous burden did not change Shah Shuja's fortunes right away. He was forced to pay Ranjit 20,000 rupees and was still not immediately released. Ranjit had heard that he retained some valuable treasures and seized them, along with anything else the unfortunate Afghan still held.

Finally, Shuja managed to escape and make his way to Ludhiana, a territory of the British. From them he received an annual pension of 60,000 rupees and was ultimately restored to the throne of Kabul. Of course, he was deposed a second and final time.

* * *

The famed "Koh-i-Noor" was once again in India. It was Ranjit Singh's most prized gem and he seized on every occasion to display it. W. G. Osborne visited the Maharajah in July 1838, and reported seeing the diamond. He valued it at £3 million, an inordinate sum but one indicative of the esteem in which this gem was held.

The following year Ranjit fell ill. When all cures had failed, including a compound of powdered gems, Ranjit decided to make peace with his gods and ordered that the stone be given to the famous shrine of Juggernaut. The crown jeweler refused to carry out this request without Ranjit's written authorization. Before it could be obtained, Ranjit Singh died, making the "Koh-i-Noor" a permanent fixture in the Lahore jewel chamber.

The third possession of the "Koh-i-Noor" in India was a short one. Ranjit Singh's demise prompted his sons to embark on an orgy of self-destruction. One conspiracy to gain the throne followed another, each foiled by the army, until only Ranjit's two-year-old son, Dhuleep Singh remained to inherit his father's throne.

Ranjit Singh's empire boasted a powerful Sikh army whose prowess had been honed in Ranjit's' many expansionist wars until it was one of the finest native fighting forces in India. Fearful that this army would also remove Dhuleep Singh, a regent named Jhindan decided to distract it by sending it across the Sutlej River against the

British in 1845. The Sikhs were defeated and the British occupied Lahore.

A protectorate was established and an indemnity of 55 million rupees for the costs of the war was levied. Following more unsuccessful rebellions, the Sikhs surrendered on March 12th, 1849. This time the British annexed all the Punjab and imposed stiff peace terms. The twelve-year-old Dhuleep Singh was forced to abdicate. The territory was placed under direct British rule, and the "Koh-i-Noor" was demanded as a gesture of goodwill to Queen Victoria.

It was turned over to Sir John Lawrence, one of three ruling council members, for safekeeping. Sir John promptly forgot about it but the Queen did not. Some six weeks after the gem had been entrusted to him Sir John received a letter while sitting in conference. The Governor General was enquiring why the "Koh-i-Noor" had not been dispatched to the Queen. For a moment Sir John was nonplussed. Then he remembered what he had done with it and calmly excused himself.

He hurried home and enquired of his body servant what had happened to the small package in a vest pocket. The servant promptly fetched the package, and when ordered by Lawrence to open it looked up and said, "But Sahib, it's only a piece of glass."

The diamond was promptly dispatched to England on the ship Medea under the protection of two British officers. On July 3rd, 1850, it was formally presented to Queen Victoria. Although the Queen was pleased, her consort, Prince Albert, expressed disappointment in its lack of luster. His opinion was confirmed by many who came to view the "Koh-i-Noor" at the Crystal Palace Exposition in 1851.

Prince Albert convinced the Queen that the diamond should be recut to give it more fire and brilliance. The Amsterdam firm of Coster was retained. A brilliant form was agreed upon. The Coster firm sent two experts, Messrs. Fedder and Voorsanger, to London to carry out the cutting. Prince Albert placed the diamond in the dop, the Duke of Wellington set the four-horsepower engine for the grinding wheel and everyone sat back anxiously to await the result.

After thirty-eight twelve-hour days of nerve-wracking effort, during which the work was reported almost daily in the English press, the cutting was completed. The diamond's 186 1/16 carats had been reduced by well over one third to 108.93. Prince Albert thought little had been gained in luster. Nevertheless, he paid Coster his £8,000 and placed the diamond among the crown jewels. Queen Victoria, however, began to wear it on public occasions.

Showing a deference, and possibly an uncharacteristic remorse, for the manner in which the diamond had been acquired, the Queen was careful not to wear the diamond in the presence of seventeen-year-old Dhuleep Singh who was living in London.

The Queen had taken a liking to the young prince and followed his education and growth with interest. On one occasion she placed the recut stone in his hand and asked whether he would have recognized it. After gazing at it soundlessly for a quarter of an hour, he returned it, stating that he was pleased to be able to personally place it in her hands. However, his true feelings were more readily expressed to others, calling the Queen "a receiver of stolen property."

At first such remarks were made in private, for Dhuleep was dependent on the good will of the British for the funds necessary to maintain him in the manner of a prince. In 1857 he gave half-hearted support to the British during the Indian Mutiny, an act crucial to ensuring the allegiance of the Sikhs to Britain. He spent money lavishly on a Georgian country estate and on entertaining and maintaining several mistresses in high style.

These expenses led him into financial difficulty when the Indian government ignored his request for an increase in his allowance. He finally resorted to the press, addressing a long letter to *The Times* in which he claimed he had been unlawfully deprived by the British of lands and possessions, including the "Koh-i-Noor". He demanded recompense. When his demands were rejected Dhuleep rallied the Sikhs to his cause and left for India. But the British held him when his ship stopped in Aden to refuel.

Completely irate, Dhuleep wandered through Europe refusing to accept his pension from the British. While in Russia he angered them further by unsuccessfully attempting to enlist the support of the Tsar in his cause to regain his lost throne. At last Dhuleep decided to make his peace with the British. He left his villa in Nice and drove to Grasse where Queen Victoria was vacationing. In private audience with her he burst into tears and begged her forgiveness for his past behavior.

The Queen still harbored a soft spot for this unfortunate victim of British imperialism, and restored him to official grace. In 1893, once again respectable, but still without the "Koh-i-Noor", Dhuleep Singh died peacefully in Paris.

At her death Queen Victoria willed the "Koh-i-Noor" to her daughter-in-law, Queen Alexandra, who wore it for her 1902 coronation. The coronation of Queen Mary in 1911 saw the diamond in her crown along with two of the "Cullinans". In 1937 it was transferred to the Queen Mother's Crown for her coronation and is still seen on state occasions.

Legend has it that for females the "Koh-I-Noor" was good luck. It is said that for this reason the Kings of England have never worn the diamond. The belief persisted in India for many years that this stone retained its malevolent powers and that misfortune would follow its possessors, male or female, until it was restored to the line of Vikramaditya.

Some Indians have attempted to reclaim it for their country. Prior to the coronation of Queen Elizabeth II it once again entered the headlines. An MP in the Indian Parliament asked whether his government proposed to take steps to reclaim the diamond and other art treasures looted by the British.

Emotional support was raised in India, and indignation in Great Britain. An Indian government official finally laid the matter to rest by stating that since the diamond was not an art object the government had no plans to ask for its return. This statement, together with a tart editorial in the *Daily Express*, argued that if the diamond belonged anywhere outside London it should be in Lahore, which was Pakistan. This should have settled the matter.

But the "Koh-i-Noor" has not rested quietly anywhere for long. Perhaps that *Daily Express* editorial set the Pakistanis to thinking how they could lay claim to the diamond. On September 7th, 1976, India and Pakistan began a new tug-of-war over the "Koh-i-Noor". Pakistan made an official request to the British for its return. This was followed by a counterclaim from India.

Again, at the beginning of the 21st century, India is staking its claim to this awesome stone. One would imagine that these countries face enough conflict without incurring more through possession of this perverse diamond. It is almost certain that the "Koh-i-Noor" will remain the center of contention for as long as it exists.

Of all the diamonds related in these pages, none more clearly fits Streeter's description with which this book is opened, "...making life a curse where it had been a blessing,..." than the "Koh-i-Noor".

A Diamond Is Forever

*I*n 1825, not long after the establishment of British rule at the Cape Colony, a missionary named John Campbell noted in his diary: "One of our people on first coming to this river collected many kinds of bright stones. He is now looking them over and throwing many of them away, having better knowledge. Age and experience discover many things to be trifles, which in youthful days were highly esteemed."

How wonderful hindsight is. It's easy for us to see that if Campbell had been less skeptical and believed a bit more in the provenance of his God he, or his church, might have been able to proselytize the whole world, funded by the "trifles" so nonchalantly discarded. For they were diamonds. Ironically, Campbell scrawled across a crude map he was making of the area, "Here be diamonds."

Forty-two years would pass before the first authenticated diamond was found, and that quite by accident. In 1866 young Erasmus Jacobs, the son of a Boer farmer, discovered a bright pebble laying near the banks of the Orange River. Intrigued by the stone, he took it home for his children to use in a game called Five Stones.

Several months later Schalk van Niekerk, who had originally owned the farm, visited the Jacob's. Mrs. Jacobs casually mentioned the stone, and van Niekerk asked to see it. The stone was found in the dust of the yard where the children had abandoned their game. Van Niekerk had a vague feeling that it was valuable and offered to buy it. Mrs. Jacobs laughed and told him he could have it for the taking. After all, there were millions where that came from, why should it have any value?

Thus were discovered the most extensive diamond fields ever found. Van Niekerk showed the stone to an acquaintance, John Robert O'Reilly. At first O'Reilly was skeptical. But he agreed to show several dealers in Hopetown. They declared the stone a topaz. However, one man, Lorenzo Boyes, Clerk to the Civil Commissioner of Colesberg, tested the stone's cutting properties on the bottom of a glass tumbler, and became convinced it was indeed a diamond.

Although such a test was by no means proof, Mr. Boyes knew to send it to Dr. William Atherstone, one of the few mineral experts in the colony. Dr. Atherstone carried out tests and confirmed that the stone was a diamond of 21.5 carats. It was later valued by Louis Hand at £500 in the rough.

For verification, Atherstone forwarded the gem to the Cape Colony Colonial Secretary, Mr. Richard Southey. When all tests proved positive he sent the gem to England for one final test by the Crown Jewelers, Messrs. Garrard & Co. It was genuine. A crystal replica of the anticipated polished gem was shown at the Paris Exhibition of 1867.

During testing the Cape Colony Governor, Sir Philip Wodehouse, had been kept abreast. He now offered O'Reilly £500 for the diamond. The offer was accepted. Boyes received £25 plus an IOU for a commission. O'Reilly never honored it. He claimed to have given half the £500 to van Niekerk but there is no record that the Jacobs family received anything for their find.

The diamond was cut into a 10.73-carat brilliant and passed through the hands of several owners during which time it acquired the name "Eureka", a particularly appropriate name under the circumstances. In 1967 it returned home, when purchased by De Beers Consolidated Mines Limited, and was presented to the Speaker of the House of Assembly as a gift to the people of South Africa.

The second major find, an 83.5-carat rough also involved van Niekerk and marked the beginning of the great South African diamond boom. This stone was found by a Griqua, named Zwaartbooi. Since the stone had been found on Griqua territory, Zwaartbooi did not immediately admit to it, fearing it would be confiscated by the chief of the Griquas.

After moving to a Boer farm outside Griqua territory he finally entrusted it to a friend, Willem Piet, for sale. Piet went looking for van Niekerk who was locally renowned for his first discovery. When van Niekerk saw the stone he offered 500 sheep, ten oxen and a horse, which Piet immediately accepted. This stone yielded van Niekerk an undreamt of profit. He sold it for £11,200 to Lilienfeld Brothers.

James Wykeham had also tried to purchase the stone, and was bitterly disappointed. He contested the sale on the grounds that it was not Zwaartbooi's to sell since it had been found on Griqua territory. In the course of the legal battle that followed, Wykeham actually had Zwaartbooi kidnapped twice to "convince" him to change his story about where the diamond had been found. But Zwaartbooi stuck to his story. Eric Bruton wrote that "[O]ne letter...suggests there was only one way to solve the problem, to 'get possession of Swartboy (sic) and bring him kindly over to your side or else fix a 50 lb. Wgt. to his neck and drop him in a fish pond'...."

But Wykeham's claim came to naught. The diamond, now 47.69 carats in its cut form, dubbed "The Star of South Africa", was eventually sold in London to the Earl of Dudley for £25,000, and again in 1974 for £225,000.

When word of the finds leaked out a rush was on that rivaled the American gold rush twenty years earlier. Prospectors flocked to Africa from all over the world, followed by tradesmen, prostitutes and riff raff of all descriptions. Boomtowns sprang up along the Orange River, its tributaries, and the lands adjacent to them. The countryside soon took on the appearance of a battlefield; pockmarked by holes made at the hands of inexperienced prospectors.

This influx inevitably contained thieves, tricksters and charlatans. As in India and Brazil, a common method of theft was to swallow a stolen gem or secret it in a self-inflicted wound. Not all attempts were successful; one native digger was caught with about £1,000 of stones he had swallowed.

Another became so ill from an infected leg wound that he was forced to go to a doctor for treatment. Imagine the doctor's surprise when he lanced the infection and found a small fortune in diamonds hidden within. One thief smuggled stolen stones in a hollowed-out false eye and was never apprehended.

Other tricksters used more subtle methods to cash in. They would meet each boatload of incoming prospectors and single out the most greedy and gullible. These men would be approached with an offer.

If the victim agreed to purchase he would be directed to a rendezvous on some dark night. In the light of day his "bargain" turned out to be a cheap glass imitation. Of course the victim could not inform the police. Some would do it to the next guy to recoup their losses.

The techniques of American gangsters got into the picture too. A well-known American crook named Harry Raymond adopted the alias Adam Worth for his African exploits. Worth had left America for London with a New York detective close on his heels. As the net began to close in he managed to bilk a pawnbroker of £20,000 before slipping away for Africa.

With his now ample funds Worth set himself up in Cape Town as a glib, handsome man-about-town. In its boomtown atmosphere this personable young man ingratiated himself with the town's most influential citizens and hit upon a scheme to make his fortune. Worth learned from his new friends that the rough diamonds from the diggings were shipped overland by cart to a railhead about seventy miles from Cape Town. From there they were carried by train to the Cape Town post office to await shipment to England. He familiarized himself with the route, as well as the layout of the post office, then put his plan into action.

Worth rode along the railway to a point about 20 miles from Cape Town. There he and his men tampered with the rails. The valuable cargo missed the boat for England and had to be stored in the post office to await the next steamer.

Worth and his men bided their time, then broke into the post office and made off with the bags of diamonds. While police scoured the countryside searching for the thieves, Worth made his way to

London where he set up shop as a legitimate diamond dealer and thus disposed of his loot at its full value.

* * *

At best, the country in which diamonds were found was harsh. Water was scarce. Reaching the diamond fields was long and arduous by oxcart. It took as much as two months at the beginning of the rush. The dream of unprecedented wealth lured prospectors on. By 1870 nearly 10,000 claims were being worked along the Vaal River alone.

Many claims were soon abandoned, particularly those in the interior where little water was available to wash the diggings. Many men returned to the more lucrative claims near the rivers. However, the best of these were occupied, leaving prospectors claimless, moneyless and without any chance of making their fortunes.

Under these circumstances many took to illegal means to make their fortunes. Some bought up useless or worked out claims, sprinkled them with a few genuine diamonds and resold them at handsome profits. Others jumped claims or did away with their rightful owners.

Not just individuals, but governments, began to cast covetous eyes on the riches of southern Africa. The Boers of the Transvaal Republic usurped all the lands north of the Vaal River from the Griquas. Not content with claiming these, they decided in 1870 to give a mining concession to a group of their own citizens, overriding the previous claims of the individual prospectors.

These prospectors formed a Diggers Republic in much the same way that the Boers had founded their own republics. Under the leadership of Stafford Parker, ex-seaman, ex-policeman and leading claimholder, the Diggers Republic set about putting its own house in order. Under Parker's stern hand the lawlessness was brought under control. Thieves were flogged, dunked in the river, or paraded through the camps wearing signs labeled "thief," depending on their offences. And, with the threat of incursions by the Boers, military service became compulsory.

The diggers' army was put to the test when President Pretorious of the Transvaal marched on them with an armed force and the concessionaires to whom his government had awarded the mining rights.

203

When the Transvaal force was confronted by the diggers it beat a hasty retreat. A similar occurrence took place when a commando group from the Orange Free State, the second Boer republic, tried to enforce its claims on the south bank of the Vaal.

Even the British government, which had abandoned the Boer republics, got into the act. Their attempt to disarm the diggers failed, so they persisted through more subtle measures. The Griqua chief, Nicholas Waterboer, was convinced by the British to let them take over his lands.

In 1871 the Griqua territories, containing the Diggers Republic, became a Crown Colony. Although many of the diggers wished to fight on, Parker convinced them of the futility of taking on the mighty British Empire. The Diggers Republic came to an end.

With so many men scouring the earth it was not long before the surface diggings ran dry. Although many gave up, some prospectors persisted, digging deeper. It was in this manner that the first pipe of diamond-bearing blue clay was uncovered at Koffiefontein farm on the banks of the Riet River.

Deep digging was costly. Huge amounts of overburden, itself often containing diamonds, had to be removed. Sophisticated machinery was necessary to remove and process the blue clay. This required risk capital. In 1891, when individual diggers could no longer profitably work their claim, they sold their rights to a company formed by Alfred Mosely.

This sort of thing took place at all pipe locations: Dutoitspan; Bultfontein; Jagersfontein, which yielded the immense 995.20-carat "Excelsior" diamond in 1893; as well as the most productive of mines, Kimberley, containing £600 million of diamonds. Together with the De Beers mine, this makes up the Vooruitzicht field.

* * *

In such an entrepreneurial climate only the hardiest men—one might say the most unscrupulous—reached the top. Two men destined to become giants of the diamond world were Cecil Rhodes and Barney Barnato. More dissimilar characters are difficult to imagine. Yet, between them diamond mining and marketing were shaped into their present form.

On the first of September 1870, seventeen-year-old Cecil Rhodes saw Africa for the first time. In poor health, he had come from England to join his elder brother, Herbert, who owned a farm in Natal. However, his brother had, like so many others, dropped everything to try his luck in diamonds. He'd been relatively successful.

At first Cecil resisted the diamond fever that surrounded him. He devoted himself to his brother's farm. To supplement its meager income he sold gold shares on commission. In 1871 his brother returned and the two ran a rather unsuccessful cotton-growing enterprise. But the lure of diamonds was an irresistible magnet to someone who had tasted success and Herbert soon returned to them, leaving Cecil to wrap up their affairs and follow.

Cecil Rhodes arrived in the fields in November 1871. His one attempt at mining was a failure, and he was soon selling ice cream and water to make a living. Cecil watched, listened and learned. Most of the little money he made was reinvested in the De Beers mine. The rest he used to pay his way to England, and at the age of 21, take a law degree at Oxford.

Rhodes returned to Africa in January 1874 and along with his partner, Charles Rudd, purchased a pump to hire out to prospectors to keep their deep diggings dry. This was just before the government raised the number of claims a person could hold to ten.

The diggings were getting out of hand. As they went deeper the narrow walls between claims began to crumble, making it nearly impossible to tell where one claim ended and another began. It was almost as though the earth was denying man's attempt to rob it of its riches.

The claims resembled the lair of a monstrous spider whose spinnings—the guy wires and cables—formed an intricate and dangerous web throughout the fields. Many prospectors could no longer afford the heavy capital necessary to work claims, and sold them to Rhodes. In 1880 he formed the De Beers Mining Company Ltd. and, bought out struggling claim holders. In 1887, he gained complete control of the diggings at De Beers.

But Rhodes was not the only entrepreneur with the skill and audacity to capitalize on the diamond boom. Barney Barnato was the working man's answer to Cecil Rhodes. Where Rhodes was sickly, tall, fair, well educated and introverted, Barnato was healthy, short, dark, poorly educated and extroverted. He, like Rhodes, had come to Africa to join his brother.

Barney found his brother nearly destitute and was forced to turn his hand to anything that could earn him a meager living. Fortunately, he had an uninhibited self-assurance. Prize fighter, vaudeville entertainer, even scullery duties were undertaken; anything that would tide him over until the morrow.

But Barney was also shrewd. He knew that with a bit of skill a more certain financial future could be his. Determined to learn diamond dealing, he became friendly with some diggers and pumped them for information on how *kopje wallopers*, or diamond dealers, judged and paid for the stones.

He soon realized that the buyers knew little more than the diggers about the value of the stones in which they dealt. Somehow or other he managed to scrape together capital to form a partnership with another dealer, Louis Cohen.

A quick look at how Cohen and Barnato started their partnership gives some insight into the business practices and scruples of the diamond dealers. Barney was always on the lookout for a deal. One day he came across Cohen negotiating a purchase with a digger and realized Cohen knew even less than he.

Barney introduced himself as a prospective buyer and asked to see the stones Cohen had just bought. After a thorough examination he returned the diamonds, commenting that since the full price had been paid Cohen could not expect a profit. Cohen was convinced that he purchased the stones for less than their true value. Barney sympathized with him.

"I'll tell you what. I know one of the best buyers. Let's take the stones to him and see what he says," Barney suggested.

Cohen agreed and the two marched into the buyer's office, Barney secure in the knowledge that any good buyer would first offer less than he knew the stones to be worth. Sure enough, when Cohen asked £30, the buyer looked askance and made a counter offer of £20.

Cohen was confused. The opinion of his new friend had been confirmed. Instead of bargaining for a higher price, or obtaining another opinion, he began to waver. After all, two buyers had now said the stones were worth only what he had paid for them.

Barney pulled Cohen aside. He convinced Cohen that he was a good salesman and got him to agree to share any profit he might make on the stones. Then he went back to the buyer and bargained until he received a better price. Cohen was so impressed that he proposed a partnership. Barney agreed. The partners' capital consisted of £60 from Cohen, and £30 and forty boxes of Havana cigars from Barney.

Their first days in business were not successful. Competition among the buyers was keen and Barney soon realized he was wasting time on unsuccessful diggers. Then he had an idea.

He watched one successful kopje walloper who made his purchasing rounds in a pony cart. The pony knew the round and stopped automatically at each customer. Barney offered twice the price the pony was worth. The dealer greedily accepted this windfall. Barney then began the pony's memorized rounds an hour earlier, catching the first and best choice of the stones everyday.

Cohen was later to claim that Barney was "...a decidedly unscrupulous character, who had, nevertheless, a grain of gold in his nature." Cohen himself was no angel. He had arrived in Cape Town, accompanied by his cousin Louis Woolf, with £25 in his pocket. Within a few days he had squandered much of this on women and gambling.

Finally, he departed for the diamond fields with his cousin, who had been more careful with his money. The two became diamond dealers but Cohen was a novice and made terrible purchases. When their funds were down to five pounds, the partnership was dissolved and Cohen was on his own with two pounds to his name.

On his first day alone Cohen began a tour of the diggings, desperately trying to find a bargain that would at least keep him in business and buy him a meal. After six hours, tired, hungry and disconsolate, he stopped to rest at the diggings of a Boer. After watching for a while he inquired whether the digger had any stones to sell. Hardly looking up, the Boer replied that he hadn't found anything for weeks.

Just as Cohen was about to renew his rounds, the digger stood up and shouted, "I have one!," holding up a large, beautiful stone.

Then he took out a battered tobacco tin, placed the stone in it and put it in his pocket. Cohen jumped at the opportunity and asked if he might examine the stone. But the digger ignored him.

He finally engaged the Boer in general conversation, and learned that the man was superstitious. He stood up, as though preparing to leave and said that he thought it odd that the digger should allow his good fortune to slip away.

Intrigued, the Boer stopped digging, leaned on his shovel and asked Cohen what made him say that.

In his most gentlemanly manner, Cohen said he thought it was obvious. The digger had had no luck until he came along. Wasn't that enough to prove that Cohen was lucky?

The digger thought about that for a moment and agreed. Cohen asked again if he might see the stone, stating that he was a major diamond dealer and expert. The digger handed it over. Cohen examined it declared that although not pure, the stone might have some little value. After weighing it on his pocket scales he asked the Boer how much he wanted for it. Cohen was aghast at the asking price of £150 but managed to bargain this down to £130. Then he asked if he might weigh the stone in his office. The trusting Boer agreed.

Cohen hurried away, certain he had a bargain but unable to figure out how to finance it. Then he hit on a plan. He headed for a diamond merchant and offered the stone for £300. Now he had to convince the digger that he still had the stone in order to conclude their negotiations.

As he hurried back to the Boer he picked up a pebble and placed it in the tobacco box. When he arrived at the digging he rattled the box and made another offer of £100. To his surprise, and immense relief his offer was accepted with no questions asked. It was in this manner Louis Cohen got his start as a kopje walloper.

Business did not prosper forever for Cohen and Barnato. The diggings around Kimberley seemed to be running out of diamonds. Many miners were convinced that when they had reached the hard blue ground their claims were worked out. With the steady decline in available diamonds Barnato and Cohen liquidated their partnership. This setback must have seemed a bitter pill for Barney to swallow.

He soon bounced back. He and his brother formed The Barnato Brothers, and paid attention when the geologists' predicted even larger fortunes in diamonds in the blue ground. Scraping funds wherever they could be found, they bought every claim they could near the center of the Kimberley Mine.

In 1880 they formed the Barnato Diamond Mining Company and controlled the center of the mine. Exhibiting the courage of their convictions, the brothers were the first to sink a shaft into the mine's center in 1883.

In 1887 Barnato and Rhodes confronted each other. Rhodes was chairman of De Beers Mining Company Limited and Barnato controlled the Kimberley Mine.

The town of Kimberley was spawned by four nearby pipes; Kimberley, De Beers, Dutoitspan and Bultfontein, and they were the most influential men at it. A third group, the Compagnie Française des Mines de Diamant du Cap de Bon Esperance, held the balance of power. Barnato knew that if he wished to come out on top, he had to gain control of the French company.

But Rhodes made the first move. With the financial backing of Alfred Beit and the London Rothschilds he offered £1,400,000 for the Company. Barney accused Rhodes of encroaching on his territory, and impulsively made a counter-offer of £1,750,000.

Rhodes knew competition would only push the price of the French company's shares up until neither he nor Barney could benefit. So he proposed that they cooperate. In return for Barnato's agreement to a lower price, he promised to resell the French company to Barnato Brothers for a fifth interest in the Kimberley Mine plus £300,000. Certain that he had the better part of the deal, Barney agreed. This was his first mistake in dealing with Rhodes.

As soon as the deal was consummated, Rhodes bought the remaining independent shares in the Kimberley Mine. He already had a fifth interest and this would give him control of it. A fierce financial battle ensued. It forced up the share prices for all the companies involved. It coincided with a slump in diamond sales, from overproduction. The price of diamonds plummeted disastrously, reaching a low of 10 shillings per carat.

Rhodes exhibited the shrewdness that would ultimately result in his ascendancy over the diamond fields. He had come to the conclusion that to maintain the high price of diamonds, one had to control their supply onto the market. This meant holding back large quantities. It was a lesson Barney Barnato had yet to learn...in fact, he was never to appreciate its full importance.

A prominent group of diamond merchants, Barnato included, was invited to Rhodes' office to bid on about 220,000 carats of rough diamonds sorted into 160 piles of various qualities. One can only imagine the sight! The participants themselves had never seen so many diamonds assembled in one place.

Rhodes told the merchants that the value of the diamonds in the depressed prices of the day was about £500,000 but that he would accept no less than £700,000. Then he withdrew to let the merchants decide.

After lengthy discussion and argument, the merchants agreed to Rhodes' price and an apportionment of the stones. The Barnato Brothers claimed the largest portion.

Rhodes' admonished them not to depress the market further by reselling the stones right away. Then he reached down and tilted the table. The merchants stared in amazement as the neatly sorted piles tumbled in one cascading mass into a bucket concealed beneath.

"I've always wanted to see a bucketful of diamonds," Rhodes is reported to have said. Then he calmly suggested that he help Barney carry the bucket back to the Barnato Brothers' office.

Barney knew what was behind Rhodes' theatrics. In addition to getting £700,000 to buy Kimberley Mine shares, Rhodes had reduced Barney's share-buying power by the amount of his diamond purchase. Furthermore, Barney and the other purchasers would not be able to recoup the price they paid for their portion for at least the six weeks it would take to re-sort them. The stones would be kept off the market for that period.

Barney had to grudgingly admire Rhodes' coup. But it did not keep him from contesting every step Rhodes took to gain ascendancy over the diamond fields. Although he ultimately lost control of the Kimberley Mine, Barney remained a worthy competitor against Rhodes' attempts at amalgamation.

Rhodes decided that their deadlock had to be broken. So he invited Barney to lunch in the Kimberley Club, a bastion of Kimberley's English-speaking elite and an inner sanctum into which the nouveau riche merchant had never been invited. Barney, reveling in his new status, behaved so outrageously at this and later meetings that some club members tried to have him barred.

Rhodes calmly persisted in his proposal to merge their companies. He pointed out that Barney would be the largest shareholder of the new company and, in addition, could become a member of the club. Rhodes also promised to support him as a candidate for the Cape Colony Parliament.

Barney, understandably suspicious of Rhodes' desire to be chairman of the board of the company, held out for life governorship on the board. The agreement was nearly wrecked by F. S. Philipson-Stow, a large stockholder in De Beers Mining Company. He was so angered by Barney's behavior at the Kimberley Club and during the negotiations that he threatened to resign rather than serve with him. Only Rhodes' powers of persuasion, supported by the remaining governor, Alfred Beit, saved the day.

Barney's reservations about Rhodes' as Chairman of the Board of the new De Beers proved well founded. Although Barnato had the most shares, Rhodes had the power. It had implications above and beyond the mining of diamonds. The new company's charter permitted it to "take steps for good government of any territory, raise and maintain a standing army, and undertake warlike operations."

As Chairman of the Board, Rhodes was soon to invoke these charter elements to further his personal ambitions. At the age of 37, he became Prime Minister of Cape Colony.

Barnato, having reached his own pinnacle in diamonds, went on to new enterprises, developing the Rand gold fields. From his lowly beginnings he had risen to one of the most powerful, and certainly richest, men in South Africa. But the demands of running an empire took their toll.

In 1897, his favorite nephew, Woolf Joel, a partner to whom Barney looked for guidance, was murdered in his office. A second nephew, Solly Joel, became involved in a plot to overthrow the Boers in Johannesburg. The plot failed and Solly was arrested by the Boer authorities. Barney was by now mentally and physically exhausted. Unable to sleep, miserable and despondent, he finally accepted his doctor's advice and set off back to London.

During the trip he seemed to regain his good spirits and love of life. But just four days sail from London, he was strolling the deck of the liner in animated conversation with Solly Joel, who'd been released on Barney's good name.

Without warning, Barney dashed for the ship's rail and climbed over. Solly managed to grab his coat and, for a moment, held him dangling against the side of the ship. Barney slipped out of the coat and dropped into the sea. A ship's officer dived after him and nearly lost his own life. At the age of 44 Barney Barnato became yet another victim of the diamond's power over greedy men.

What happened to Cecil Rhodes? As Prime Minister of Cape Colony he was implicated in the events that led to the attempted overthrow of the Boer republics. Following votes of censure by Parliament for his part in these events, he resigned as Prime Minister in 1896 but retained his seat in the Cape Colony Parliament.

Rhodes' strategy against the Boers precipitated hostilities that flared into the Boer War. In 1899 the Boer's declared war on Great Britain and laid siege to several important British outposts, including Kimberley. The siege lasted from 1899 to 1900 during which time Rhodes took control of Kimberley's defenses. He opened up the Kimberley and De Beers mines to shelter women and children from the Boer siege guns, and turned the mines' into workshops for producing guns and munitions.

After General French lifted the siege of Kimberley, Rhodes' health began to fail. He retired to his cottage at Muizenberg where he died in 1902 just before the war's end.

* * *

In the years following Rhodes' death a few more pipes were discovered in South Africa. Production was now taking place within the jurisdiction of the Government of South Africa. It was possible to practice Rhodes' theory of controlling production to meet demand and stabilize diamond prices. This tactic was a great success, until the advent of diamond mining in other African countries.

On May 1st, 1883, a strip of African coast running from the

mouth of the Orange River to the border of present-day Angola was bought from the Bethany Hottentot chief by a German explorer named Lüderitz. Fearing that the Hottentots would not honor his purchase, Luderitz turned to the Cape Colony for protection. This request was turned down so he approached his homeland, Germany, which declared the area a German Protectorate.

Diamonds were discovered there in 1908. In order to protect the find from an onslaught by individual prospectors, the Germans declared the whole coastal strip "forbidden territory," and in 1909 gave the mining rights to the Deutsche Diamanten Gesellschaft. A selling arm, Diamant Regie, was established in Berlin to market the diamonds.

The war changed all that. The Germans were overthrown in 1915 and the Government of South Africa took jurisdiction over South-West Africa. After the war, the South African government allowed selected German companies to mine the area.

During this period a man destined to follow in Cecil Rhodes' footsteps appeared on the scene. Ernest Oppenhiemer arrived at Kimberley in 1902 as a buyer for a major London diamond merchant. He became mayor of Kimberley, a Member of Parliament and earned a Knighthood for raising a regiment during the Great War.

In 1917 he formed the Anglo-American Corporation of South Africa, with large infusions of American and British capital, to exploit the gold deposits in the South African Rand. He extended his business interests into diamonds in 1921, by setting up the Consolidated Diamond Mines of South West Africa Limited. Then he gained control of the South-West African deposits. He also became a director of De Beers.

During 1925 major diamond deposits were found at the mouth of the Orange River. Oppenheimer, by then chairman of De Beers, bought out the company working the site and transferred its stocks to De Beers, gaining control of private diamond mining in South-West Africa. Oppenheimer was in a position to exert a major controlling interest on the production and sale of the bulk of the world's diamonds.

Then the depression hit. The situation was aggravated by the fact that the South African government's diamond holdings were outside

213

the Diamond Corporation's control. The government blocked the transfer of the Corporation's diamonds to banks to be used as loan securities, and diamond deposits were discovered in other African countries.

The situation deteriorated so badly that between 1929 and 1932 sales of the Diamond Corporation fell from sixty-one million dollars annually to nine. Kimberley took on the appearance of a ghost town as mines shut down.

The South African government began to realize its tactics were benefiting no one, least of all itself. So the Diamond Producers Association was introduced. It established production quotas for South Africa and its territories, including the government. This provided an outlet for the sale of roughs.

Oppenheimer took it a step further by persuading all producers that their interests lay in combining forces to regulate production. Eric Bruton describes the organizations Oppenheimer set up to realize these aims:

> In 1934, the Diamond Trading Company was formed to carry out the actual selling of diamonds. This and the D.P.A. became the nucleus of what eventually became known as The Central Selling Organization, a group of marketing companies through which all the principal diamond producers sell diamonds on a cooperative basis...now renamed The Diamond Trading Company Limited.
>
> All diamonds that the C.S.O. handles are first sent by the mines to the D.P.A. offices in Johannesburg or to the Diamond Corporation offices in London. They are divided into two groups—gem and industrial—each of which is sold through different organizations.

These organizations have managed to survive intact to the present day, a living tribute to Ernest Oppenheimer, whose foresight helped establish the diamond as the king of gems in the 20th century. Through his marketing techniques the romance and glamour of the diamond has spread around the world, aptly summed up in De Beers famous words, "A Diamond Is Forever."

Diamond Princes: The Indian Maharajahs

For centuries man has been regaled by legends and songs about the fabulous wealth of the Orient. No land has contributed more to those legends than India, whose very name conjures visions of treasure. The "Koh-i-Noor", the "Regent", the "Sancy" and countless others originated there, particularly in the mythic mines of Golconda, whose name has come to symbolize untold wealth.

Much of its treasure has since been dispersed throughout the world, but enough remains in India to bedazzle the eyes and minds of the most jaded travelers.

Neither the rapacity of Nadir Shah nor the greed of Western imperialists was enough to divest India of its riches. In particular the maharajahs—India's kings and princes—were able to build enormous collections. During his visit to India in 1875 the Prince of Wales was amazed by the wealth of India's royal houses.

"There were howdahs of gold on the elephants worth forty thousand pounds, princely barges shaped like swans, palanquins of precious metal, chairs of ivory, fans of peacock feathers, umbrellas of cloth of gold, carpets of pearl and turquoise." The Maharajah of Rewa wore a turban of dazzling diamonds before the Prince. The Maharajah of Gwalior had a special palace built for his visit, "...with gold bed and toilet articles, baths of solid silver, perfume bottles labeled 'Prince of Wales Own Bouquet,' ten thousand pounds of lighting fixtures, and a Persian carpet in the drawing room that could hold two thousand people standing."

In the late nineteenth and early twentieth centuries many Indian princes lived a more secure life under their British protectors. No longer frightened of their neighbors or required to spend vast sums to protect their lands, they channeled their revenues into luxury seldom equaled.

Central to that lifestyle, for many, were fortunes in jewelry and gems. Jagatjit Singh, Maharajah of Kapurthala, owned the world's largest topaz, which he wore as a belt buckle, "...and a noteworthy ornament for his turban made of 3,000 diamonds and pearls."

The Maharajahs of Patiala were renowned collectors of fine gems. In the 1870s, the diamonds of Empress Eugenie of France were purchased for £300,000. And for many years a diamond called "Sancy" resided in their vaults. It was only in 1944 that the Gemological Institute of America was able to differentiate between the two "Sancy" diamonds. The Patiala Sancy weighed 60.4 carats while the true one weighed only 55.

Another diamond confused with a famous look-alike is the "Darya-i-Nur (Dacca)". The East India Company first exhibited it in 1851 at the Crystal Palace. It was later sold to the Nawab of Dacca who attempted to sell it in 1955 and again in 1959. Its present whereabouts is unknown.

Royalty on the Indian sub-continent have restricted their gem purchases to Indian stones, but not exclusively. One of the most famous South African diamonds was the "Jonker". At the time of its discovery in 1934 only three other diamonds known to history, the "Cullinan", "Excelsior", and "Great Mogul", were larger than its 726 carats in the rough. It was sold by its discoverer, Jacobus Jonker, to the Diamond Corporation for £63,000.

Here, the ubiquitous Harry Winston entered the picture, purchasing the "Jonker" for an undisclosed amount and placing it on exhibition in America. In 1936 Winston had the rough cut into twelve gems, the largest of which weighed 149.2 carats. This finished diamond was also put on exhibition.

In 1949 it was sold to King Farouk of Egypt, and again ten years later to Queen Ratna of Nepal. In addition to the cut "Jonker", four diamonds totaling 56.42 carats from the rough were sold to the Maharajah of Indore.

* * *

Not every Indian prince of the last century spent his life in luxury. Man Singh, Maharajah of Jaipur, ascended to the Rajahship of Jaipur in 1922 at a time when the powers of Indian princes were quite extensive. He hired capable administrators to run his domains and delegate power.

During World War II he served as an officer in the Life Guards and was appointed President of Rajasthan at the partition of India in 1948. He then became ambassador to Spain.

Although a progressive and enlightened prince, Man Singh did not eschew all trappings of royalty. He loved to display his jewels. Included in them were three emeralds, the largest of which weighed 490 carats, and a triple-stringed necklace of spinal rubies, each of which was "bigger than a pigeon's egg."

He held an annual party on the roof of his palace, unsurpassed in its brilliance. All the white decorations, including carpets, and a silver chair cushioned in brocade matched the full moon. Guests were dressed in white, and only diamonds were permitted, shimmering from breast and brow.

Among his most prized possessions was an extensive collection of illuminated paintings worth millions that he bequeathed to his people. At the time of his death in England, in 1970, Maharajah Man Singh was said to be the third richest man in England.

In the summer of 1930 A. Monnickendam reports that he was invited to the English residence of the Maharajah Ranjit Singh of Nawanagar. The invitation came without explanation. He was picked up by the Maharajah's Rolls Royce, entertained at a lavish luncheon and escorted to a large room where the reason for the invitation was revealed.

The Maharajah was handed a large, gold jewel box. When he opened the box Monnickendam was amazed to see "...a magnificent diamond of about 130 carats set in a pendant."

The maharajah asked for his appraisal. "On examination I found it to be absolutely perfect, and of the finest color and quality," Monnickendam writes. "In fact it resembles the famous Regent diamond in every way....When I told him that it was one of the finest stones in the world, and that it must be a famous stone, he told me that the diamond came from the Russian Crown Jewels." Monnickendam valued the diamond at £250,000 and later heard that the Maharajah had been able to purchase it for £100,000.

In 1970 a diamond of 148 carats, called the "Nawanagar", was still in the possession of the Maharajah of Nawanagar. It's believed that this is the same diamond Monnickendam saw.

* * *

Perhaps the Indian princes best known to the Western world are the Aga Khans. They are hereditary rulers of the Muslim Ismaili sect with followers in India, Pakistan, East Africa and Central Asia. These princes engaged in a ritual dating to the times of the Great Moguls that symbolized their wealth and power as perhaps no other event could have done.

The most famous enactment of this ritual took place on March 10th, 1946, in Bombay. Aga Sir Sultan Mohomed Shah, Aga Khan III, climbed into an ornate, canopied chair on one side of a huge balance scale. He sat serenely while diamonds cascaded from cases onto the counterbalance, slowly raising his 243 pound bulk. When the marker indicated equilibrium, 545,600 carats of industrial diamonds, loaned by the London diamond syndicate, were deposited on the counterbalance. This ceremony celebrated the Aga Khan's diamond jubilee as Ismaili leader, and was repeated later the same year in Dar-es-Salaam. The value of the diamonds was contributed in cash, gold and gems by the Aga Khan's followers and turned over to charity.

Since partition, the power, prestige and wealth of most Indian princes declined, due to the financial demands of India's democratic socialist government. But many new "princes of commerce" have risen in their wakes, some as interested in gems as their royal predecessors. To them have fallen the finest fruits of the world's diamond market.

The "Jahangir", an 83-carat, drop-shaped diamond, so named

for the inscription of the Mogul emperor's name it carries, dangled from the beak of the peacock on the famed Peacock Throne. It was owned by the Maharajah of Burdwan and sold in 1954 to the Greek shipping tycoon, Stavros Niarchos. Three years later it was auctioned at Sotheby's for £8000 to an Indian businessman.

After having seen their country plundered of so much of its gemological treasures, it must be particularly satisfying for an Indian to turn the tables. Two such incidents concern some the finest diamonds of Brazilian origin. The first of these is "The Star of the South" which, at the time of its discovery in 1853, was the second largest diamond ever found in Brazil.

Its 261.88 carats must have been literally unbelievable to the female slave who found it in the Bagagem Mines. For her honesty—the stone certainly would have been difficult to conceal—she was given her freedom and a small annuity.

At first it was sold for the ridiculously low price of £3000 but several transactions later it realized £40,000. Cut by the famous Dutch diamond cutter, Coster, to 128.8 carats, it now revealed a beautiful pink color. It was displayed at the London Exposition of 1862 and sold, five years later to Khande Rao, the Gaekwar of Baroda. It then became the property of a Bombay businessman, Rustomjee Jamsetjee.

The second Brazilian diamond to find its way to India is the famed "English Dresden". It acquired its name from E. H. Dresden, the English purchaser of the stone. This diamond was also found at the Bagagem mines, in 1857. After having Coster cut the 119.5-carat rough to a pear shape of 76.5 carats, Dresden put the gem up for sale.

Streeter claims that although "...the quality of the stone is superior to the 'Koh-i-Nur'" it was difficult to sell.

But in 1864 an English merchant from Bombay took a fancy to it. Unfortunately for both him and Dresden, he entrusted the purchase negotiations to a middleman who succeeded in convincing Dresden that his client would pay £32,000 instead of the asking price of £40,000. Dresden agreed, and the middleman took the diamond to his client in Bombay, then pocketed the difference.

The curse that afflicts owners of great diamonds now exerted its influence on the Bombay merchant. His business transactions took a turn for the worse, leaving him penniless. He took to his bed where he soon died. His executors were undoubtedly happy to salvage something of his property, selling the diamond to the Gaekwar of Baroda for £40,000.

By now it was 1934, this was the last time this diamond was known to be among the Baroda jewels. It was acquired by another Indian businessman, Cursetjee Pardoonji.

* * *

Of all the Indian families of the past century, royal or common, two deserve special note for amassing some of the fortune in gems still in today's India. The first were the Nizams of Hyderabad. It seems appropriate that rulers of the lands containing the mines of Golconda should have become the richest men of their day.

By any standards Osman Ali, 7th Nizam of Hyderabad (1911-67), was as enigmatic and eccentric as he was rich. His youthful looks and stature led many to underestimate him. One overlooked his expressionless, staring eyes.

In private he was the most austere of men in his habits, wearing a simple cotton, pajama-like garment, slippers from the local bazaar and an ancient tattered fez. He restricted personal expenditures to about thirty-five pence a day.

Yet in public his manner and appearance were meticulously correct, befitting an Indian prince. He was not only a Hindu prince to his subjects but a Muslim religious leader revered throughout the Muslim world. He was a collector, amassing more than two hundred limousines. He used only two regularly.

His palaces boasted "...one of the world's finest collections of Grecian silver, jade so rare it could scarcely be valued...all distributed about his palaces more for forms sake than for ostentation." He was meticulously clean, washing his hands after handling every letter or state paper.

He nevertheless bequeathed a hoard of gems to his son, which Osman Ali built into a formidable collection. One of the diamonds he inherited was the "Jacob" a 100-carat stone reportedly found in the toe of one of his father's old slippers. He had it set in gold filigree for use as a paperweight!

The same story is told in connection with the famous "Nizam". Found in the Golconda mines about 1835, the "Nizam", at about 440 carats in the rough, was the largest diamond ever discovered in India. At its 277-carat cut weight it is certainly the largest Indian polished. What such a gem's value would be today can only be guessed. But in 1874 Louis Dieulafait estimated it at £200,000. Balfour claims that it was this stone used as a paperweight.

The 7th Nizam was not content to collect gems; surely there must be some practical purpose to which they could be put. Many— let us hope the smaller and less pure—must have been used in his practice of *unami*, the ancient Greek medical system based on "...the action of powdered jewels administered in infusions of herbs or in syrups. A teaspoonful of crushed pearl mixed with honey...was a remedy for ailments of the heart."

At his death in 1967 it was claimed that the Nizam of Hyderabad was the richest man in the world. While this may be disputed, there is no doubt that he had more cash, £24 million in gold bars and gold coins plus further millions in bank notes, and readily convertible wealth than any man living. In jewelry alone his estate was valued at over £30 million!

Since 1967 much of the Nizam's property has been sold to meet tax demands. But his fortune in jewels is believed to be intact. How long it will last is open to question. On September 20th, 1979, this treasure was scheduled for auction. But, for a third time since 1967, the auction was challenged in court and annulled on the ground of undervaluation. Let us hope that this treasure trove will be preserved for posterity.

* * *

The Baroda dynasty was nearly as rich as Hyderabad, and much more notorious. This reputation grew with the accession of Khande Rao as Gaekwar of Baroda in 1856. Capricious is a mild word to describe the Gaekwar's escapades. He "...once accumulated sixty thousand pigeons of all breeds, had his priests conduct a marriage ceremony over a pair of them, and gave a vast banquet with fireworks afterward. He lost interest when a palace cat carried off the bridegroom and turned to organizing a battle between five hundred nightingales."

The Roman circus could not exceed in horror the events organized by the Gaekwar. Fights between various combinations of men and beasts were organized for his entertainment. On the winners of the human conflicts he might bestow as much as £4000.

Khande Rao amassed the wealth of the house of Baroda. Gems and jewels poured into his vaults. His purchases included the "Akbar Shah" for £25,000 and "The Star of the South" for £80,000, which he mounted in a necklace along with the "English Dresden".

Not even Baroda's coffers were bottomless. Such expenditure had consequences. He raised taxes and when this did not suffice, he issued a proclamation to his administrators to relinquish all bribes they had received in the preceding ten years. He soon accumulated £200,000, from those he did not even suspect of corruption.

At first, the British overseers of Baroda turned a blind eye on these activities. However, when Khande Rao died in 1870, he was succeeded by his brother, Mulhar Rao. Compared to Mulhar Rao, Khande Rao had been benign. The new Gaekwar's first act was to imprison Khande Rao's commander-in-chief and place him on a diet of pepper and saltpetre "...which pickled him in fifteen days."

Taxes became exorbitant and women of all ranks were snatched from the streets to grace the Gaekwar's harem. Anyone foolish enough to complain about these acts was subjected to the most hideous tortures, such as dragging through the streets tied to the hind leg of an elephant. If one survived this treatment "...he was revived with a drink of water. His head was then placed on a stone and...stepped on..." by the elephant.

The British could not ignore such activities. A particularly zealous Resident, Colonel Sir Robert Phayre reported the Gaekwar to higher authorities, who sent him a letter of rebuke. Not long afterward Colonel Phayre reported an attempt to poison him by powdered diamond in his morning drink, and accused the Gaekwar of perpetrating this act.

Although the Gaekwar knew that Colonel Phayre was likely to soon be dismissed, thus eliminating the motive for such an act, he was brought to trial. The six-man court was evenly split. Nevertheless, the government of India decided that enough was enough.

In 1875 a twelve-year-old named Sivaji Rao was adopted by Khande Rao's widow and became the Gaekwar. During his minority he was surrounded by English tutors and administrators so that when he took over his lands he was a thoroughly Westernized, model Indian prince. Maharajah Sivaji Rao was the complete antithesis of those before him.

Baroda's prosperity was restored and his own wealth increased. He had only one wife, as far as is known, no mistresses, and led a life of devotion to his country. He established the first high school, free compulsory education, and the first state library system in India. On religious and social matters he was a liberal. By his death in 1939 he had truly brought Baroda into the twentieth century and was much mourned by his subjects.

He was succeeded by a grandson, Pratap Sinha, who, at thirty-one, was a "...hedonist with a fair claim to be the last of the big spenders." He inherited a £60 million fortune, and devoted his days to horse racing and luxurious European spas favored by other idle rich. He married a woman whose tastes exceeded his own. In 1948 he was said to have spent £2 million during a six-week stay in New York City.

In 1950, with Indian princes of like mind, he formed the Union of Princes in an attempt to protect his privileges. But this attempt was doomed to failure; there was little appreciation for these "leeches on society" in the new, socialist India. In April 1951 the government stripped him of his titles and privileges, stopped his annuity and gave his title to his son, Fateh Sinha.

But Pratap Sinha was far from poor. He retained vast estates and one of the finest stables of horses in England. An enormous portion of the fabled Baroda treasury disappeared with him when he left India. He took a pearl necklace worth £500,000; a £400,000 diamond necklace; the "Eugenie"; "The Star of the South"; "English Dresden"; and "Moon of Baroda" diamonds—all of which later turned up in private collections.

Pratap Sinha died peacefully in the summer of 1968. With him ended an era unlikely to ever be duplicated again.

Diamond of Despair: The "Hope"

$\mathcal{P}$ossibly no diamond has a more notorious reputation than the "Hope". Misfortune or violent death have dogged the footsteps of nearly everyone who has come in contact with it.

The "Hope" first appeared in the mid-seventeenth century when Tavernier brought it back from India. At that time a disgruntled English cutter claimed Tavernier had stolen it from a temple where it had been one of the eyes of a statue of the Hindu god Rama-Sita. Rama-Sita's revenge is said to account for all the misfortune that has followed the diamond's owners. Tavernier fell from grace along with his king, was defrauded by his nephew, and finally died alone—some say devoured by wolves—in the wilds of Russia.

However he acquired the diamond, Tavernier did not hold onto it for long. At 112.5 carats, it was the largest of 1,167 diamonds sold to Louis XIV in 1668. It cost 220,000 livres, or nearly one quarter of the total bill for the diamonds. Such a diamond had never been seen in Europe. Its color, generally described as sapphire blue, is one of the rarest to be found in diamonds.

So enamoured was Louis of this beautiful gem that he officially designated it the "Blue Diamond of the Crown" and in 1673 ordered it recut by his crown jeweler. The result was a heart-shaped stone of

67 1/8 carats, which he often wore. Then his early military success-es soured and financial and political troubles plagued him. His mis-tress, Madame de Montespan convinced the King to allow her to wear it. Not long thereafter she fell from favor and retired to a convent.

For Louis XVI and Marie Antoinette the blue diamond was also bad luck. The queen loaned it occasionally to her favorite friend, the Princess Lamballe. All three lost their heads to the guillotine in the French Revolution.

Even the rogues of the Revolutionary government could not con-trol the "French Blue." Having confiscated all the jewels of the King and Queen, they placed them in the Garde Meuble. From there they were stolen. While many of the jewels were recovered, the blue dia-mond, valued at £120,000 in the 1792 inventory of the French Crown Jewels disappeared from France.

What happened in the ensuing thirty-eight years was long unknown; even now there are doubts. Such a unique stone could not be easily disposed of; its size and color were a dead give-away.

Some say that it was carried to Spain by Grade Meuble thieves and cut to hide its true identity. In support of this theory is a 1799 portrait by Goya in which Queen Maria Luisa of Spain proudly sports a sizeable, gorgeous blue diamond. A dissolute and domineering queen, Maria Luisa contributed to the downfall of Spain at the hands of Napoleon I and was exiled with her husband.

The blue diamond reappeared in Amsterdam in the hands of a diamond cutter named Willem Fals. Some claim it was he who re-cut the gem to elude claims by the French government. In any case, he held it only a short time. His son, Hendrik, stole the diamond and fled to England, leaving his father to die penniless. Hendrik found a buyer in Lord De Beaulieu and then, out of remorse for what he had done, committed suicide. De Beaulieu sold the diamond to Mr. Daniel Eliason, a London diamond merchant, and died the next day under strange circumstances.

From this point the history of the blue diamond is more authen-tic, although the claims about its curse are less so. In 1930 Eliason put the diamond up for sale. Its history of bad luck must have inter-fered with its sale since it brought only £18,000.

Now cut, the diamond weighed 44.5 carats. Although some

claimed this stone was a remnant of the "Blue Diamond of the Crown", that could not be verified. In an amazing bit of gemological sleuthing, Edwin Streeter claimed that his stone, the 13.75-carat "Brunswick Blue", and a 1.25-carat gem he bought, comprised the main parts of the original "Blue Diamond of the Crown". Streeter's theory is generally believed.

The diamond's purchaser in 1830 was Henry Philip Hope from whom it acquired its present name. Henry Philip died in 1839 and passed the diamond on to his nephew, Henry Thomas Hope. The diamond seems not to have worked its pernicious powers against the first Hopes. The third family member was not so lucky.

Lord Francis Hope inherited it on his father's death. In 1894 he married a successful Australian actress named May Yohe and gave her the diamond to wear. From then on everything seemed to go wrong for Lord Francis and his wife. Miss Yohe's acting career declined miserably, then her marriage to Lord Francis ended in divorce. Over the succeeding years May Yohe was heard many times to attribute her misfortunes to the curse of the cold blue diamond she'd been foolish enough to ignore.

By 1906 Lord Francis was feeling the wrath of the diamond outside his personal life. He was in dire financial straits, and gladly sold the diamond to meet the pressing demands of creditors. Its purchaser was a London diamond merchant named Weil who immediately resold it. The "Hope" was now in the hands of New York jeweler, Simon Frankel.

The diamond's reputation was worldwide. Frankel suffered great financial difficulties finding a buyer brave, or foolish, enough to think he could control its powers. But he finally did so in Mr. Jacques Colot, a French gem dealer.

Colot probably bought the stone because he already had another buyer lined up, the Russian Prince Kanitovski, and could get rid of it before it affected him. But Colot was mistaken. Shortly after disposing of the "Hope" he committed suicide.

Kanitovski was no more fortunate than the diamond's previous owners. He lent the diamond to his mistress, Mademoiselle Lorens Laduc of the Folies Bergeres. On the first night that she wore it on stage the Prince, in an inexplicable rage, shot her from his box. Within a few days he was the victim, assassinated by political terrorists.

The "Hope" next came into the possession of one Simon Montharides, a Greek jeweler, who resold it to Abdul Hamid II, the notorious Sultan of Turkey, for £80,000. The ink was hardly dry on the transaction before Montharides, his wife and son skidded, and hurtled to their deaths over a cliff in his car.

Abdul Hamid had entrusted his new acquisition to the keeper of his jewels. Soon this man was murdered. His successor met a similar fate at the hands of a Constantinople street mob. Then the diamond worked its deadly charm on the Sultan's favorite, Salama Zubaya.

Without asking the Sultan's permission, Salama decided that the diamond should be used to enhance her beauty. When the Sultan heard of this he went into a fit of rage and shot her. This act was one of many that marked the bloody reign of Abdul Hamid. Confronted with plots and revolution on all sides, he decided to dispose of this curse and in 1908 put it up for sale. Less than a year later he was deposed.

The next unfortunate owner was a Spaniard, Señor Selim Habib, who drowned in the wreck of the French liner Seine, after selling the diamond. The "Hope" passed into the hands of the renowned Paris jeweler, Pierre Cartier. For some reason it seems to have left Cartier unaffected. In 1911 he sold it to the American, Mrs. Evalyn Walsh McLean, for £30,800.

Mrs. McLean, a millionairess in her own right, and wife of Ned McLean whose father had founded the *Washington Post*, recalled, in an article in *The Saturday Evening Post* in 1935, how she acquired the "Hope". While on a trip to Paris with her husband she was approached by Cartier, who reminded her that she had admired the great blue diamond when she had visited Constantinople.

Mrs. McLean remembered it well and listened with growing curiosity as Cartier related its devastating history. "...that it was supposed to be ill-favored and would bear bad luck to anyone who wore or even touched it. That Selim Habib was supposed to have been drowned when his ship sank after he had disposed of the gem. We all knew about the knife blade that sliced through Marie Antoinette's throat. Then, too, Lord Francis Hope had plenty of troubles that, to a superstitious soul, might seem to trace back to a heathen idol's wrath or something similar. May Yohe, Hope's wife, eloped with feckless Captain Putnam Bradley Strong. Maybe that was not bad luck, precisely, but it was embarrassing at least.

"Bad luck objects," Mrs. McLean said to Cartier, "for me, are lucky."

Mrs. McLean never fully understood how wrong she was. She agreed to buy the 'Hope' and told her mother-in-law. Her mother-in-law almost fainted. When she recovered she told her daughter-in-law, "It is a cursed stone and you must send it back. Worse than being freighted with bad luck is the buying of it—a piece of recklessness." When the purchase became known Mrs. McLean even received letters from May Yohe who "...blamed the diamond which she, as Lady Francis Hope, had often worn. She begged me to throw it away and break the spell."

But all these warnings went unheeded. Mrs. McLean kept the diamond. She must have been a little concerned with the reputation, for at one stage she asked her maid to find a priest to bless it. A cleric was finally located who would carry out the rite. Mrs. McLean related, "The priest donned his robes and put my bauble on a velvet cushion. A brewing storm began to break. Lightning flashed. Across the street a tree was struck and splintered. Maggie was half frantic with her fear, and beads were clicking through her fingers. I wished that day I could have such faith in things I cannot see. The priest's words, that I could not understand—he spoke in Latin—gave me strange comfort. Ever since that day I've worn my diamond as a charm. I like to pretend that the darn thing brings good luck. As a matter of fact, the luckiest thing about it is that, if I ever had to, I could hock it."

Mrs. McLean was reported to have worn the diamond day and night, even hiring a detective to accompany her swimming. Such protection cost her nearly £5000 per year.

But Mrs. McLean was no more able to elude the diamond's curse than its previous owners. In 1918, while she was attending the Kentucky Derby, her eight year old son, Vinson, escaped from the bodyguard in Washington, D.C. and ran into his street. He was killed instantly. Not long after this her husband took to drink, lost *The Washington Post*, went mad and soon died.

An overdose of sleeping pills killed her daughter. Still, Mrs. McLean never attributed her misfortune to her diamond.

At her death in 1947 the "Hope" was purchased from her estate for nearly £36,000 by Harry Winston. For years it traveled around the U.S. with other of his famous gems. Its virulent reputation did not put off five million people from coming to see it. And for once in its troubled history it served a good cause, raising over one million dollars for charity. One might even think that by putting the stone to such worthy use Winston escaped the diamond's curse.

A diamond with such a history was not easy to dispose of. Finally, in 1957, Winston donated it to the Smithsonian Institution in Washington, D.C. to serve as the centerpiece for a collection of gems intended to rival those in the Tower of London. There it sits to this day, imprisoned behind bulletproof glass, gleaming before millions of visitors who seem drawn by its perverse reputation.

Perhaps it awaits its chance to be released and wreak its vengeance once again on those foolish enough to underestimate its powers.

Appendix

The below listed charts indicate the value of the pound sterling vis-a-vis the French franc and other currencies in relation to the U.S. dollar. The period covers the years from 1792 to the present. As we go to press in the late spring of 2001, the pound is worth approximately $1.68.

Year	$/G8P	FRF/$	DEM/$	ITL/$	JPY/$	CHF/$	EUR/$
1792	4.44						
1793	4.70						
1794	4.82						
1795	4.36	2.99					
1796	4.51	2.94					
1797	4.37	2.90					
1798	4.36	2.90					
1799	4.44	2.90					
1800	4.46	5.07	3.17				
1801	4.36	5.21	2.74				
1802	4.47	4.54	2.74				
1803	4.66	4.51	2.86				
1804	4.53	4.78	2.82				
1805	4.40	4.33	2.86				
1806	4.40	4.81	2.99				
1807	4.46	4.52	3.00				
1808	4.88	4.09	2.92				
1809	4.44	4.34	2.86				
1810	4.11	4.63	2.70				
1811	3.73	4.66	3.09				
1812	3.77	4.36	2.15				
1813	3.90	5.09	2.40				
1814	4.48	5.66	2.56				
1815	4.75	4.50	2.84				
1816	4.57	5.40	2.59	5.90	5.31		
1817	4.53	5.37	2.55	5.96	5.37		

KEY:
GPB=British Pound
FRF=French Franc
DEM=German Mark
ITL=Italian Lira
JPY=Japanese Yen
CHF=Swiss Franc
EUR=European Community Union Euro

Diamonds: Famous and Fatal

Year	$/G8P	FRF/$	DEM/$	ITL/$	JPY/$	CHF/$	EUR/$
1818	4.34	5.50	2.73	5.87	5.46		
1819	4.53	5.40	2.91	6.03	5.36		
1820	4.62	5.55	2.87	5.97	5.52		
1821	4.93	5.20	2.85	5.60	5.15		
1822	4.99	5.21	2.84	5.52	5.12		
1823	4.79	5.34	2.80	5.76	5.22		
1825	4.84	5.34	2.83	5.57	5.29		
1826	4.97	5.24	2.73	5.23	5.18		
1827	4.94	5.12	2.79	5.14	5.07		
1828	4.87	5.20	2.83	5.22	5.15		
1829	4.86	5.25	2.71	5.35	5.22		
1830	4.73	5.24	2.79	5.44	5.21		
1831	4.88	5.17	2.86	5.25	5.12		
1832	4.83	5.34	2.93	5.38	5.28		
1833	4.66	5.47	2.87	5.53	5.42		
1834	4.71	5.37	2.80	5.45	5.32		
1835	4.84	5.26	2.81	5.35	5.21		
1836	4.79	5.26	2.70	5.40	5.23		
1837	5.07	5.14	2.76	5.22	5.11		
1838	4.89	5.16	2.73	5.28	5.13		
1839	4.85	5.21	2.74	5.30	5.16		
1840	4.82	5.17	2.78	5.34	5.12		
1841	4.84	5.25	2.80	5.31	5.19		
1842	4.72	5.42	2.85	5.50	5.36		
1843	4.82	5.32	2.79	5.38	5.27		
1844	4.88	5.22	2.77	5.29	5.22		
1845	4.80	5.27	2.87	5.53	5.24		
1846	4.72	5.39	2.79	5.50	5.36		
1847	4.89	5.23	2.85	5.35	5.19		
1848	4.81	5.26	2.84	5.44	5.23		
1849	4.82	5.26	2.77	5.52	5.23		
1850	4.86	5.19	2.74	5.34	5.15		
1851	4.91	5.14	2.73	5.21	5.12		
1852	4.89	5.13	2.69	5.23	5.11		
1853	4.85	5.13	2.74	5.27	5.11		
1854	4.81	5.19	2.77	5.30	5.16		

Year	$/G8P	FRF/$	DEM/$	ITL/$	JPY/$	CHF/$	EUR/$
1855	4.82	5.20	2.70	5.34	5.17		
1856	4.84	5.15	2.74	5.32	5.13		
1857	4.85	5.23	2.73	5.44	5.20		
1858	4.87	5.14	2.72	5.23	5.14		
1859	4.86	5.16	2.84	5.22	5.14		
1860	4.62	5.40	2.75	5.54	5.38		
1861	4.84	5.21	2.06	5.31	5.20		
1862	6.47	3.85	1.81	3.96	0.60	3.85	
1863	7.39	3.41	2.74	3.50	0.54	3.41	
1864	4.83	5.17	2.75	5.33	0.90	5.16	
1865	4.84	5.12	2.73	5.28	0.92	5.17	
1866	4.81	5.13	2.77	5.66	0.92	5.19	
1867	4.90	5.13	2.78	5.80	0.91	5.17	
1868	4.87	5.15	2.77	5.58	0.94	5.19	
1869	4.86	5.15	2.78	5.53	0.92	5.18	
1870	4.87	5.23	2.74	5.54	0.90	5.15	
1871	4.88	5.28	2.82	5.60	0.91	5.18	
1872	4.89	5.23	4.12	5.89	0.91	5.19	
1873	4.88	5.17	4.14	6.10	0.97	5.17	
1874	4.90	5.13	4.16	5.77	0.97	5.13	
1875	4.89	5.15	4.15	5.65	1.00	5.15	
1876	4.84	5.19	4.21	5.77	0.98	5.19	
1877	4.86	5.19	4.22	5.73	1.04	5.19	
1878	4.88	5.19	4.20	5.55	1.08	5.19	
1879	4.84	5.20	4.20	5.95	1.09	5.19	
1880	4.82	5.24	4.22	5.56	1.11	5.21	
1881	4.85	520	4.21	5.40	1.11	5.20	
1882	4.85	5.08	4.19	5.31	1.13	5.23	
1883	4.85	5.20	4.20	5.25	1.10	5.25	
1884	4.85	5.22	4.21	5.29	1.14	5.27	
1886	4.84	5.23	4,21	5.31	1.27	5.28	
1887	4.87	5.22	4.20	5.34	1.30	5.25	
1888	4.89	5.18	4.17	5.30	1.32	5.19	
1889	4.85	5.18	4.20	5.35	1.27	5.20	
1890	4.86	5.20	4.21	5.44	1.20	5.21	
1891	4.84	5.18	4.20	5.55	1.30	5.20	

Year	$/G8P	FRF/$	DEM/$	ITL/$	JPY/$	CHF/$	EUR/$
1892	4.89	5.16	4.17	5.46	1.45	5.14	
1893	4.87	5.17	4.18	6.18	I.80	5.17	
1894	4.88	5.15	4.18	5.69	2.08	5.19	
1895	4.89	5.14	4.20	5.70	1.93	5.17	
1896	4.87	5.16	4.19	5.64	1.94	5.19	
1897	4.86	5.19	4.19	5.58	2.06	5.21	
1898	4.85	5.21	4.22	5.73	2.03	5.24	
1899	4.89	5.16	4.21	5.76	2.02	5.21	
1900	4.85	5.16	4.20	5.66	2.03	5.19	
1901	4.86	5.14	4.18	5.36	2.03	5.18	
1902	4.88	5.14	4.19	5.23	2.00	5.18	
1903	4.84	5.19	4.22	5.25	2.04	5.20	
1904	4.88	5.15	4.18	5.23	2.04	5.17	
1905	4.86	5.14	4.18	5.22	2.01	5.16	
1906	4.84	5.20	4.22	5.27	2.03	5.20	
1907	4.87	5.17	4.20	5.27	2.03	5.18	
1908	4.87	5.15	4.20	5.24	2.02	5.16	
1909	4.88	5.16	4.19	5.20	2.02	5.16	
1910	4.86	5.20	4.20	5.21	2.03	5.20	
1911	4.87	5.18	4.20	5.22	2.03	5.19	
1912	4.87	5.18	4.20	5.26	2.02	5.21	
1913	4.86	5.21	4.21	5.23	2.03	5.22	
1914	4.88	5.14	4.48	5.30	2.04	5.21	
1915	4.73	5.84	5.15	6.57	2.03	5.29	
1916	4.76	5.84	5.69	6.86	1.96	5.03	
1917	4.76	5.71	5.70	8.28	1.93	4.36	
1918	4.77	5.45	8.37	6.33	1.89	4.85	
1919	3.81	10.82	47.62	13.08	1.98	5.38	
1920	3.49	16.89	72.99	28.58	1.99	6.49	
1921	4.16	12.75	190.19	22.70	2.09	5.15	
1922	4.61	13.83	7352.94	19.88	2.05	5.28	
1923	4.36	19.05	440.5 mil.	23.04	2.13	5.72	
1924	4.70	18.52	4.20	23.25	2.60	5.16	
1925	4.85	26.77	4.20	24.81	2.32	5.18	
1926	4.85	25.32	4.20	22.55	2.04	5.18	
1927	4.88	25.38	4.19	18.59	2.17	5.18	

Year	$/G8P	FRF/$	DEM/$	ITL/$	JPY/$	CHF/$	EUR/$
1928	4.85	25.58	4.20	19.10	2.18	5.19	
1929	4.88	25.39	4.18	19.10	2.04	5.14	
1930	4.86	25.45	4.19	19.09	2~02	5.16	
1931	3.37	25.49	4.23	19.57	2.30	5.13	
1932	3.28	25.62	4.20	19.57	4.82	5.20	
1933	5.12	16.34	2.68	12.16	3.25	3.30	
1934	4.95	15.16	2.47	11.71	3.47	3.09	
1935	4.93	15.15	2.47	12.38	3.48	3.08	
1936	4.91	21.42	2.46	19.01	3.51	4.35	
1937	5.00	29.46	2.48	19.01	3.44	4.32	
1938	4.67	37.99	2.47	19.01	3.68	4.42	
1939	3.93	44.90	2.49	37.25	4.27	4.46	
1940	4.04	49.19	2.49	43.18	4.27	4.31	
1941	4.04	44.94	2.50	52.78	4.27	4.31	
1942	4.04	129.83	2.49	111.76	4.27	4.30	
1943	4.04	67.88	2.49	237.50	4.27	4.29	
1944	4.04	55.36	2.49	237.50	4.27	4.29	
1945	4.03	55.19	10.00	237.50	50.00	4.29	
1947	2.50	119.30	10.00	585.00	238.00	4.14	
1948	3.03	119.30	3.33	660.00	220.00	3.99	
1949	2.38	214.34	3.33	665.00	327.00	4.30	
1950	2.52	349.50	4.20	700.00	360.00	4.31	
1951	2.45	349.50	4.20	690.00	360.00	4.37	
1952	2.73	349.50	4.20	634.00	360.00	4.28	
1953	2.78	349.50	4.20	629.00	360.00	4.29	
1954	2.72	349.50	4.18	638.50	360.00	4.28	
1955	2.77	349.50	4.20	635.50	360.00	4.28	
1956	2.75	349.50	4.20	627.75	360.00	4.29	
1957	2.86	350.00	4.20	624.89	359.66	4.29	
1958	2.80	419.10	4.18	624.00	359.70	4.31	
1959	2.80	488.00	4.17	620.60	358.20	4.32	
1960	2.80	4.94	4.17	620.60	358.20	4.31	
1961	2.81	4.97	4.00	620.60	358.20	4.32	
1962	2.80	4.90	4.00	620.60	358.20	4.32	
1963	2.80	4.89	3.98	622.38	358.40	4.32	
1964	2.79	4.90	3.98	624.80	358.30	4.32	

Year	$/G8P	FRF/$	DEM/$	ITL/$	JPY/$	CHF/$	EUR/$
1965	2.80	4.90	4.01	624.70	358.93	4.32	
1966	2.79	4.95	3.98	624.45	361.25	4.33	
1967	2.41	4.91	4.00	623.86	361.70	4.33	
1968	2.38	5.07	4.00	623.50	357.70	4.30	
1969	2.40	5.82	3.69	625.50	357.65	4.32	
1970	2.39	5.53	3.65	623.00	357.53	4.32	
1971	2.55	5.22	3.27	593.61	315.01	3.91	
1972	2.35	5.12	3.20	582.41	301.66	3.77	
1973	2.32	4.70	2.70	608.27	280.27	3.25	
1974	2.35	4.44	2.41	648.09	301.02	2.54	
1975	2.02	4.47	2.62	683.99	305.16	2.62	0.86
1976	1.70	4.97	2.36	872.60	293.08	2.45	0.88
1977	1.91	4.70	2.10	871.08	239.98	1.99	0.81
1978	2.03	4.17	1.82	831.00	194.30	1.62	0.72
1979	2.22	4.02	1.73	804.00	240.30	1.60	0.69
1979	2.38	4.55	1.97	930.00.	203.10	1.79	0.76
1981	1.91	5.69	2.24	1193.00	219.80	1.79	0.92
1982	1.61	6.74	2.38	1371.00	234.70	2.01	1.03
1983	1.45	8.34	2.73	1656.00	231.70	2.18	1.21
1984	1.16	9.65	3.16	1936.00	251.60	2.60	1.41
1985	1.44	7.51	2.45	1668.00	200.25	2.06	1.13
1986	1.47	6.38	1.92	1339.00	157.47	1.61	0.93
1987	1.87	5.33	1.57	1160.00	121.01	1.27	0.77
1988	1.81	6.06	1.77	1308.00	124.93	1.50	0.85
1989	1.61	5.77	1.69	1267.00	143.85	1.54	0.84
1990	1.93	5.10	1.49	1127.50	135.40	1.27	0.73
1991	1.87	5.20	1.52	1151.25	124.80	1.36	0.75
1992	1.51	5.53	1.62	1475.00	124.80	1.47	0.83
1993	1.48	5.92	1.74	1717.50	111.80	1.49	0.89
1994	1.56	5.34	1.55	1622.00	99.70	1.31	0.81
1995	1.55	4.90	1.44	1584.40	103.35	1.15	0.76
1996	1.70	5.19	1.54	1519.00	115.90	1.34	0.81
1997	1.65	6.02	1.80	1769.00	130.61	1.46	0.91
1998	1.66	5.59	1.66	1648.94	113.20	1.38	0.85
1999	1.61	6.54	1.95	1931.73	102.36	1.60	1.00